Rethinking the School Curriculum

In 2000, the school curriculum in England was equipped with an extensive set of aims for the first time in the country's history. In this book leading experts in the teaching of school subjects examine the significance of the new aims for the reform of the curriculum.

In two general introductory chapters John White discusses the aims and how they might be realised in schools, and draws conclusions about how government policy on the curriculum should proceed. The remainder of the book focuses on subject specific areas and how these could and should be developed to produce a more relevant and enjoyable curriculum experience for pupils, including more opportunities for choice of activities.

This honest portrayal of the school curriculum today and how it could be developed in line with the new aims set by the government will be of particular interest to those studying education with a particular focus on the areas of curriculum, assessment, school management, philosophy of education and the history of education.

John White is Professor of Philosophy of Education at the Institute of Education, University of London and has written extensively on the subject of the National Curriculum.

Contributors: Peter Gill, Michael Hand, Terry Haydn, Edgar Jenkins, Richard Kimbell, David Lambert, Bethan Marshall, Dawn Penney, Charles Plummeridge, John Steers, Keith Swanwick, and Kevin Williams.

Rethinking the School Curriculum

Values, aims and purposes

Edited by John White

 RoutledgeFalmer
Taylor & Francis Group

LONDON AND NEW YORK

First published 2004
by RoutledgeFalmer
11 New Fetter Lane, London EC4P 4EE

Simultaneously published in the USA and Canada
by RoutledgeFalmer
29 West 35th Street, New York, NY 10001

RoutledgeFalmer is an imprint of the Taylor & Francis Group

Typeset in Bembo by
Wearset Ltd, Boldon, Tyne and Wear
Printed and bound in Great Britain by
TJ International Ltd, Padstow, Cornwall

British Library Cataloguing in Publication Data
A catalogue record for this book is available from the British Library

Library of Congress Cataloging in Publication Data
A catalog record for this book has been requested

ISBN 0-415-30679-5 (pbk)
ISBN 0-415-30678-7 (hbk)

Contents

Contributors

Peter Gill taught physics and mathematics in schools for eighteen years, including four as Head of Science at a large comprehensive. He joined King's College London in 1990 and for several years was responsible for the PGCE in mathematics. His research work and publications involved the learning of mathematics in other contexts, particularly science. He left King's College in 2001, and while retaining links with the university, now works as an independent educational consultant and writer.

Michael Hand is Lecturer in Education at the Institute of Education, University of London. He has written on a number of topics at the interface of religion and education, including religious upbringing, spiritual education, the problem of indoctrination and the justifiability of faith schools.

Terry Haydn is a Senior Lecturer in Education at the School of Education, University of East Anglia. He worked as a head of history at an inner-city school in Manchester for many years, before moving to the Institute of Education, University of London. He is co-author of *Learning to Teach History in the Secondary School*; *Citizenship Through Secondary History*; and *History, ICT and Learning*, and has published several papers in the area of citizenship education, the use of new technology in schools and assessment issues in education.

Edgar Jenkins was until recently Director of the Centre for Studies in Science and Mathematics Education at the University of Leeds where he is Emeritus Professor. He is the author of numerous articles and books and for ten years edited the international research review journal, *Studies in Science Education*. He currently edits the series *Innovations in Science and Technology Education*, published by UNESCO and his most recent book (with J.F. Donnelly) is *Science Education: Policy, Professionalism and Change* (2001).

Richard Kimbell taught design and technology in schools and in teacher education before founding the Technology Education Research Unit (TERU) at Goldsmiths College London, where he holds a professorship, in 1990. He has undertaken curriculum and assessment research projects for Research Councils (e.g. ESRC), industry (e.g. LEGO, Apple), for government departments (e.g. DflD, DfES) and for external agencies (e.g. the Design Museum, Engineering Council). He is Editor-in-Chief of the *DATA* journal, and his latest book, *Assessing Technology: International Trends in Curriculum and Assessment*, won the 'Outstanding Publication of the Year' award from the Council for Technology Teacher Education at the International Technology Education Association 1999, in Minneapolis, USA.

David Lambert taught geography in comprehensive schools for twelve years, before his appointment as Lecturer in Geography Education at the University of London Institute of Education, becoming a Reader in 2001. His *Cambridge Geography Project* won the 1992 *TES* school-book of the year award. He has published widely in the field of geography education including (with Paul Machon) *Citizenship through Secondary Geography* for RoutledgeFalmer (2001). He is currently Chief Executive of the Geographical Association.

Bethan Marshall taught English, media and drama for nine years in London comprehensives before taking up a lectureship in teacher education at King's College London. She combined this job for five years with that of English advisor working in both the secondary and primary phases. She has written and commented extensively on English teaching in both academic journals and the media, as well as in her book *English Teachers – The Unofficial Guide*. She also writes and researches in the field of assessment.

Dawn Penney is a Senior Lecturer in the School of Education, Edith Cowan University, Perth, Australia. Since 1990 Dawn has been engaged in critical policy research, focussing on contemporary developments in physical education. Dawn is co-author with John Evans of *Politics, Policy and Practice in Physical Education* (1999, E&FN Spon, an imprint of Routledge) and editor of *Gender and Physical Education. Contemporary Issues and Future Directions* (2000, Routledge).

Charles Plummeridge is Reader Emeritus at the Institute of Education, University of London. He has taught music in primary and secondary schools and continues to be heavily involved in community musical activities. His publications cover various aspects of music education and he has a particular interest in curriculum issues. He has recently contributed to the *Revised Grove Dictionary of Music and Musicians* and has edited, with Chris Philpott, *Issues in Music Teaching*, published by Routledge/Falmer.

John Steers trained as a painter and a potter. After teaching art and design in secondary schools in London and Bristol, he was appointed General Secretary of the National Society for Art Education in 1981. He was the 1993–1996 President of the International Society for Education through Art. He is a Senior Research Fellow at the University of Surrey, Roehampton, and a frequent contributor to the *International Journal of Art & Design Education*.

Keith Swanwick is Emeritus Professor of Education at the Institute of Education, University of London. Previously Professor of Music Education, from 2000 to 2002 he was also Dean of Research. His books include: *Popular Music and the Teacher* (1968); *A Basis for Music Education* (1979); *Discovering Music* (with Dorothy Taylor) (1982); *Music, Mind and Education* (1988); *Musical Knowledge: Intuition, Analysis and Music Education* (1994); and *Teaching Music Musically* (1999, Routledge).

John White is Professor of Philosophy of Education at the Institute of Education, University of London. His recent books include *Education and the Good Life: Beyond the National Curriculum* (1990), *Education and the End of Work* (1997), *Do Howard Gardner's Multiple Intelligences Add Up?* (1998), *Will the New National Curriculum Live Up To Its Aims?* (with Steve Bramall) (2000), *The Child's Mind* (2002).

Kevin Williams is Head of Education at Mater Dei Institute, Dublin City University and a past-president of the Educational Studies Association of Ireland. His publications include the jointly edited collection *Words Alone: The Teaching and Usage of English in Contemporary Ireland* (2000, University College Dublin Press) and *Why Teach Foreign Languages in Schools? A Philosophical Response to Curriculum Policy* (2000, London, Philosophy of Education Society of Great Britain).

Preface

The world over, school curricula are based on a set of familiar school subjects – often such items as mother tongue, mathematics, science, history, geography, a foreign language, art, music, physical education. In all countries, those who want their educational system to prepare children for a flourishing personal and civic life have serious reservations about the status quo, in particular, the tendency of the conventional curriculum towards compartmentalisation and atomisation and also its contribution to pupil disaffection and rejection of learning.

Since 2000 the English educational system has had a standard for measuring the success of traditional school subjects in meeting broader aims. This takes the form of an extensive new official statement on the 'Values, aims and purposes underpinning the school curriculum' – the first such statement of aims in English history. In this book leading experts in different curriculum areas apply this standard to the teaching of their own subject.

An honest picture of shortfalls is combined with imaginative proposals for a better match between their subjects and the new aims. Both tend to point in the same direction. In one way, this is not surprising, since the present authors have worked closely together for over a year, sharing ideas and collectively refining the work into an authoritative set of proposals for future policy reform. Their focus is on the English system, but since the general aims of its curriculum can be applied to most others, their diagnoses and solutions have global resonance.

1   Introduction

John White

The year 2000 was revolutionary for education in England. For the first time in the country's history all state schools were given a common framework of curricular aims. This book looks at the implications of this revolution for the school curriculum itself – not least for the subjects that make it up. Nearly all of these were part of the curriculum before 2000. At that time they were not directed by a national framework because there was no such framework. How closely have the new overall aims matched the aims of the subjects? How far should the latter now evolve so as to improve the match? How far indeed should the curriculum be planned on a subject basis at all? School subjects are, after all, only vehicles to achieve certain ends: they are not self-justifying entities. Now that we have a set of overarching aims, could these be realised by other kinds of curricular vehicle?

Further questions arise about the validity of the new aims themselves. However close the fit may be between subjects and overall aims, nothing is gained if the aims themselves are faulty. One of the topics this book covers is the adequacy of the post-2000 aims. Another, just heralded, is the extent to which subjects or other vehicles are the best way of trying to meet these aims. But its main thrust is an examination of the current school subjects, the adequacy of their objectives and *modi operandi* in the light of the new aims framework.

Although the book is about recent developments in England specifically, its theme is far from parochial. The question 'What should be the aims of school education?' is fundamental to any system. So are the questions 'By what means may aims be best realised?' and 'How good is the match between system-wide aims and the specifics of different curriculum subjects?'. Many, if not most, countries have official statements of aims. Many, if not most, also build their curriculum around a familiar set of subjects, including native language and literature, mathematics, science, history, geography, one or more foreign languages, music, art, physical education. What links are there between recommendations about general aims on the one hand and requirements in the different subjects on the other? Are the latter explicitly derived from and justified by the former? Or are the overall aims more like high sounding national mission statements which can be ignored in practice? Are the familiar subjects included because it is *taken as read* that these are what the school curriculum must consist of?

At one level the book concentrates on fundamental issues of this sort. At another, it is intended as a contribution to the next stage of curriculum reform in England. Global and national themes interconnect and illuminate each other throughout its length. England is unusual among countries due to its belated adoption of overall aims. This means that its recent and continuing experience of curriculum reform allows globally important issues to be raised in unusual starkness.

The new aims for the school curriculum

Before 1988 maintained schools in England were responsible for their own curricula and the aims underlying them. That year saw the introduction of the National Curriculum. This was based on ten foundation subjects – English, mathematics, science, technology, history, geography, a modern foreign language, music, art, physical education.

It is hard to say for certain why these were chosen, since no rationale was provided for them. Richard Aldrich has drawn attention to the very close similarity between the 1988 list and the subjects prescribed for the newly introduced state secondary (later grammar) schools in 1904 (Aldrich, 1988, p. 22). The National Curriculum gives every appearance of having been lifted from what was originally traditional grammar school practice.

Whatever its origin, it was *not* derived from a set of underlying aims. Not that it was entirely bereft of aims. After 1988 it had two:

* [to] promote the spiritual, moral, cultural, mental and physical development of pupils at the school and of society;
* [and to] prepare such pupils for the opportunities, responsibilities and experiences of adult life.

Uncharitable commentators may find these a trifle on the thin side. Certainly it is impossible to read into these bland truisms anything like a justifying rationale for the ten foundation subjects.

In the late 1990s pressure grew for the purposes of the National Curriculum to be more clearly spelt out. The discussions which the Qualifications and Curriculum Authority (QCA) had around this time with teachers, teaching organisations, local authorities and researchers showed that many believed that current statutory arrangements, including the National Curriculum, lacked a clear vision of what the parts, individually and collectively, were designed to achieve. This reinforced the QCA's view, and that of its predecessor the School Curriculum and Assessment Authority (SCAA), that there needed to be 'a much clearer statement about the aims and priorities of the school curriculum' (SCAA, 1997).

This statement materialised in the opening pages of the *Handbook* for teachers on the National Curriculum post-2000. This comes in two volumes, one for primary teachers, the other secondary. I shall call these HPT and HST respectively). The main section is called 'The school curriculum and the National Curriculum: values, aims and purposes'.

Values, aims and purposes

Values and purposes underpinning the school curriculum

Education influences and reflects the values of society, and the kind of society we want to be. It is important, therefore, to recognise a broad set of common values and purposes that underpin the school curriculum and the work of schools.

Foremost is a belief in education, at home and at school, as a route to the spiritual, moral, social, cultural, physical and mental development, and thus the well-being, of the individual. Education is also a route to equality of opportunity for all, a healthy and just democracy, a productive economy, and sustainable development. Education should reflect the enduring values that contribute to these ends. These include valuing ourselves, our families and other relationships, the wider groups to which we belong, the diversity in our society and the environment in which we live. Education should also reaffirm our commitment to the virtues of truth, justice, honesty, trust and a sense of duty.

At the same time, education must enable us to respond positively to the opportunities and challenges of the rapidly changing world in which we live and work. In particular, we need to be prepared to engage as individuals, parents, workers and citizens with economic, social and cultural change, including the continued globalisation of the economy and society, with new work and leisure patterns and with the rapid expansion of communication technologies.

Aims for the school curriculum

If schools are to respond effectively to these values and purposes, they need to work in collaboration with families and the local community, including church and voluntary groups, local agencies and business, in seeking to achieve two broad aims through the curriculum. These aims provide an essential context within which schools develop their own curriculum.

Aim 1: The school curriculum should aim to provide opportunities for all pupils to learn and to achieve

The school curriculum should develop enjoyment of, and commitment to, learning as a means of encouraging and stimulating the best possible progress and the highest attainment for all pupils. It should build on pupils' strengths, interests and experiences and develop their confidence in their capacity to learn and work independently and collaboratively. It should equip them with the essential learning skills of literacy, numeracy, and information and communication technology, and promote an enquiring mind and capacity to think rationally.

The school curriculum should contribute to the development of pupils' sense of identity through knowledge and understanding of the spiritual, moral, social and cultural heritages of Britain's diverse society and of the local, national, European, Commonwealth and global dimensions of their lives. It should encourage pupils to appreciate human aspirations and achievements in aesthetic, scientific, technological and social fields, and prompt a personal response to a range of experiences and ideas.

By providing rich and varied contexts for pupils to acquire, develop and apply a broad range of knowledge, understanding and skills, the curriculum should enable pupils to think creatively and critically, to solve problems and to make a difference for the better. It should give them the opportunity to become creative, innovative, enterprising and capable of leadership to equip them for their future lives as workers and citizens. It should also develop their physical skills and encourage them to recognise the importance of pursuing a healthy lifestyle and keeping themselves and others safe.

*Aim 2: The school curriculum should aim to promote pupils' spiritual, moral, social
and cultural development and prepare all pupils for the opportunities, responsibilities
and experiences of life*

The school curriculum should promote pupils' spiritual, moral, social and cultural
development and, in particular, develop principles for distinguishing between right
and wrong. It should develop their knowledge, understanding and appreciation of
their own and different beliefs and cultures, and how these influence individuals
and societies. The school curriculum should pass on enduring values, develop
pupils' integrity and autonomy and help them to be responsible and caring citizens
capable of contributing to the development of a just society. It should promote
equal opportunities and enable pupils to challenge discrimination and stereotyping.
It should develop their awareness and understanding of, and respect for, the environments in which they live, and secure their commitment to sustainable development at a personal, local, national and global level. It should also equip pupils as
consumers to make informed judgements and independent decisions and to understand their responsibilities and rights.

The school curriculum should promote pupils' self-esteem and emotional well-
being and help them to form and maintain worthwhile and satisfying relationships,
based on respect for themselves and for others, at home, school, work and in the
community. It should develop their ability to relate to others and work for the
common good. It should enable pupils to respond positively to opportunities, challenges and responsibilities, to manage risk and to cope with change and adversity. It
should prepare pupils for the next steps in their education, training and employment and equip them to make informed choices at school and throughout their
lives, enabling them to appreciate the relevance of their achievements to life and
society outside school, including leisure, community engagement and employment.

The interdependence of the two aims

These two aims reinforce each other. The personal development of pupils, spiritually, morally, socially and culturally, plays a significant part in their ability to learn
and to achieve. Development in both areas is essential to raising standards of attainment for all pupils.

(DfEE/QCA, 1999, pp. 10–12)

It should be apparent from this how much more determinate are these aims than the
platitudinous ones of 1988. True, some of the 2000 aims need further precision, but
overall they do present a picture of the kind of pupil that the school curriculum can
ideally help to foster. They draw attention to the personal qualities pupils require, as
well as intellectual equipment in the shape of knowledge and skills. Broadly speaking,
the ideal pupil is an informed, caring citizen of a liberal democratic society. He or she is
an enterprising, independent-minded, contributor to the well-being of the national
community and all its members, respectful of differences of culture and belief, aware of
transnational and global concerns and with an understanding of major human achievements in different fields.

Some 60 per cent of the specific aims mentioned are about the pupil's personal qualities, as distinct from skills or types of knowledge or understanding. The detailed items
in these three categories are:

personal qualities: valuing ourselves, our families and other relationships, the wider groups to which we belong, the diversity in our society and the environment in which we live; the virtues of truth, justice, honesty, trust and a sense of duty; enjoyment of and commitment to learning; confidence in one's capacity to learn; an enquiring mind; capacity to think rationally; sense of identity; appreciation of human aspirations and achievements; thinking creatively and critically; being innovative and enterprising; integrity and autonomy; responsible and caring citizens; challenging discrimination; respect for the environment; commitment to sustainable development; making informed judgements as consumers; self-esteem; emotional well-being; respect for oneself; respect for others; being able to relate to others; being able to manage risk, cope with change and adversity; making informed choices at school and throughout pupils' lives; having the will to achieve; curiosity about themselves and their place in the world; attitudes needed to foster the inner life; willingness to participate, work with others for the common good; financial capability; qualities associated with enterprise education (confidence, self-reliance, learning from mistakes); entrepreneurial characteristics of tenacity, independence.

skills: essential learning skills of literacy, numeracy and ICT; physical skills; six key skills; five thinking skills.

knowledge and understanding: knowledge and understanding of the spiritual, moral, social and cultural heritages of Britain's diverse society and of the local, national, European, Commonwealth and global dimensions of pupils' lives; acquiring a broad range of knowledge and understanding (so as to enable pupils to think creatively and critically); knowledge and understanding of pupils' own beliefs and cultures; recognising the importance of pursuing a healthy lifestyle; understanding the environments within which one lives; self-understanding; understanding necessary to making moral judgements; understanding relevant to making financial decisions, running mini-enterprises, sustainable development.

It should not be surprising that personal qualities are so prominent in this scheme. Since the view of education in the document is about promoting a certain kind of society, it is understandable that it should concentrate on cultivating citizens of an appropriate sort. This means delineating the type of people these citizens will be.

The skills, knowledge and understanding these citizens will need is a further matter. To some extent these can be derived from the personal qualities themselves. One example in the document is the claim that developing a sense of identity requires one to have knowledge and understanding of diverse cultural heritages. Another, not explicitly mentioned in the document, but in line with it, is that autonomy, which has to do with making informed choices about important goals in one's life, requires knowledge and understanding of the various options among which one is to choose.

One further preliminary point: the section on 'Values, aims and purposes' at the beginning of the *Handbook* is not the only place in it where overall aims are mentioned. They also appear a few pages further on in the section called 'Learning across the National Curriculum' (DfEE/QCA, 1999, pp. 19–23 (HPT), 21–25 (HST)). This consists of a heterogeneous collection of general objectives which the different curriculum subjects are intended to serve. Here is an indication in note form of the aims covered in these four pages:

growth of a sense of self; curiosity about oneself and one's place in the world; fostering the inner life; concern for others; making responsible moral decisions; responsibilities and rights of being members of families and communities; making an active
contribution to the democratic process; understanding and respecting cultural traditions, one's own and others; appreciating and responding to a variety of aesthetic
experiences; acquiring 'key skills' of communication, application of number,
information technology, working with others, improving own learning and performance, problem solving; acquiring 'thinking skills' of information-processing, reasoning, enquiry, creative thinking, evaluation; learning to make sensible choices about
managing money; in the context of enterprise education, developing confidence,
self-reliance and willingness to embrace change; acquiring the understanding, skills
and attitudes required to participate in decisions to do with sustainable development.

A fuller discussion of the overall aims comes in Chapter 2. As has been made clear,
the aims are set out in lists of items. No rationale for these is given. In the next chapter
we explore how well the items hang together in a coherent pattern and whether any
adequate justification can be provided for them. For the moment they will be taken as
read. This is not a wholly arbitrary decision. Intuitively at least, they appear to be on
the right lines, at least if one is working within a broad liberal democratic compass.
Although we have to go beyond intuitions into more rigorous assessment, the aims as
stated will be taken as baseline for the rest of this chapter.

From aims to curriculum

Having discussed the aims themselves, I now turn to how schools are to realise them.
Here it is crucial to hold on to the fact that the aims are for the whole school curriculum, not just the National Curriculum. The *Handbook* states that 'the school curriculum
comprises all learning and other experiences that each school plans for its pupils'
(DfEE/QCA, 1999, p. 10). As far as school subjects are concerned, this covers work in
religious education as well as in the National Curriculum areas (religious education has
been a compulsory subject in state schools since 1944). The *Handbook* definition also
transcends the timetabled curriculum. It can cover what a school plans through the way
it structures its 'ethos': its encouragement, for instance, of respect for others in the classroom and in the playground. In sum we can distinguish between general aims and the
school curriculum (in this wide sense) as the vehicle intended to realise them.

Curriculum planning cannot sensibly start with the curriculum. Given that the curriculum is a vehicle, or collection of vehicles, intended to reach a certain set of destinations, we have to begin with the destinations themselves. Once we have these, we have
at some point to work out what kind of vehicles are best to help us attain them in
particular circumstances.

Suppose, as suggested, we take as read the overall aims. How is it best to try to
realise them? Can we go straight to the curriculum in its broad sense? The curriculum
consists of *experiences*, the planned pupil experiences intended to realise the aims. Possible examples of these – generated both via timetabled activities and via whole school
processes (school ethos) – are as follows:

Pupils are encouraged to:

•   listen to things (stories, instructions, others' views);

- look at things (diagrams in books, writing on the board, videos);
- reason things out (how to solve a problem in maths);
- how to create more interest in the School Council;
- imagine things (what it is like to be in someone else's shoes);
- contemplate things (poems, paintings, aesthetic features of the school environment);
- feel various emotions (compassion, suspense, delight, imagination-mediated fear);
- try to remember things (past feelings, geographical facts);
- exercise their bodies.

These and other types of experience constitute the school curriculum as the *Handbook* defines it. What connection is there between things like these and the overall aims? Well, why do we want students to look at things, think about things, feel things and so on? Sometimes these have a partly intrinsic justification: the delight that young children feel in listening to a story is an end in itself. But teachers also have intentions for their pupils which go beyond immediate experience. They are interested in more long-lasting mental states: they want the children to come to believe, know and understand things; to acquire mental or physical skills, like reasoning historically or climbing ropes; to acquire or deepen dispositions or habitual ways of behaving, like controlling fears or resentments, being cautious in their thinking, having an appropriate kind of confidence or self-esteem.

This brings out the fact that there are two importantly different kinds of ingredient in the mental life of the child (or, indeed, of anyone) (see also White, 2002, Chapter 1). On the one hand there are conscious occurrences (experiences of listening, thinking, moving one's limbs); and on the other continuing mental states (understanding, knowing how to swim, being kind). The continuing mental states exist even when there are no present conscious occurrences. A child can understand fractions without having anything to do with fractions at the moment. She still understands them when she is having her tea, perhaps even when she is asleep. The same goes for skills and for personal qualities. A child can know how to dive without actually diving; and is still a kind person when she is on her own and there is no one around to be kind to.

The experiences – the conscious occurrences – which constitute the school curriculum are vehicles intended to bring about continuing mental states such as knowledge and understanding, skills and dispositions (personal qualities). These are the curriculum's aims. Indeed, as we have already seen, the overall aims in the *Handbook* fall under these headings. General aims take more and more determinate forms the closer one gets to the pupil's experience. At the experiential end they are maximally determinate. Take the class of young children delightedly listening to a story. What does their teacher plan that they learn, over and above, that is, intending them to have an experience enjoyable in itself? One of the things she wants is for them to enjoy experiences *of this sort*, that is to get into the habit of wanting to hear simple stories like this. We can call this an 'immediate' aim – the aim a teacher (or whole school) has in engaging learners in a particular activity. Behind the immediate aim lie aims of increasing generality. She wants them to enjoy simple stories of this sort not only through hearing them, but also through reading them. She wants them to enjoy literature in general. She wants them to develop a deeper understanding of human nature or a more refined aesthetic sense. Of course she is also likely to have other aims in reading the story – to do, for instance, with sharing enjoyable experiences with others or introducing more advanced vocabulary.

These aims also fit in a range from immediate to very general. In addition, all the aims mentioned interconnect and are inextricable from each other in practice.

At the more general end of the continuum we reach the kind of overall aim that we find in the *Handbook* or similar documents. In between the highly general aims and the teacher's immediate aims are aims of varying levels of generality or specificity. Curriculum planning consists in mapping out, and relating to each other, aims across the whole range, from the most general to the most immediate. At the immediate end, the teacher's, it also includes working out experiences – specific forms of listening, looking, thinking and so on – designed to realise these aims.

Curriculum planning, therefore, is a collaborative enterprise at different levels. As is often the case, not least in post-1988 England, governments lay down overall aims (e.g. developing self-understanding). They also lay down aims at the next levels of specificity, aims for and within particular curriculum areas (e.g. understanding aspects of one's own society's history which help one to understand oneself; more specifically again, understanding the significance of the rapid rise in the population since the late eighteenth century). Teachers specify these further at the level of the school and the classroom.

In Chapter 2 I will be saying more about curriculum planning, both in general and in relation to developments in England. As well as looking more closely at the justification of overall aims, I will go further into ways in which they may be realised, concentrating especially on what can and should be done via whole school processes and, within timetabled activities, what can be done without using school subjects as a framework.

Matching school subjects to overall aims

I now narrow the focus on to the curriculum subjects themselves, specifically the subjects of the English National Curriculum plus religious education (RE).

The *Handbook* on the National Curriculum, separate booklets on all the National Curriculum subjects (which cover most of the same ground as the *Handbook*), and a booklet on the RE curriculum are constructed on a subject basis. As we have seen, the overall aims at the beginning of the *Handbook* in principle cover non-subject-based learning. In actuality, however, virtually the whole of the government documentation just mentioned is about the aims of the different *subjects*, their programmes of study, their contribution to learning across the curriculum and their attainment targets.

The explanation for this is obvious enough. When the *Handbook* appeared in 1999, nearly all the curriculum subjects with which it deals (with the exception of personal, social and health education (PSHE) and citizenship) had already been compulsory elements since 1988. The government had to work with what was already in place.

This is understandable, but it does give rise to a question. The *Handbook* introduced a set of overall curricular aims. Presumably some coherence is intended between these new aims and the documentation on the aims, programmes and attainment targets of the various subjects. Presumably these latter features are seen as ways in which the overall aims are to be made more determinate in the way described in Section 3. The question is whether these presumptions are justified. To what extent do we find a good match between the overall aims and the specific requirements laid down for the different subjects?

I explored this question in detail in a project, so far unpublished, undertaken in 2001 for a national educational agency. I took all thirteen current subjects, including RE and the two newcomers PSHE and citizenship, looked at their aims, programmes of study,

Table 1 Compulsory subjects of the English school curriculum, including the National Curriculum, from 2003

	Key Stage 1	Key Stage 2	Key Stage 3	Key Stage 4
Age	5–7	7–11	11–14	14–16
Year groups	1–2	3–6	7–9	10–11
National Curriculum subjects				
Core subjects				
English	•	•	•	•
Mathematics	•	•	•	•
Science	•	•	•	•
Other subjects				
Design and technology	•	•	•	
Information and communication technology	•	•	•	•
History	•	•	•	
Geography	•	•	•	
Modern foreign languages			•	
Art and design	•	•	•	
Music	•	•	•	
Physical education	•	•	•	•
Citizenship			•	•
Religious education	•	•	•	•

attainment targets and contribution to learning across the curriculum and tried to establish how far there is a match or mismatch between these specific items and the overall aims. To what extent are the subjects, as officially conceived, suitable instruments for realising the general aims?

The short answer is that the results are patchy. Very broadly speaking, the best match tends to be found in subjects only recently introduced into the curriculum: design and technology, ICT, citizenship and PSHE. Many longer established subjects tend to be problematic in various ways. These include art and design, English, geography, history, mathematics, modern foreign languages, music, physical education, RE, science.

There is not space to run through all the results, but below are some examples. In citizenship there is a good match. Its aims are stated as follows:

> **Citizenship** gives pupils the knowledge, skills and understanding to play an effective role in society at local, national and international levels. It helps them to become informed, thoughtful and responsible citizens who are aware of their duties and rights. It promotes their spiritual, moral, social and cultural development, making them more self-confident and responsible both in and beyond the classroom. It encourages pupils to play a helpful part in the life of their schools, neighbourhoods and communities and the wider world. It also teaches them about our economy and democratic institutions and values; encourages respect for different national, religious and ethnic identities; and develops pupils' ability to reflect on issues and take part in discussions.
>
> (DfEE/QCA, 1999, HST p. 183)

If we compare these with the overall aims, we see close links between them. There is the same concern with personal qualities like self-confidence, responsiveness to others' needs, civic involvement, respect for cultural differences, reflectiveness, as well as with the knowledge and skills needed to sustain them. The programme of study for citizenship is also in sync. It is not difficult to see how the overall aims map on to such randomly selected items as learning about the criminal justice system or the significance of the media in society, learning to 'negotiate, decide and take part responsibly in both school and community-based activities' (KS 3 *Handbook* for Secondary Teachers (HST) pp. 184–185). The whole tone of the citizenship documentation is pupil-centred, in that, like the overall aims, it keeps firmly in mind the ideal of a certain kind of person and the skills and understanding which such a person must have.

The same is true of design and technology. As with citizenship its own aims look outwards, beyond its own confines, towards wider personal and social horizons picked out in the overall aims:

> **Design and technology** prepares pupils to participate in tomorrow's rapidly changing technologies. They learn to think and intervene creatively to improve quality of life. The subject calls for pupils to become autonomous and creative problem solvers, as individuals and members of a team. They must look for needs, wants and opportunities and respond to them by developing a range of ideas and making products and systems. They combine practical skills with an understanding of aesthetics, social and environmental issues, function and industrial practices. As they do so, they reflect on and evaluate present and past design and technology, its uses and effects. Through design and technology, all pupils can become discriminating and informed users of products, and become innovators.
>
> (DfEE/QCA, 1999, HPT p. 90, HST p. 134)

Further specification is given to these aims in the programme of study. This includes such items as learning 'to generate ideas for products after thinking about who will use them and what they will be used for' (KS 2 HPT p. 94); learning 'to select appropriate tools and techniques for making their product' (KS 2 HPT p. 94), learning 'to identify and use criteria to judge the quality of other people's products' (KS 3 HST pp. 136–137).

Gaps in matching

With most of the longer-established subjects, there is much less room for confidence about a good match with the overall aims. Subjects where the match is – to different degrees – problematic include art and design, English, geography, history, mathematics, modern foreign languages, music, physical education, RE, science. These problems are discussed below.

Art and design

Similar points, *mutatis mutandis*, could be made about art and design, except that there is more weight here on pupils' making works of art (the musical equivalent being composition). The justification of both subjects in terms of larger aims is unclear both from the documentation and more generally. Both subjects have appeared in curricula for maintained schools since the late nineteenth century. Music grew out of 'singing' and art and design out of 'drawing', the latter included originally for 'the great mass of our working population' as 'likely to be useful to them in their future occupations as workmen and artisans' (Selleck, 1968, p. 121). Today they are both multi-faceted, sophisticated subjects, assured of a place in the curriculum, but unclear as to their over-arching purposes.

English

One of the overall aims states that the school curriculum: 'should encourage pupils to appreciate human aspirations and achievements in aesthetic, and ... social fields, and prompt a personal response to a range of experiences and ideas' (DfEE/QCA, 1999, p. 11). This would suggest, among other things, acquaintance with literature on a human scale, not necessarily literature written in English. There is no need to dwell on the extraordinary richness of world literature, which nearly all of us access only in translation. It is not only absorbing for its own sake, but affords us the best insights we often have into other cultures and countries.

Yet because the school subject responsible for literature is called 'English', it has traditionally been taken as read that the texts it studies are those written originally in English. This tradition has come through to the 2000 curriculum, with its long statutory and non-statutory lists of works to be read at Key Stages 3 and 4. All these are texts written originally in English.

If, as seems sensible, we need to create room for world literature in schools, how should this be done? Should we stretch the label 'English' to cover it? Or should the title of the subject be changed to 'language and literature'?

Film is among the most important forms of dramatic art of the twentieth century. There is no clear place for it in the school curriculum, although it is mentioned in odd places under English. It is a visual art, but not included with other visual arts under art and design. All this may reflect the fact that the categories under which education in the arts is delivered – art and design, English, and music – date back to the nineteenth century and so do not well reflect twentieth century developments.

Geography

Unlike some other subjects, most of geography's aims closely match overall aims statements, for instance, geography:

> prepares pupils for adult life and employment. It is a focus within the curriculum for understanding and resolving issues about the environment and sustainable development. It links the natural and social sciences. Through geography pupils encounter different societies and cultures. This helps them realise how nations rely on each other. Geography can inspire them to think about their own place in the world, their values, rights and responsibilities to others and the environment.
>
> (DfEE/QCA, 1999, HPT p. 108, HST p. 154)

But with the exception of work on the environment and sustainable development, the programmes of study and attainment targets tend to focus largely on intra-subject material to do with geographical enquiry and skills. There is less than might have been

expected about cultural matters; but much about repeatable features found across different countries, in other words, about subject matter approached scientifically and in
abstraction from the child's own perspective.

History

So many of the overall aims are about pupils' roles as national and global citizens in
rapidly changing cultural, political economic, technological and social conditions. This
requires a background of understanding of recent and contemporary history. Yet the
history curriculum contains very little work on the twentieth century.

Mathematics

The first reason given for mathematics' importance is that it equips pupils with powerful tools of logical reasoning and problem-solving (DfEE/QCA, 1999, HPT
p. 60, HST p. 57). This is an ancient argument for the subject, and it assumes the
existence of general thinking skills. However, there are problems about this – akin to
problems raised, incidentally, more than a hundred years ago when faculty psychology
provided a rationalising theory for the elementary school curriculum (Selleck, 1968,
pp. 45–58). For instance, the reasoning and enquiring acquired in history classes seems
very different from the reasoning and enquiring involved in planning a family holiday.
There *may* be general skills which cover widely diverse fields, but it should not
be assumed that they exist before evidence – at present non-existent – is provided
for this.

Statutory requirements in mathematics are laid down in great detail. Fourteen pages
are devoted to its programmes of study, as compared with an average of four pages for
all subjects. From the standpoint of the overall aims, just how important are all these
statutorily required items? Students at Key Stage 3 have to recall the essential properties
of quadrilaterals like the trapezium and rhombus. When was the last occasion that any
reader of this book made use of these notions?

Modern foreign languages

The importance of MFL is said to lie in helping pupils to understand and appreciate different cultures and countries; and to think of themselves as citizens of the world
(DfEE/QCA, 1999, HST p. 162). These are goals wholly in line with the overall aims.
Yet virtually all the material in the attainment targets and programmes of study has to
do with learning linguistic skills. No attempt is made to show why the latter should be
thought an especially good means of attaining the goals just mentioned. If promoting
the understanding of other cultures is what one is after, other vehicles look much better
bets for the non-specialist: accounts of them in English, literature in translation, foreign
films with subtitles or dubbing.

Music

The attainment targets and programmes of study are inward-looking. They provide
structured progression in acquiring the various sub-skills and forms of understanding
and appreciation found within the subject – i.e. as performers, composers, listeners and

judges. Pupils are thus led into the foothills of various related specialisms, yet the overall point of this for those children who will not become specialist musicians is not clear.

Physical education

For most people good physical health is a basic need for whatever activities they wish to undertake. The overall aims acknowledge this in their reference to encouraging pupils to 'recognise the importance of pursuing a healthy lifestyle'. Sub-aims covered by this may be taken to refer to understanding how the body works, diet, sensible habits of eating and drinking, work on body image, the need for adequate exercise, care in avoiding damage to one's body, drugs education and aspects of sex education. School dinner policy can play a part in this, along with timetabled classes in various areas.

In addition some children have a more specialised interest in developing their physical skills in some more particular direction – through dance, gymnastics, games, swimming, athletics. Physical education as a curriculum subject is almost totally orientated towards such specialisms. Its contribution to more general health aims is not well worked out.

Religious education

This subject presents a quite different matching problem. No problem here of links between the aims of RE and overarching aims. The RE material is full of statements such as: 'Pupils learn about religious and ethical teaching, enabling them to make reasoned and informed judgements on religious, moral and social issues' (QCA, 2000, inside front cover).

The most natural way of taking such comments is that RE deals with ethical and moral issues as part of children's general moral education. This is in line with the tradition of religious education in this country. There was a tight link between religious instruction and moral instruction in the elementary schools of the late nineteenth century (Selleck, 1968, p. 59). Closer to home, the introduction of RE as the only compulsory subject in maintained schools after 1944 had much to do with the belief that Britain needed to 'revive the spiritual and personal values in our society and in our national tradition' (Niblett, 1966, p. 15).

The civic significance of RE may well have dwindled between 1944 and 2000, but the more general association between religious and moral education has persisted more tenaciously. Until 2000 RE was seen in many quarters as *the* locus for moral education in the curriculum. In 2000 PSHE and citizenship were added to the National Curriculum subjects. In addition to these two new subjects in the ethical/moral/civic field, *every* subject has now to declare – in its *Learning across the National Curriculum* statement – how it contributes to learning in this area.

There are thus two sources of ethical and moral education now flowing into the new curriculum, one associated with religion, the other not. How far may this lead to a confusion in pupils' minds at odds with the insistence on clear, rational thinking prominent among the new overall aims? Recent statistics suggest that Britain is now a country where organised religions play little or no part in the great majority (perhaps 80 per cent) of people's lives. If present trends continue, this majority can be expected to increase (HMSO, 2000, 13.19, 13.20).

The points just made suggest that the whole area of how ethical/moral/civic aims are to be delivered calls out for review. In particular, it needs to be asked if this area of learning should now fall outside RE's remit altogether.

Science

The documentation on this rightly makes much of such aims as understanding the impact of science on industry and the quality of life; and discussing science-based issues that may affect the future of the world. But these are not reflected in the attainment targets. Virtually all the level statements here are about mastering specific areas of knowledge and techniques of enquiry within science.

Jenner, Lavoisier and Darwin are the only names of scientists mentioned, and their theories appear only as non-statutory examples to illustrate more general points. There is next to no work on the great turning points in the history of science, e.g. the impact of Copernicus and Galileo, the scientific revolution and the enlightenment, the impact of geology and evolution theory on views about man's place in the universe, the harnessing of science in the last two hundred plus years to industrial production, military affairs, medicine, social improvement etc. There is nothing about the impact of science on religion over the past five hundred years. There is no reference to any of the human sciences.

Inward-looking tendencies

Judging by the documentation, all the subjects we have considered, with the partial exception of English and RE, have an intra-subject orientation. In other words, their main preoccupation is with helping pupils to acquire knowledge, understanding and skills in their specialised area. Thus history aims at equipping pupils with a degree of historical knowledge and understanding, as well as reasoning and enquiry skills pertinent to the discipline. The same is true, *mutatis mutandum*, for other intellectual subjects, i.e. mathematics, geography and science. In MFL, art, music and PE the emphasis is more on skills of performance and production informed by relevant knowledge and understanding.

Learning in these subjects has to do with inducting novices into their *modi operandi*. The model at work seems to be something like apprenticeship in acquiring the rudiments of competence as a geographer, historian, mathematician, scientist, musician, visual artist, linguist.

It would be quite unfair to say that these subjects profess no links with overall aims. Geography, for instance, mentions its contribution to understanding other societies and sustainable development; mathematics its application to everyday life; science its role in understanding technological aspects of industrial and social life. Despite this, the attainment targets, programmes of study, and aims statements show a marked intra-subject emphasis.

Does this matter? It may seem odd to upbraid these subjects for concentrating on their own special ways of thinking, their own special skills and facts. What could be wrong with that? In another context – specialist courses at university, perhaps – this might be unremarkable. But in the new school curriculum, overall aims come first, subjects second. Schools' first duty is not in the preparation of specialists, but with providing a sound general education in line with subject-transcending aims.

That does not necessarily mean that an intra-subject orientation is wholly to be ruled out. Among the new overall aims we find 'developing ... pupils' autonomy' and 'equipping them to make informed choices at school and throughout their lives'. There is a powerful argument that in order to choose options which include science-based or music-based careers, or indeed science or music pursued as ends in themselves, pupils have to have an appropriate understanding of the nature of science or music. The knotty question then becomes: what counts as *appropriate* understanding? How much acquaintance with science or music does one need as a basis for choice, and of what kind? Is the apprenticeship model adequate for this, or should one look for one with wider horizons? This kind of justification in terms of equipment for choice is scarcely, if at all, found in the new *Handbook*.

The most striking finding from the survey I carried out was the intra-subject orientation of so many curriculum subjects. However, in the light of the history of school subjects this is perhaps not so surprising. The intra-orientated subjects have been statutory elements in the National Curriculum since 1988, that is more than a decade before the new aims appeared on the scene. As noted earlier, the list of subjects included in 1988 is remarkably similar to the list included in the secondary regulations of 1904. In those eighty-four years the internal strength of these subjects increased and was consolidated via their statutory – and later non-statutory but by then entrenched – place in the school curriculum, via their subject-associations, and via their links with higher education. Most of them originated as school subjects in the late nineteenth century and were not then taught in universities. Promoters of these subjects sought to enhance their status by emphasising their academic rigour. This process developed further in the twentieth century via links between secondary school teachers, university teachers, subject associations and examining boards (Goodson and Marsh, 1996: an overview drawing on subject-specific works by Ball, S., Jenkins, E., Layton, D. and others). Over the years subjects which had a lowly place or no place in the 1904 curriculum joined the others on the escalator of respectability and professionalism: as mentioned already, 'drawing' was elevated into 'art and design', while music, absent in 1904 but common in elementary schools as 'singing', grew into the sophisticated, many-sided subject we know today. Achieving the status of a 'foundation' or 'core' subject in 1988 strengthened still further the power of these subjects and of their institutional links.

In 1993 Duncan Graham, the first Chairman and Chief Executive of the National Curriculum Council which preceded QCA, wrote: 'Do subjects exist to enable learning or as a vehicle for vested interests, lobbies, and departmental baronies?' (Graham and Tytler, 1993, p. 120).

The inward-looking nature of many of the subjects, their attachment to the apprenticeship model and the demands of specialisation raise questions about how far they should be allowed to continue in their present form. The arrival of the new overall aims has given us a touchstone, previously lacking, for assessing their suitability, as presently constituted, for delivering the pupil- and civic-centred education now required.

The structure of the book

Most of this book is a subject-by-subject discussion of issues raised in previous sections. Among other things Chapters 3 to 13 can be seen as putting to the test the conclusions of the project conducted for the national agency. They cover all the pre-1988 subjects now contained in the National Curriculum, as well as religious education. A chapter on design and technology has also been included in the light of the comments made about it above. The post-2000 entrants to the National Curriculum, PSHE and citizenship have not been selected and neither has ICT. The chapters on subjects are preceded, in Chapter 2, by a discussion of some key questions in general curriculum planning.

Chapter 3 looks at *Art and Design*. With notable dispassion, John Steers sees the subject as marked by a 'prevailing orthodoxy' of approach. He interprets its historical development since the eighteenth century as a process of adding elements thought to reflect 'good practice' at different times, and so generating the less than coherent and fragmented curriculum we have today. Positively, he would like to see art and design recognise the shortcomings of 'school art', which has largely lost touch with wider contemporary developments in the professional field, in favour of more flexible arrangements which bring home to both teachers and pupils that art and design 'can actually *matter* in their lives'. This involves re-addressing the balance within the subject – moving 'fine art' from its privileged position and offering older students more opportunities for choice of working in a range of media and technologies, in design and craft activities as well as in fine art. It also demands more authentic forms of assessment that go far beyond the monitoring of orthodoxy.

Richard Kimbell's discussion of *Design and Technology* in Chapter 4 is distinctly upbeat. The only curriculum newcomer in 1988 (under the title technology), it grew out of former craft subjects (e.g. woodwork and needlework) and areas of technology (e.g. electronics), drawn together and given focus through processes of designing. As an area encompassing both art and science, D&T is by its nature interdisciplinary. Despite continuing problems in the spread of good practice in the teaching of the subject, it makes procedures of values-sensitive planning and making rather than knowledge content central to its activity. This means that it conforms more closely than most other subjects to the new generic aims of the curriculum. Unlike other subjects, its attainment target is expressed wholly procedurally, in terms of how tasks are tackled. Kimbell agrees with David Hargeaves that D&T 'is moving from the periphery of the school curriculum to its heart'.

Bethan Marshall shows in Chapter 5 how current debates about the content and purpose of *English* cannot be understood without tracing the historical lineage of competing positions. The view that locates the subject among the liberal arts originated with Matthew Arnold and was developed further by Leavis. The conception of English as a vehicle of critical dissent has even older, religious, roots, but has now become secularised; while contemporary conservatives, influenced by Eliot, often associate the subject with the preservation of English culture and hold that only via adhering to a canon of national literature can its decline be prevented. Marshall goes on to link the 'Gradgrindian' nature of current policy with the anti-utilitarian critiques of Arnold and others. She favours a position which does justice both to the aesthetic aspects of the liberal arts position and to elements of the tradition of dissent, dissociating herself to a large extent from the fashionable tendency in English teaching circles to see print literacy as giving way to a more multi-modal future.

In Chapter 6 David Lambert gives a frank account of the 'identity crisis' that besets *Geography* and of its proponents' keenness to defend the 'place in the sun' which it won in the 1988 settlement against incursions from competitors in curriculum 'turf wars'. He regrets the way National Curriculum requirements have steered teachers towards conformity, noting the role of widely-used textbooks in this process. He would like there to be much more thought about the *purposes* of teaching geography so that the subject can recover a sense of direction. Potentially, geography has a huge amount to contribute to the realisation of the new overall aims of the curriculum, not least because of its interdisciplinary nature. Its future should lie in a greater responsiveness to children's needs as independent thinkers and as citizens; and in a willingness to subordinate the integrity of the subject, where appropriate, to new forms of cooperation and intermingling with other curriculum areas.

This brings us to Terry Haydn's Chapter 7 on *History*. This echoes the theme in the geography chapter about a current lack of consensus on why the subject is important. Traditionally, its purpose has been moral and civic, with a focus on the lives of great men and women. More recently, others have argued for it as a logically distinct form of knowledge. These aims have been held in uneasy tension since 1988, with political pressures in subsequent years towards the former. The current history curriculum fails to appeal to many ordinary children, is too intent on 'coverage', makes too few connections with contemporary affairs, and invites teaching to the test. The way forward lies in reversing these tendencies, and in putting more weight on differences in interpretation and revitalising the history teaching community. The gap between the generic aims and current arrangements is wide and will only be reduced once more freedom is granted to teachers.

Peter Gill begins his Chapter 8 on *Mathematics* with a dismissal of three of the most prominent arguments for the subject's being so extensively taught – its utility (beyond basic numeracy), its role in training thinking skills, and its intrinsic interest. His examination of how well it fits the overall aims also reaches largely negative conclusions. As with history, there has historically been a tension between ways of conceiving the subject, in the case of mathematics between those who see it as preparation for further work in higher education and those for whom it is a part of a child's personal development, the former being more influential. Once again, assessment arrangements come under fire as inadequate vehicles for revealing depth of understanding. Peter Gill suggests a radical overhaul of practices and regulations within the field, advocating that those who have not progressed well in the subject by the end of Key Stage 3 should be allowed to opt out.

Chapter 9 is on *Modern Foreign Languages*. Kevin Williams begins, like Gill, with a rejection of familiar vocational and other utilitarian arguments for compulsory provision. He then focuses on several valid arguments for learning a foreign language which are *not* uppermost in official justifications of the subject but which *are* closely in line with generic aims of the whole curriculum. Arguments of an experiential kind are: to provide pleasure, to form a basis for further learning, and to engender cultural decentring. Arguments connected with ethical development have to do with promoting openness to others at an individual level and, in a symbolic way, at the national. Williams holds that these arguments together justify giving all students the opportunity to learn a foreign language, perhaps more intensively and at an earlier age than usual, but that, seeing that not all students have an interest in or aptitude for the subject, they do not justify compulsory provision for more than one year.

Music is a prominent ingredient of contemporary culture. Yet, as Charles Plummeridge and Keith Swanwick argue in Chapter 10, its vitality and many-sidedness is not well reflected in school music. The National Curriculum has reinforced the traditional dominance of class teaching (which has its origins in choral singing in church), with a lesser role for instrumental tuition and extracurricular activities. Training in musicianship has been and still is the central rationale for the subject rather than a more general induction into the discourse of music. The music curriculum needs to be more closely linked with the wider musical world and to build on contemporary local initiatives based on outreach programmes and other activities. This calls for a much more flexible music curriculum reflecting the multiplicity of forms of musical experience and offering more options to secondary students. The changes would bring musical provision much closer to the new overall aims.

In *Physical Education*, too, according to Dawn Penney's analysis in Chapter 11, the National Curriculum has given further legitimation to long-standing practice. Traditionally the subject has been conceived as a collection of discrete forms of activity, most often connected with sport. This conception originated in élite public (i.e. independent) schools in the nineteenth century, élitist connotations continuing in the privileging of preparation for high-order sporting performance among the aims of the subject as practised. The original National Curriculum order for PE had wider purposes than performance, but political involvement in the early 1990s narrowed these in the direction of the tradition. The curriculum is now built firmly around performance in dance, games, gymnastics, athletics, outdoor and adventure activities, and swimming. Dawn Penney questions the rationale for this structure and favours a radical refocus on a more flexible, interconnected and inclusive curriculum geared to children's current and future lives and with greater opportunities for choice given to schools and pupils.

Religious Education is not a part of the National Curriculum but has been compulsory since 1944. In Chapter 12 Michael Hand begins by looking at the original rationale for RE at that time. He locates this in the wartime desire, given totalitarian threats, to found British democracy on firm ethical foundations, Christian-based RE being the vehicle. After the war, with the decline of confessional RE and the coming of a multicultural society, this purpose gradually gave way to two other roles for the subject – moral education of a non-confessional sort and the promotion of understanding and respect for a variety of faiths (although after 1988 Christianity regained something of its traditional privileged status). Hand argues that neither of these current rationales is strong enough to justify compulsory RE for all. But there is a *third* and more defensible rationale, yet not prominent in the documentation: pupils should be equipped to make informed judgements on the truth or falsity of religious beliefs.

Like many other subjects, *Science* is still imprisoned by its past. Edgar Jenkins shows in Chapter 13 the class-divided nature of the subject for most of the twentieth century. Science was first taught in nineteenth century public schools and then in secondary grammar schools. Courses were based on the fundamentals of chemistry and physics and, later, biology, and on extensive practical work in specialised laboratories. The legacy is that most children did little or no science until more recent times; only in 1989 did it become an established part of the standard primary curriculum. In addition, since that date, the élite tradition, with its specialist, university-oriented outlook and ritualised emphasis on laboratory activity has become further entrenched at the secondary level, leaving school science increasingly divorced from the role that science has come to play in the modern world. However, he cautions that framers of a more inclusive science curriculum should look warily on demands for science to be taught through its technological and civic applications and argues that attention should be given to developing the pedagogical and other strategies needed to introduce students to the key features of how scientists currently understand the world.

As will be apparent from this résumé of the chapters, there are many parallels across the subjects in historical development, the tenacity of custom, the focus on specialist training, social class differences in provision, disagreements about aims, the impact of the National Curriculum, the constraints of its assessment system, a desire for a reshaped curriculum which is more inclusive and in tune with the new overall aims. Chapter 14 picks out a number of these common themes and discusses lessons that can be learnt from them which may be used to formulate more adequate National Curriculum policies.

References

Aldrich, R. (1988) 'The national curriculum: an historical perspective' in Lawton, D. and Chitty, C. (eds) *The National Curriculum*, Bedford Way Paper 33. London: Institute of Education University of London.

DfEE/QCA (1999) *The National Curriculum Handbook for Primary/Secondary Teachers in England* (two versions, labelled here HPT/HST).

Goodson, I.F. and Marsh, C.J. (eds) (1996) *Studying School Subjects: a Guide*, London: Falmer.

Graham, D. and Tytler, D. (1993) *A Lesson for Us All*, London and New York: Routledge.

HMSO (2000) *Social Trends 30*, London: HMSO.

Niblett, W.R. (1966) 'The Religious Education clauses of the 1944 Act: aims, hopes and fulfilment' in Wedderspoon, A.G. (ed.) *Religious Education 1944–1984*, London: Allen & Unwin.

QCA (2000) *Religious Education: Non-statutory Guidance on RE*, London: Qualifications and Curriculum Authority.

SCAA (1997) *Second Annual Report on Monitoring the School Curriculum 1996–7*, London: School Curriculum and Assessment Authority.

Selleck, R.J.W. (1968) *The New Education: The English Background 1870–1914*, Melbourne: Pitman.

White, J. (2002) *The Child's Mind*, London: RoutledgeFalmer.

2 Shaping a curriculum

John White

Late in Chapter 1, I narrowed the focus on to the school subjects of the English curriculum. Now I widen it again to ask the following questions:

1 why have a National Curriculum in the first place?
2 what should be its aims and why?
3 how are the aims to be realised in curricular arrangements?

I discuss these both in the English context and more generally.

Why have a National Curriculum in the first place?

In England before 1988 it was theoretically teachers who decided their schools' aims and curricula. There were practical problems about this, not least the often widely different provision between schools. But there was also a more fundamental issue. *Why* should teachers have this power? Do they have an expertise which equips them to make such decisions?

Where teachers *do* have an expertise is in deciding what specific aims and what pupil experiences best suit the particular children they teach in specific circumstances and at specific times. But this does not show why they should make macro-decisions – decisions about what aims to have in the first place.

There is, indeed, a good argument *against* leaving macro-decisions in their hands. Teachers are only one section of the population, yet choices about the directions school education should take affect us all. These choices cannot help being about the kind of society there should be in the future and the kind of people who belong to it. As such they are essentially *political* decisions touching on the good life for individuals and for society. Teachers are no more professionally equipped to make such choices than computer operators or shop assistants. Army officers are not left to make decisions about whether or not to wage war: again, their professional equipment does not take them so far. It is characteristic of a democratic society that macro-decisions affecting the well-being of the whole society in education, military affairs, health, law and order and other fields are not left to *sections* of the population but are seen as belonging to the citizenry as a whole.

This is the fundamental reason in favour of putting aims and curricula – at a macro-level – under political rather than professional control. It is not an argument for central rather than local political control. Different policies are appropriate in different countries. In a small country like England where there are not major cultural differences between regions, and where political life is organised largely at national rather than local level, overall national control makes obvious sense. Larger federal democracies like the USA, Canada and Australia may be expected to give more power to states or provinces.

Do democratically elected ministers have the right to introduce *whatever* aims and curricula gain parliamentary approval? The question applied to England in 1988 when a patently inadequate National Curriculum was installed (see Chapter 1). It is clear that there must be some kind of check on ministerial and parliamentary arbitrariness.

What kind of check? To answer this, we have to go back to the rationale for a politically-imposed curriculum in the first place. It assumes a democratic society in which everybody is politically equal. Nationally determined aims and curricula are only justifiable if they are fashioned within and support such a framework.

This is a significant conclusion. It means that the answer to question 1 leads us to an answer to question 2. Aims for the school curriculum must at the very least be aims which foster a democratic society.

What should be the aims of a National Curriculum and why?

More flesh must be put on this. A democratic society is based on certain core values. The first of these we have met already: political equality. According to this, no one should be in a privileged position when it comes to decisions designed to affect the well-being of the political community. It is the principle behind one person, one vote.

There could, in theory, be democratic societies which adhere to political equality and which rigorously enforce some religious or other doctrine. Whether such societies have ever existed in fact I do not know. When we think of democracy today, in the twenty-first century, we tend to add another value to it: personal autonomy. We tend to take it as read as an ideal – not always fully realised in practice – that each person should make their own decisions about how they are to lead their lives, given that their choices are not likely to harm others. For us a democratic society is taken to be a *liberal* democracy – one in which obstacles are not put in the way of people choosing to live according to their own ideas.

A qualification is necessary. Is personal autonomy intended to be a value that *everyone* in the democratic community should follow? What about those religious people, for instance, for whom the idea of personally directing one's life is anathema since one should obediently follow the will of God? Is not liberal democracy, after all, *illiberal*? Not necessarily. There is a version of it which does not insist on autonomy for all, but leaves room for individuals to lead the life they prefer even if this excludes autonomy. This version is the taken-for-granted ideal that nearly everyone in a society like contemporary Britain lives by.

This is not the place to go more deeply into the political philosophy of democracy. But even the short distance we have travelled has taken us a long way in determining what the aims of a National Curriculum should be.

Personal qualities

It gives us, first, some insight into the personal qualities that people need to acquire. A society of political equals is one in which certain attitudes will be ruled out – élitist, racist, sexist views or any others which privilege one section of the population over another. Political equality is not a value easily confined within the frontiers of a national community: it transcends them to rule out chauvinist, racist and élitist attitudes at the international level. All these things require education. So does preparation for a life based on one's own preferences (including those which exclude further autonomous decisions). Moral aims also come into the picture here given that preferences which are harmful to others are winnowed out: children need to be brought up to allow others equal freedom to lead their own lives and to be supportive of their efforts to do so.

There is much more that could be said about the personal and social aims just mentioned. The value attached to living a life of one's own rests on a more deeply embedded value: leading a flourishing or fulfilled life. What counts as this? Does *any* kind of preferred way of life qualify, provided it is morally innocuous? Suppose a person autonomously goes for a way of life based as far as possible around watching TV game shows and playing fruit machines. If he succeeds in his ambitions, could his be a flourishing human life?

There is a key ethical issue here central to thought about education. Does the nature of the good life for the individual depend on that individual's preferences – or can we identify the ingredients of personal fulfilment independently of them? A currently influential line of thought in philosophical ethics favours the second option. The kind of ingredients that tend to be included in a list of personal goods include: accomplishing something in one's life (e.g. through the work that one does) which makes one's life meaningful rather than meaningless; living autonomously; having intimate personal relationships; understanding oneself and the world in which one lives; promoting the well-being of other people; enjoying physical pleasures of eating, drinking, sex and exercise; aesthetic enjoyment of works of art (including popular art) and natural beauty (see, for example, Griffin, 1996, pp. 29–30).

So far these aims derived from an initial commitment to a democratic society have all been about personal qualities. There is much more to be added under this rubric, especially about qualities needed to sustain one in one's pursuit of one's major personal and moral goals – like courage, perseverance, self-confidence, friendliness, appropriate management of one's bodily appetites. All these, and other virtues, too, need nurturing through education.

Knowledge and understanding

These personal qualities generate, in their turn, aims to do with knowledge and understanding. Having attitudes appropriate to politically equal citizens requires understanding what political equality is in the first place and its role in a democratic society. This in turn demands a grasp of the differences between democratic and other kinds of society and régime – not just in the abstract, but as found in the world in which we live and past worlds from which our own world has emerged.

Personal autonomy brings its own demands on understanding. Making one's own way in life depends on the existence of options among competing ways of life, activities, belief systems, careers. One task of the school is to equip pupils with knowledge about such options. If the view mentioned above is right, that one can construct a list of ingredients of human well-being independently of what any individual might prefer, then certain kinds of understanding will become more salient – e.g. about the arts, one's self and the world one lives in, close personal relationships, physical pleasures, types of accomplishment.

Moral concern for others in the community and outside it also requires knowledge – of people's psychology, their needs and preferences. All the personal qualities mentioned so far depend on a good background knowledge of the main features of one's own society and sketchier insights into other countries and communities. This includes an understanding of the technological bases of modern societies as well as of cultural matters.

Every personal quality, indeed, makes demands on understanding. A key element in personal autonomy in an age of globalisation like our own is the ability to chart one's route through life in the light of major uncertainties in the area of economic development, job markets, finance, international stability, changes in consumption, population, the natural environment. Assessment of risks and possibilities as global factors that affect one's personal choices is now a feature of all our lives (Giddens, 1991). This, too, depends on accurate information. Management of one's physical desires, to take a final example of a personal quality, requires knowledge about one's body, food values, diet, drugs, sexual relationships and much else.

A related area of knowledge that the pupil requires is about basic needs, his or her own and other people's. Whatever way of life people adopt, there are certain fundamental needs which have to be satisfied. In order to lead a flourishing life, indeed in some cases in order to survive at all, we all (normally) need clean air, food and drink, clothing, housing, reasonable health, a comfortable ambient temperature, an income, company, security against attack or disaster, non-interference by others in our plans and activities. In their own interests and in order to promote other people's, children need some understanding of basic needs, how they may be satisfied and what obstacles lie in the way of this.

Conclusion on aims

It will be helpful to take stock. From an initial commitment to the aim of preparing children for membership of a democratic society, a number of fundamental educational aims have been derived, first to do with personal qualities and then, derivative from these in their turn, to do with knowledge and understanding. The lists of items under these headings are by no means complete: it would take at least a whole book to fill out the story. But I hope at least the methodology is reasonably clear, since once it is followed, further aims can be deduced.

Much that is prominent in actual curriculum objectives is absent from the account so far. Among other things, I have said nothing about basic skills of numeracy and literacy. But it would not be difficult to show how these can be generated from what has been spelt out so far.

Are there important aims which have been omitted and are not somehow embedded in the 'democratic' aim? Has justice been done to scholarly aims traditionally held to be important – a good understanding of the worlds of the mathematician, scientist or historian; or an appreciation of major human achievements in intellectual and artistic, engineering and other fields?

While mathematical, scientific and historical understanding is obviously embedded in, or derivable from, many of the aims described above, there is nothing in them about specialised training in these disciplines on an apprenticeship model. It is not clear what valid justification of this could be given in a general education.

Some appreciation of major human achievements across time is important as a facet of self-knowledge, where the focus is on oneself as a member of the human species. Democratic citizenship is not lived in a time-bubble of the present. Part of living together as free and equal beings is a celebration of the past achievements which have shaped our own world and bequeathed it many blessings.

The post-2000 aims: how well do they measure up?

I come back to the overall aims in the *Handbook* discussed in Chapter 1. How well do they match the account sketched out in the last section?

Their main shortcoming is that they simply comprise lists of items and lack an explicit rationale. The items are contained in two places – the statement on 'Values, aims and purposes' and the later section on 'Learning across the National Curriculum' – but are not logically related to each other. The lists of items are collected in sub-groups in both sections, but these do little to reveal their logical structure. In addition, not all the aims are on the same logical level:

- some are clearly vehicles for attaining wider aims in the list (e.g. those to do with literacy, numeracy, ICT, physical skills).
- others concern personal qualities and achievements desirable in pupils' lives as a whole (e.g. a sense of identity, emotional well-being, financial capability, the appreciation of human aspirations and achievements, thinking creatively and criti- cally, an ability to relate to others). These may be valuable in themselves and/or as means to further ends.
- at the most general level, there are aims to do with self-fulfilment, the pupil's well- being, concern for others, citizenship. These would appear to provide justifications for aims at lower levels.

It would be helpful if the aims could be arranged more systematically so as to show inter-relationships and patterns of justification.

This more systematic arrangement should go hand-in-hand with an explicit rationale. Presumably the aims included in the lists have been included for considered reasons. These reasons need to be spelt out in a coherent argument. This is important partly because some of the terms used are abstract or equivocal and the precise sense in which they are to be understood needs to be made clear. Examples are 'the well-being of the individual', 'equality of opportunity', 'spiritual development', 'cultural development'.

Finally, some of the aims may be logically confused. Those included under 'Think- ing skills', for instance. In discussing mathematics in Chapter 1 I mentioned the seduc- tiveness of thinking that there are general thinking skills, widely transferable across domains (see also Johnson, 2001). The *Handbook* includes 'reasoning skills' and 'creative thinking skills' and *apparently* (it is not altogether clear) treats them as general. But the kind of reasoning found in mathematics (or formal logic) is importantly different in many ways from that involved in designing products in design and technology (for one thing, the former is theoretical reasoning, the latter practical). There is no reason, as far as I am aware, to hold that creative (imaginative) thinking in formulating scientific hypotheses will transfer to the creative thinking of the story writer.

So much for defects in the post-2000 aims. Their strength lies in the ease with which they could be given a logical arrangement and rationale closely matching the 'democratic' account of the last section.

While in other contexts aims-statements have focussed on breadth and depth of learning for its own sake, or on the needs of the economy, or on preparation for leadership or for followership, the post-2000 aims return again and again to the flourishing of a certain sort of liberal democratic society. They stress the equal promotion of each citizen's well-being, acknowledging that this has to be based, at least for the most part, on self-understanding, autonomy and informed choice among options, including those to do with work, personal finance, relationships, beliefs and activities pursued for their own sake. At the same time these aims see citizens as not selfishly concerned with their own ends but as sensitive to their relationships with others and to others' needs, at various levels from intimate, through local and national, to regional and global. The democratic community is multicultural, hence aims to do with intercultural understanding and respect.

Other aims recognise the need for a strong economy and sustainable development in a healthy democracy and prepare pupils to make contributions to these. This acknowledges the need to prepare pupils for social and economic change. A broad understanding of aspects of the natural and human worlds is clearly necessary if all these purposes are to be met. It is also necessary for the wider aim of encouraging pupils to appreciate human aspirations and achievements in general.

It may be, of course, that I am reading too much into the statements about overall aims and urging an idiosyncratic interpretation of my own. I do not think this is so, but will have to leave it to readers to consider the full list of aims and draw their own conclusions.

How are the aims to be realised in curricular arrangements?

The post-2000 aims are a good first shot, for England and indeed for other countries should they wish to take them up, at a defensible set of educational objectives for a democratic society. They need recasting so as to remove deficiencies. In that way their rationale will become more patent and distinctions between more and less fundamental aims more clearly identifiable.

Suppose we assume this recasting. How can the aims be expected to have a bearing on curricular arrangements? I take it they are *indeed intended* to have a bearing on them – and not meant to be by-passable mission statements.

Planning the curriculum in the abstract must *begin* with overall aims. It cannot start with the status quo, for the question immediately arises whether current practices are defensible, and this takes one back straightaway to underlying aims. Curriculum policy-making in the short term cannot *in practice* begin with a blank sheet: it has to take into account, for instance, that so many thousands of teachers of secondary geography or music are now in post. But the compromises that will have to be struck can only rationally be struck against the background of some kind of more ideal picture and this is what I am concerned with here.

Filling in this picture in any detail would be a long task and here I can only give a sketch. For a fuller account, see the pamphlet which I co-authored for the Institute for Public Policy Research some years ago, called *A National Curriculum for All* (O'Hear and White, 1991).

I shall assume that, once recast, the aims will have gone some way to make general statements more determinate. When the *Handbook* talks, for instance, of education 'as a route to ... the well-being of the individual' (p. 10), how is this well-being to be understood? Has it to do with success in whatever goals one sets oneself? Or are there constraints on these goals? I have broached this issue above and will not now go further into rival philosophical positions. The only claim I am making is that *in some way* there needs to be greater determinacy at points like this. No doubt whatever resolution is arrived at will be controversial: few perspectives on human well-being will be acceptable to all parties. There is no undisputed starting-point for the aims of education: in the end decisions will have to be political decisions. As democratic decisions, they are in principle reversible. That is not to deny that in drawing up the aims effort should be made to make them as defensible as possible.

The recast aims will also indicate where one aim demands another. Being a 'responsible and caring citizen', for instance, requires understanding something both about democratic government in general and also about various economic and social features of one's own society in particular. This is a simple instance of how aims connected with personal qualities carry demands about aims to do with knowledge and understanding. Similarly, when the *Handbook* states that the school curriculum 'should prepare pupils for the next steps in their education, training and employment and equip them to make informed choices', this requires some understanding of the range of employment options.

Further specification is possible beyond points like this. How is one to categorise the range of employment options? The deductive method I have just been relying on needs to be supplemented by more empirical methods – bearing in mind that there could be several equally acceptable ways of grouping items.

Without proliferating examples further, I hope it is clear how a much fuller account of overall aims can be worked out. Just *how* full it needs to be is a further question. On the one hand, the state is properly responsible only for the broad framework, not for the details. On the other, sometimes statements can be too general. Suppose, for instance, national aims only go so far as to mention 'making informed choices about careers'. As it stands, this could cover the kind of careers education that used to be found in some secondary modern schools, introducing working class children only to a range of working class jobs. In this particular case, other aims, for example about equality of opportunity, could come in to prevent such a narrowing. In other cases, more specification at national level might be required. The issue is a difficult one on which to adjudicate in the abstract and would need case by case decisions.

Let us suppose that problems like this one are behind us and we have a full and reasonable set of national aims. Somehow these will have had to be grouped in logically arranged categories along the way. There is no one way of doing this and again I have no nostrums in the abstract. In the IPPR pamphlet mentioned above Philip O'Hear and I broke things down after the following pattern (with further categories under each heading):

a   personal qualities

  i   personal concerns
  ii social involvement and concern for others
  iii critical and reflective awareness

b   knowledge and understanding

  i   social
  ii scientific
  iii personal

c　experience of the arts

d　practical competencies

    i　communication and literacy
    ii　physical movement, health and safety
    iii　planning and organisation
    iv　social interaction

Let's take it, then, that the aims have worked out in appropriate detail and are arranged in sensible categories. The next question is this. How are the aims to be realised? Via what vehicles can the experiences planned for pupils (the essence of the curriculum on the *Handbook* definition (see p. 6)) be shaped in accordance with the aims? Here there are two main possibilities: timetabled activities and whole school processes. I begin with the latter.

Whole school processes

As we saw in Chapter 1 (pp. 4–5), in the *Handbook* there is a preponderance of overall aims to do with personal qualities. Whole school processes can assist timetabled activities in helping to foster these. Together, they can help to build up dispositions in pupils to think and act on a day-to-day basis in accordance with these values.

From a functional point of view, whole school processes are as much vehicles for realising aims as timetabled activities. So there is as much reason to introduce mandatory and recommended procedures for these as for the timetabled curriculum.

Examples of relevant whole school processes are policies and practices on:

- regular staff (including on occasion non-teaching staff) discussion about overall aims: their nature, rationale, means of realising them.
- collective decision making across the staff on the whole timetabled curriculum plan.
- assessment and recording/reporting progress.
- the school as a model of a democratic workplace.
- acquainting pupils with the overall aims and discussing with them their nature and rationale.
- the encouragement of informed choices at school.
- making learning enjoyable for all pupils.
- teacher–pupil, teacher–teacher, and pupil–pupil relationships and attitudes.
- setting and maintaining a code of conduct.
- reaching consensus with parents about overall aims: their nature, rationale, means of realising them at home and at school.
- encouraging pupils and rewarding them for success in realising overall aims.
- relationships with the local community which support the overall aims.
- promoting equal access to learning.
- developing a social life and extra-curricular programme.
- establishing and supporting interactive styles of teaching and learning.

For further details on whole school processes, see O'Hear and White (1991), pp. 17–19.

Timetabled activities

The timetabled curriculum is not necessarily confined to school subjects. We need to know the most appropriate vehicles for realising the aims and should not assume that these will always be discrete subjects – let alone the current subjects of the National Curriculum. Topic-based or integrated courses; various practical activities; periods of free private study; wider groupings such as 'the arts' rather than music; visual arts and literature as separate subjects, are all in the ring, as well as forms of classroom organisation and pedagogy. On the other hand, subjects do reflect to some extent logical differences in the organisation of knowledge and awareness; and they have behind them years of experience in internal structuring and sequencing of learning. It makes sense to draw on their strengths while avoiding their weaknesses. Perhaps the most serious of the latter is their tendency over time to become worlds of their own, battlemented against their neighbours and wider social demands. Newer National Curriculum subjects like design and technology, PSHE and citizenship are freer from this criticism, being all well in mesh with the wider aims. This is also true of social studies, which is not currently a subject of the English school curriculum, but has a strong claim to be included.

In remodelling the school curriculum to fit the new aims, there is a strong case for reviewing and reorganising the current subject-based programmes of study so that they find their proper place among other curricular vehicles. This is not a task that I can broach here. For one thing, it must be built on the recast aims which have still to be worked out. Meanwhile, some indication of how planning may proceed in further detail can be found in the IPPR pamphlet (O'Hear and White, 1991, pp. 19–22). Those pages spell out one way in which subjects and other vehicles can work together in realising aims.

Conclusion

This chapter has looked at fundamental questions about who should determine the aims of the school curriculum, what these aims should be, and how they can be realised in curricular arrangements. Although the issues are important for any educational system, the chapter has discussed them in the context of English education, providing a critique of current developments as well as indications of how things can be improved.

The focus throughout has been on state-wide prescriptions drawn from official documentation. These take us only so far towards the planned pupil experiences which lie at the heart of the curriculum. A crucial further step is found in the curricular arrangements made by schools and teachers when they interpret (or sideline?) official pronouncements in the light of local circumstances. It is at this stage that planned pupil experiences come centrally into the picture.

To what extent pupils' experiences actually match up to teachers' intentions is a further question. They may include feelings of disaffection, low self worth or distaste towards a subject; and if these become habitual, what children may end up acquiring may be beliefs and personal qualities that are the opposite of what their teachers want – beliefs that academic study is a waste of time, or personal qualities like poor self-esteem.

This chapter has had a wider focus than Chapter 1. That raised questions about the adequacy of the present subjects of the English school curriculum; historical and other obstacles in the way of their meeting more general aims; and how they might move forward. In the next, central, chapters of the book these issues are pursued in more depth, subject by subject. The starting point here is the official curriculum. The essays that follow are sensitive to the differences between what is laid down in government documentation, curricular arrangements made by teachers, and the actual as well as the planned experiences of pupils.

References

DfEE/QCA (1999) *The National Curriculum Handbook for primary/secondary teachers in England*.

Giddens, A. (1991) *Modernity and Self-identity: Self and Society in the Late Modern Age*, Stanford: Stanford University Press.

Griffin, J. (1996) *Value Judgement: Improving our Ethical Beliefs*, Oxford: Clarendon Press.

Johnson, S. (2001) *Teaching Thinking Skills*, Impact Pamphlet No 8: Philosophy of Education Society of Great Britain.

O'Hear, P. and White, J. (1991) *A National Curriculum for All: Laying the Foundations for Success*, London: Institute for Public Policy Research.

3 Art and design

John Steers

Background

It might be expected that the National Curriculum statutory Order for Art in England, introduced in 1992 and subsequently twice modified, was the considered outcome of a rare opportunity to consider the philosophy, purpose and content of the subject from first principles. What emerged from the Art Working Group was a rational but far from radical conceptual framework that essentially codified an existing tradition. This was distorted by the National Curriculum Council to create an artificial divide between theory and practice with two attainment targets, 'Investigating and Making' and 'Knowledge and Understanding'. The revised curriculum introduced in 2000 had a single attainment target, 'Knowledge, skills and understanding' with four strands. Strand 1, 'Investigating and making art, craft and design', strand 2, 'Exploring and developing ideas' and strand 3, 'Evaluating and developing work'. The remaining strand, 4, 'Knowledge and understanding' is expected to inform all these processes.

The development of the National Curriculum for art and design has been a process of compromise and précis apparently designed to make it fit a similar basic template as other subjects. Embedded within it is a traditional, modernist approach to teaching and learning in this subject with roots in two sets of ideas. The first stems from a tradition of working from direct observation and an emphasis on process, promoted strongly by the Art Advisers Association in the 1970s and early 1980s, sanctioned by HMI, and perpetuated in secondary schools by the examination boards. The second important influence comes from domain-based curriculum models that emerged first in the United States in the late 1960s and which later informed the development of assessment criteria for the GCSE in the mid-1980s. These strands now have coalesced in a predominant approach where children and young adults all too often produce work that is formulaic in subject, style and concept.

Arguably, the introduction of the National Curriculum did little to change pre-existing practice, especially in secondary schools, except to cause a decline in design and craft activities and make critical and contextual studies a required element of the subject. Hughes, reflecting on the need to reconceptualise the art and design curriculum, described it as an arbitrary set of practices passed down over the years and, through process of accretion, absorbed to form the canon of the subject:

> The result is a set of procedures, processes and practices which are a kind of historical trace of past theories of art education, child development or art, craft and

design practice, all existing simultaneously and each exemplified by activities which jockey for time and space.

(Hughes, 1998: 45)

The subject literature for the past decade or so includes frequent critical references to a prevailing orthodoxy of approach. Binch describes how the GCSE examination introduced in the mid-1980s, with its strong emphasis on 'process' often led to a single classroom methodology, particularly in secondary schools, where the starting point is usually investigation and research. This is followed by development of ideas, some 'experimental' activities and the completion of a 'finished' piece of work. Whilst the investigation and research could be into any relevant matters, including the work of artists, craftspeople and designers, or into concepts, issues and ideas, Binch notes that:

> it is most commonly based upon objective drawing and visual analysis. The predominant sources of reference are collections of objects set up in the art room. The model reinforces the insular nature of 'school-art' and, even when reference is made to external sources, it is usually based on the same methodology of objective drawing and visual analysis.
>
> (Binch, 1994: 124)

The high stakes education system makes teachers adept at finding effective prescriptions for their students that enable them to satisfy the QCA's assessment objectives. This approach often produces 'safe' work of a kind on which teachers can rely for the award of good examination grades. Thus teachers try to meet the demands of league tables, inspection, and appraisal for threshold payments. Work that is seen to be well rewarded by the system is rapidly imitated and what once was a genuinely innovative or creative approach is reduced in no time to cliché or pastiche.

This phenomenon is not new – the history of art education in schools is littered with examples of 'school art'. It is easy to recall a sequence of once fashionable and ubiquitous images: monotone drawings of Che Guevara; work dependent on the Sunday newspaper colour supplements; studies of sections of vegetables and fruit; baseball boots and trainers; images from 'in' record sleeves; crushed Coca-Cola cans; rubber plants; reflections in stainless steel kitchen utensils – to that long-running all-time favourite, the sliced pepper. What these 'school art' exercises have in common is their almost total lack of any relationship to contemporary art and design activity beyond the school art room. A key concern, therefore, is the apparent lack of alternatives to these tired and derivative approaches.

Art and design education needs to change if it is not to atrophy through its sheer indifference to students' own interests and concerns (and to those of parents, higher education and employers). The National Curriculum has not faced this challenge and, despite the subject's re-designation in the 2000 version as 'Art and Design', there is strong evidence of recent retrenchment in a limited fine art approach (Mason and Iwano, 1995). The National Curriculum removes any real incentive to explore new approaches or visions of the art and design curriculum – its very existence proclaims that the problem of what to teach has been finally codified, there is no need to look further. And yet:

> we are still delivering art curricula in our schools predicated largely upon procedures and practices that reach back to the nineteenth century – procedures and

practices which cling to a comfortable and uncontentious view of art and its purposes. As a result, secondary art and design education in England and Wales is, in
general, static, safe and predictable.

(Hughes, 1998: 41)

In the present education climate, with an often corrosive emphasis on quasi-
vocational utility, assessment, league tables, monitoring and inspection, it is hard to
convince government of the need for radical change. There are conflicting calls from
within the field to adopt new approaches to art education to take account, for example,
of new technologies. Or perhaps to embrace media education; align art education with
postmodern trends in arts practice; to adopt a multicultural approach; celebrate diversity
or to place primary emphasis on the transmission of an ill-defined cultural heritage.
There is little coherence to these proposals and there is a danger that, as so often in the
past, any 'development' will consist of grafting additional concerns onto an already
shaky conceptual framework.

A brief history of art and design education

There is evidence that art and design education has evolved through an often uncritical
process of adding extraneous elements to a particular view of what at the time constituted 'good practice'. The extent of international influences may seem surprising –
there has been interchange of ideas and practices for more than a century facilitated,
partly, by international organisations such as the International Society for Education
through Art (InSEA).[1] It is possible to discern traces of the French atelier system, the
Weimar Bauhaus, Scandinavian craft activities, and the last vestiges of liberal, child-
centred ideas of education with a lineage from Rousseau, through Pestalozzi, Froebel
and Cizek to Richardson and Read. Very little stemming from these various philosophies will be encountered in a pure form, instead half-grasped beliefs with their
origins in a variety of rationales filter their way into the classroom.

The aims, values and content of art education have always been contested.
Thistlewood identifies the key paradox in competing conceptions of art and design
education as 'a matter of strategic economic necessity; [or] . . . as comparable to other
arts and humanities and worthy of disinterested study for its own sake' (Thistlewood,
1992: 8). Macdonald (1970) similarly recognises that art and design can be an instrument of either a utilitarian or liberal education, with ensuing pedagogy tending to
emphasise either systematic training or individual freedom of expression. Thistlewood concludes that histories of art and design education seldom reveal clear historical pathways because the various elements are so tightly interwoven and
contradictory: 'design versus fine art; instruction versus freedom from instruction;
the object versus the conceptual experience' (Thistlewood, 1992: 9). He argues that
it is difficult to ignore the fact that fundamental, irreconcilable disagreements about
policies, rationales and justifications have been usual. 'Revolution versus convention;
child-centrality versus subject centrality; the expressive versus the utilitarian – in
some form or other they feature in every account of what has taken place before
now' (Thistlewood, 1992: 8). What are the priorities at the start of the twenty-first
century – perhaps education *in* art, education *for* art, or education *through* art or some
combination of these?

The first meeting of the Society for the Encouragement of Arts, Manufactures and

Commerce in 1754 provides early evidence of a utilitarian approach when it was decided to give rewards to encourage drawing:

> And it being the Opinion of all present that ye Art of Drawing is absolutely Necessary in many Employments, Trades, and Manufactures, and that the Encouragement thereof may prove of great Utility to the public, it was resolved to bestow Premiums on a certain Number of Boys or Girls under the Age of Sixteen, who shall produce the best pieces of Drawing, and shew themselves most capable, when properly examined.
>
> (Macdonald, 1970: 36)

The nineteenth century saw a rapid increase in the growth of art institutions, the first training school for art teachers, the first government art examinations and teaching certificates, the first state art education in the public day schools, and the first art masters' association.[2] The Board of Trade promoted the Schools of Design to ensure a supply of skilled artisans for manufacturing industry. Drawing was seen as the central tool for improving ability and it was taught in a strictly curtailed imitative manner where accurate replication was the criterion for success. Drawing was also encouraged in elementary schools from the 1830s and lessons were usually dependent on copying from exemplars such as the government 'Drawing Book'. If its primary purpose was utilitarian there was also some recognition also of how it might support other learning:

> Drawing has hitherto been looked upon as a polite accomplishment, in which it is graceful to be proficient ... It however affords great aid in defining, expressing and retaining certain ideas ... and must assist in the formation of habits of attention from the circumstances of its requiring so much care and accuracy.
>
> (Central Committee of Education (1836) in Macdonald, 1970: 153)

In 1852 the Board of Trade established the Department of Practical Art and a national system of art education was set up of such thoroughness and rigidity that it truly merited the name 'cast iron'. A course of instruction was introduced for training teachers and pupil-teachers for the public day schools:

> The Primary or First Grade Course for schools was strictly utilitarian and started with linear geometry and perspective, then continued with outlines of simple objects from the flat copy. After this the children were allowed to copy solid geometrical shapes, and then returned to the flat copy to draw outlines of the human figure and animals. The final achievement was drawing flowers in outline and painting them, both from flat copies.
>
> (Macdonald, 1970: 167)

A dual purpose was made clear by HM Inspectors of Education:

> The kind of drawing which it is proposed to teach, is, in the strictest sense, an education of the eye, and of the hand, such as may indeed be the first step in the career of a great artist, but must at any rate enable the common workman to do his work more neatly and better.
>
> (Committee of Council on Education (1857–1858), in Macdonald, 1970: 168)

A utilitarian grip on the art and design curriculum persisted well into the twentieth century and the 'Kensington system of art-teaching' went mainly unchallenged throughout the Empire. However one vociferous critic was John Ruskin who opposed the division between training for the applied arts and education for fine art. He had non-conformist views on the art education of young and he advocated parents allowing their child:

> To scrawl at its own free will, due praise being given for every appearance of care, or truth, in its efforts ... it should have colours at command; and, without restraining its choice of subject ... it should be gently led by the parents to try to draw, in such childish fashion as may be, the things it can see and likes – birds, or butterflies, or flowers or fruit.
>
> (Ruskin, 1857: vi)

Nevertheless Ruskin warned that in later years the indulgence of using colour should only be granted as a reward, after a child has shown care and progress in its pencil drawings. Perhaps more 'child-centred' than most of his contemporaries, he was not so radical in his views that he failed to urge constant, careful imitation and observation. But Ruskin was famously clear about the purpose of art education:

> I would rather teach drawing that my pupils may learn to love Nature, than teach the looking at Nature that they may learn to draw. It is surely also a more important thing, for young people and unprofessional students, to know how to appreciate the art of others, than to gain much power in art themselves.
>
> (Ruskin, 1857: xii)

In Germany in the first years of the twentieth century, Bruno Paul held the view that art schools had a responsibility, both to artists and society, to provide vocational training that would enable students to be socially useful. After the Great War, Paul merged the Berlin Academy of Art with the School of Decorative Art and declared that all students, whether they intended to become fine artists or artist craftspeople or designers should be trained in essentially the same way. Between 1919 and 1933 the staff of the influential Weimar Bauhaus included Josef Albers, Johannes Itten, Paul Klee, Wassily Kandinsky, Laslo Moholy-Nagy, Marcel Breuer and Mies van der Rohe. The vision of Walter Gropius, its founding director:

> was to unite all arts and crafts to create a new architecture that comprised a living environment; to break down the false separation between the applied arts and the fine arts, between art and utility; and to train artists in the creative possibilities of machine design.
>
> (*Encyclopaedia Britannica*, 1998)

When the Bauhaus was closed by the Nazis in 1933, many of the staff went to work in the United States, but their ideas were taken up in the United Kingdom in the 1950s and 1960s by the 'Basic Design Movement'. A group of artist teachers, who included Richard Hamilton, Victor Pasmore, Harry Thubron and Tom Hudson, sought to understand and explore the underlying 'grammar' and 'formal elements' of art and design through precise analysis of visual phenomena. Basic design courses were first established in art schools but their influence spread to general education, partly through publications such as de Sausmarez's '*Basic Design: The Dynamics of Visual Form*' (1964). One legacy of this movement in the National Curriculum is the emphasis on the so-called 'formal elements' of art and design.

The philosophy of the Child Art Movement of the 1930s can be traced to Jean Jacques Rousseau and the idea that each child needs a special type of education suited to individual needs and development – liberal ideas that in turn were espoused by Pestalozzi and Froebel. By the early twentieth century the Austrian Franz Cizek could declare that 'Child Art is an art which only the child can produce' – recognition that children's work could be worthy of being seen as 'art' in its own right was a milestone in the history of art education. Cizek believed that children should be allowed freedom of expression and preserved from adult influences. Yet the work that he exhibited in London in 1908 was sophisticated and highly disciplined, often in the demanding form of woodcuts and papercuts. 'It was their sheer competence which astonished British and American art teachers, many of whom thought that a well-shaded group of solids was the apogee of child art' (Macdonald, 1970: 345).

The 'New Art Teaching', initiated by two London County Council inspectors, Marion Richardson and R.R. Tomlinson, flourished between 1930–1939. Richardson opposed Cizek's ideas, considering the results of his approach most unchildlike. She searched for a more psychologically relevant art education, more suited to the child's individual development stage and realised that children need positive stimulation by the teacher before they can understand how to express their own ideas. She developed a range of strategies for enabling children to develop their own imagery including 'mind pictures', where children painted from mental images rather than observation. It is child-centred ideas of art education that unjustly seem to give rise to a persistent view which equates art education with promoting an undisciplined 'free for all' where 'anything goes'. Roger Scruton who claims that rigorous education separates past 'geniuses' from today's 'creative' artists provides a typical recent example. In polemic devoid of evidence he states:

> Children write poetry before they have memorised a single line of it, dance before they have learnt a single step, paint and daub without the faintest knowledge of figurative drawing. . . . grammar, spelling and punctuation are downgraded in the interest of self-expression.

> (Scruton, 2001: 6)

The central argument in Herbert Read's seminal text '*Education through Art*' is now often taken for granted. But the self-proclaimed anarchist Read saw it as nothing short of revolutionary. He wrote:

> We declare that our foremost aim is 'the establishment of an education in art which will develop the imaginative and creative powers of children', and that, to the outside world, must seem as harmless as any cause that ever brought two or three people together. But those who have followed through the implications of this aim know that it is packed with enough dynamite to shatter the existing educational system, and to bring about a revolution in the whole structure of our Society.

> (Read, 1965:1)

The competing ideologies of child-centred art educators and the proponents of the new basic design movement clashed at a Society for Education through Art conference in 1956 where the protagonists;

> almost came to blows over their respective views of the purpose and content of art and design education. In one sense it was the old being replaced by the new, but in another, the inevitable changes being brought about by different needs and contexts both within and outside art and design. Herbert Read had been the champion of child centredness . . . but was also a figurehead for the new Basic Design and was seen according to the different camps as traitor or prophet.
>
> (Swift, 2000: 4)

Not for the first time, neither side could be said to have won the debate. Rather, aspects of both approaches settled down to take their place in the confused matrix of art and design education. For a period in the 1960s to mid 1980s 'Design Education' offered a new rationale to be integrated into art and design. The work of Peter Green at Hornsey College of Art, and Bruce Archer and Ken Baynes at the Royal College of Art's Design Education Unit was particularly important in this respect, as was the influence of the Design Council. Design was seen as a critical area of experience and learning in the contemporary world which needed a cross-curricular approach in schools, and one in which art and design was expected to make a significant contribution. Baynes' (1985) seminal paper 'Defining a Design Dimension of the Curriculum' provides a full account of some subtle ideas that deserved to have flourished more, but they were discarded in the development of the National Curriculum.

A recent significant development in art and design education has been the introduction of 'Critical and Contextual Studies'. This originates in ideas about extending the range of art and design education beyond practical making.[3] An early reference can be found in a US Department of Education publication (1970), where four objectives for art education were identified. These were developing the ability to:

1   perceive and respond to aesthetic elements in art.
2   recognise and accept art as a realm of experience and participate in activities related to art.
3   know about art.
4   form reasoned critical judgments about the significance and quality of works of art.

In the USA, Elliot Eisner's influential *Educating Artistic Vision* (1972) advocated production, art criticism and art history as the three major components of the art curriculum and his ideas soon had a following in the United Kingdom. In the States they were formative in the development of *Discipline Based Art Education*, a curriculum model with four domains: art production, art criticism, art history and aesthetics. Brian Allison was instrumental in bringing these ideas to the United Kingdom and he also advocated a four-domain curriculum model: Expressive/Productive; Perceptual; Analytical/Critical and Historical/Cultural (Allison, 1982). Allison's ideas had first surfaced in a 1977 Schools Council (1977) document where the aims of art education were summarised as 'making, looking at, thinking about, feeling about, knowing about and responding to art, craft and design'.

In turn, new domain models emerged, most of which were variations on a theme of combining art appreciation with art making. In 1986 the Secondary Examinations Council GCSE Grade Criteria Working Party proposed a three-domain model comprising a Conceptual Domain, a Productive Domain and a Critical and Contextual Domain concerned with those aspects of art and design which enable candidates to express ideas and insights which reflect a developing awareness of their own work and that of others. This model clearly influenced the ideas of the National Curriculum Art Working Group whose initial proposals for a three-attainment target curriculum model ('Understanding', 'Making' and 'Investigating') were scuppered by the then Secretary of State Kenneth Clark.

Critical and contextual studies had been accepted into the mainstream following the work of the Critical Studies in Art Education project (1981–1988), the principal outcome of which was publication of Rod Taylor's influential book *Educating for Art* (1986). Taylor's energetic and charismatic promotion of his ideas ensured its legacy was considerably less ephemeral than most curriculum development projects. However, it was also an idea whose time was right because resource pressures in schools were making it impossible to sustain the more formal approach to teaching the history of art, design and architecture required by the CSE and GCE 'O' and 'A' level examinations.

This brief synopsis of the history of art and design education would not be complete without mention of the SCDC/NCC 'Arts in Schools Project' which coincided with the development of the National Curriculum. The project was led by Ken Robinson, and as some years earlier in the Gulbenkian Report 'The Arts in Schools' (Robinson, 1982), he appeared to set out a generic case for the inclusion of 'the arts' rather than specific arts disciplines in the curriculum (National Curriculum Council (1990)). For reasons that were as much strategic than philosophical, this was bitterly opposed by the majority of the art and design community. A vigorous debate ensued that was eventually resolved in favour of separate disciplines by a narrow majority in the House of Lords on the eve of enactment of the Education Reform Act.[4]

Some years prior to the introduction of the National Curriculum, Maurice Barrett was able to identify six distinct rationales underpinning art education in secondary schools – fine art; art and craft; design education; conceptual; visual education; and graphicacy. Similarly the American, Edmund Feldman (1982), identified four varieties of art curriculum – technical, psychological, anthropological or aesthetic. Today, debates about postmodern approaches to art and design education, the role of new media and technologies, and cultural and visual literacy are more evident in other countries than in the United Kingdom.[5] Such diversity is no longer in evidence in English schools because the ability of art and design teachers to determine their own priorities and rationales has been lost. The National Curriculum sets out *what* should be taught and although, in theory, *how* it should be taught is not prescribed, the assessment and monitoring regime creates considerable wash back on classroom practice. It should be recognised that the National Curriculum for art and design, at best, can only offer a *single* view of the subject. Inevitably, other equally valid visions or contributions to thinking about the subject are lost from sight.

The National Curriculum 2000

The 2000 curriculum includes for the first time a statement about the supposed importance of each subject:

Art and design stimulates creativity and imagination. It provides visual, tactile and sensory experiences and a unique way of understanding and responding to the world. Pupils use colour, form, texture, pattern and different materials and processes to communicate what they see, feel and think. Through art and design activities, they learn to make informed value judgements and aesthetic and practical decisions, becoming actively involved in shaping environments. They explore ideas and meanings in the work of artists, craftspeople and designers. They learn about the diverse roles and functions of art, craft and design in contemporary life, and in different times and cultures. Understanding, appreciation and enjoyment of the visual arts have the power to enrich our personal and public lives.

(DfEE, 2000)

The single attainment target 'Knowledge, Skills and Understanding' might easily be used for any subject in the curriculum. The four strands lack the clarity of most of the curriculum domain models described above. Indeed the strands – 'Investigating and making art, craft and design', 'Exploring and developing ideas', 'Evaluating and developing work' – all involve complex interwoven and over-lapping processes which cannot help but be 'informed' in different ways by the final strand, 'Knowledge and understanding'.

Since the 1991 report of the Art Working Group, revisions of art and design in the National Curriculum have been more a process of précis than development, driven by alleged manageability issues. Overall the 2000 document is as arid as its predecessors and the rationale statement is innocuous, neither inspiring nor particularly illuminating. It offers no coherent explanation of *why* studying art and design is important, but assumes it is self-evident that the listed activities should be a significant part of the general education. It attempts to encompass existing safe 'good practice' in the fewest possible words but lacks any clear theoretical or philosophical coherence. Economic or vocational arguments for studying art and design are ignored and the 'visual arts' are favoured over craft or design. It pretends that all the long-standing 'fundamental, irreconcilable disagreements about policies, rationales and justifications' have been resolved. Thus no competing visions or rationales are necessary – this is finally *it*, art and design education comprehensively sorted, packaged and made ready for use by classroom operatives.

In 1995 Ross (1995: 273) claimed that an overwhelming feature of the English National Curriculum Orders for art is that they only make sense to practitioners who do not need them. Only those who already know something about progression and development are able to supply the differentiating detail to understand the descriptors. He argued that:

In almost every case the specification of elements in the programmes as stages in a sequence of learning is a blatant sham. The intended effect of the typographical layout is to persuade by impression rather than substance. The intention is to create an illusion of progression – in other words, to fabricate a *fiction*. It is my belief that the whole project translates into a fiction – a set of inscriptions that are no more than that. They rely for their force upon the mere fact of having been written down. They claim the authority of a financial spreadsheet. Not only might the exercise be misconceived ... because learning in the arts is not like this, it fails even on its own terms because when it is rendered as articulate statement, it is self-evident (and pretentious) nonsense.

Little has changed with the 2000 curriculum for which the QCA has published exemplary schemes of work to 'support' art and design. While there may be some teachers, especially in primary schools, who need support and guidance for teaching art and design, there is no lack of such material available from local authority, commercial and subject association publications and on-line curriculum resources. Instead of the flexibility the QCA claims it wants to encourage, it is already evident that its detailed scheme of work for art and design is becoming *the* scheme of work for the subject in many primary schools (HMI, 2001). Rather than providing guidance, it is adopted in its entirety if only as a safeguard against criticism from Ofsted. There appears to be no plan to revise the scheme of work so the danger exists of the published cycle being repeated annually and, to compound the orthodoxy problem, it is highly unlikely that other publishers will take the financial risk of competing with the 'official' scheme.

National curricula, *per se*, are designed to define and standardise what knowledge should be transmitted and invariably concentrate on what is to be *taught* rather than *learnt*. The attainment targets concentrate on relatively easily defined competencies, processes and skills, reinforced by guidance on planning and by formal assessment. Elliot Eisner (1985: 387) argues that trying to produce curriculum materials that are intended to be teacher proof is a mistake: 'teachers need materials that stimulate their ingenuity rather than materials to which they are subservient'. Another American observer, Brent Wilson (1995: 346), suggests that all too often national curricula for art 'fragment the outcomes of art education into discrete bits. They fail to distinguish between outcomes of greater and lesser importance.' The 2000 version of the curriculum provides a case in point.

It is not a question of returning to a non-existent Golden Age of art education. However, history shows that in the past ideas about how best to teach the subject were not just contested but alternative, experimental approaches were continually explored. Instead of encouraging this creative flux, the National Curriculum and formal assessment acts as a drag anchor on development – a modernist or formalist framework is retained which limits the scope of the subject and reinforces orthodoxy. Little attempt has been made to consider postmodern perspectives or to debate and define what art and design education is actually *for* at the start of the twenty-first century. There is little incentive or opportunity to explore radical alternatives since the QCA has an effective monopoly of curriculum development – it may take as long to shake off this stranglehold as it did in the nineteenth century to loosen the iron grip of the South Kensington system. What is at stake here is a choice between atrophy and a vital and relevant future for teaching and learning in art and design. It is a future that will require well-trained creative teachers with the confidence to take creative risks and create a climate in which the creativity and imagination of their students can flourish.

Towards revitalised art and design education

In 1998–1999, with the prospect of a review of the National Curriculum ahead, the National Society for Education in Art and Design (NSEAD) with the support of the Arts Council of England convened a working group to consider reform art and design education. A series of seminars on 'The Art Curriculum and the Postmodern World' contributed to a special 'Directions' issue of the international *Journal of Art and Design Education*.[6] Central to this publication was 'A Manifesto for Art in Schools' (Swift and Steers, 1999) which drew wide – and not far from unanimous – support at well-attended national conferences convened to debate the issues. Sir William Stubbs, then chair of the QCA and rector of The London Institute of Art and Design, addressed the last of these seminars.

The manifesto defined three fundamental principles of a postmodern art and design curriculum – *difference*; *plurality*, and *independent thought*. It was emphasised that through their application in art and design practice and theory:

> knowledge and knowing will become understood as a negotiation of ideas which arise from asking pertinent questions, and testing provisional answers rather than seeking predetermined ones. The emphasis is on the learner and learning, negotiating what they learn, learning how to learn, and understanding knowledge as a multiplicity of changing hypotheses or theories which are subject to evidence, proof, argument and embodiment.
>
> (Swift and Steers, 1999: 7)

Consideration of *difference* becomes a locus for action and discussion at a personal and social level. *Plurality* points to a variety of available methods, means, solutions and awareness for approaching any issue. *Independent thought* develops individuality, the capacity to challenge received opinion, and fosters creativity through introspection into the nature of learning and teaching in art. Understanding these principles is as vital for learners as it is for teachers.

Perhaps needless to say, the manifesto's arguments were rejected by QCA and they resulted in no discernible influence on the 2000 curriculum following the introduction of which, the problems remain the same as those set out in the manifesto. So do the solutions. The first essential is to re-design the preparation and development of teachers to give them the confidence to embody and promote risk-taking, personal enquiry, and creative action and thought throughout their teaching career.

Second, it is vital that there should be more opportunities for learners to understand art and design as something that can actually *matter* in their lives and has *relevance* to present and future action. There needs to be more choice, autonomy and empowerment through the development of a more critical, enquiring reflexive and creative mindset to assist self-generated and self-aware learning. Instead of the drab routines of 'school art', the curriculum should be planned to raise consciousness of real personal and social issues, and their representation in past and present art forms through an essentially intercultural curriculum. Gundera and Fyfe demand development of strategies for intercultural visual literacy and warn that positive action needs to be undertaken urgently:

> There has to be a constant and fundamental reappraisal of the histories and national identities into which we have all been inducted with such care. . . . Art education remains tied to a hegemonic canon, shut up in a cultural prison, which recognises only its own art forms, or, if it recognises those outside it, interprets them according to its own values. Opening the prison demands an intercultural curriculum, a multifaceted and multifocal curriculum, which redefines the canon of art history

and presents the traditions of the world within their own standards, not those of the Eurocentric tradition.

(Gundera and Fyfe, 1999: 87)

Design education should focus on addressing real needs, while the mainstay of art activity should be what it has always been – what it is to be human. The universal themes of birth, death, love, war, gender, disease, spirituality and identity can be re-examined in the context of our rich and varied postmodern, post-colonial, multi-ethnic and multi-faith society.

Third, all pupils, including the most able, should be encouraged and entitled to study art and design throughout their compulsory schooling. There should be more flexibility to specialise within the discipline at Key Stage 3 and greater opportunities to make a well-informed choice about whether to continue with it as an examination subject at Key Stage 4. The choice and type of study available across all forms of art and design must be broadened without the present implied hierarchy that places 'fine art' at the apogee. There should be opportunities to choose to study a range of media and technologies, all underpinned by diverse but well articulated rationales. This requires the development of a variety of curricula permitting a choice of either broadly focussed studies within the inevitable resource constraints, or more in-depth approaches to specialisms within the wider curriculum area. Instead of the statutory and monolithic National Curriculum, *multiple visions* of the art and design curriculum should be encouraged and developed. The many-sided traditions that consciously, or more often sub-consciously, have influenced current practice can be reviewed, up-dated and augmented if still relevant. Thus diverse aims, practices and purposes would be designed to encourage difference, plurality and independence, perhaps through modules related to age, ability or intention, or through specific approaches to specific areas of study (for example, new media, the built environment, or three-dimensional design) or a combination of these. The present orthodoxy of theory always informing practice should not be taken for granted, and older students should have the choice of studying art and design theory without necessarily having to engage in studio work.

The largely unquestioned assertion that necessarily 'art and design includes craft' should be challenged. While it is evident that there are ways in which these disciplines are interdependent and interrelated, it can equally be argued that they are distinct practices with different theoretical bases. It has been noted that in the last decade both design and craft activities in school art departments have declined. Perhaps from Key Stage 3 onwards, in addition to a general course, there should be the possibility of specialising in art, or design, or craft.

Fourth, for these ideas to take root in schools, it will be necessary to reconsider the values implicit in current assessment and examination practices, to whom the results of such practices are addressed and for what purpose, and their respective usefulness. Instead of the imposition of an assessment template that is common to all subjects, there is a need to recognise authentic subject specific assessment approaches appropriate to varied aims and rationales within each subject area. Assessment criteria need to be re-examined to expose the mainly hidden inferences that reinforce present orthodoxies, such as 'accuracy', 'likeness', 'perspective', 'expressive', 'original', unless these are clearly stated and explained. More consideration should be given to self-assessment and terminal 'tests' should be rejected in favour of procedures that require students to engage in longer term, more complex and challenging projects, working in teams when it is appropriate to do so. Authentic assessment would depend mainly on portfolio evidence of development, written or recorded student reflections and teacher–student dialogue. Assessment in this area is a matter of informed *judgement* rather than the application of fallible standardised criteria; objectivity in art judgements is based on the comparative and experiential knowledge of the assessors, on connoisseurship, rather than limited prescription.

A secure place for art and design in schools has been a seductive, if illusory, goal that many in the field thought might be achieved through its recognition in National Curriculum legislation. But time and resources remain limited – for most students there are approximately 400 hours for formal art and design education in the years of compulsory schooling. The average amount spent on the subject in state-maintained schools is £1.18 at Key Stage 1 and £1.29 at Key Stage 2 per pupil per year, rising to a paltry £2.68 at secondary level (Edwards *et al.*, 2001). While the future of art and design education depends on expanding the range and variety of what might be studied, it is hardly realistic just to bolt on a few extras to an under-resourced and shaky curriculum framework. It is evident that merely modifying or replacing the curriculum Orders for Art and Design will not resolve all the problems that have been identified; the interconnectedness of teaching, learning, subject knowledge, assessment, and the preparation and development of teachers has to be recognised and properly resourced.

In sum, more decision-making and authority for teachers and learners is needed within a climate of enquiry, creative risk-taking and opportunity. This means re-addressing the content of art education, encouraging development of diverse approaches and finding improved ways to promote curriculum innovation – requiring greater flexibility than is allowed by the present statutory curriculum. Investment in creative, sometimes risky, curriculum development is essential in order to develop varied but rigorous and effective teaching and learning strategies. The QCA could evaluate such endeavours but should not seek to control them. The education and in-service development of must include the essential theoretical and philosophical underpinning needed to sustain them in practice. Reappraisal is needed of all forms of assessment and evaluation, including teacher appraisal and the priorities of school inspection. Only then will the fundamental values of art and design have a realistic opportunity to integrate with the current and future interests of students and of society in meaningful ways for the subject and individuals while contributing fully to the values claimed for the National Curriculum.[7]

Notes

1   The International Federation for Teaching of Drawing and of the Arts Applied to Industry held its first congress in 1900 and its successor the International Society for Education through Art (InSEA) was founded in the 1950s.
2   The Society of Art Masters was founded in 1888. It is the direct antecedent of the present day National Society for Education in Art and Design.
3   Several accounts can be found in the *Journal of Art and Design Education* Volume 12, No. 3, 1993, Abingdon: Carfax.
4   For further discussion of the Arts in Schools debate see the following papers in the *Journal of Art and Design Education*: Steers, J. (1991) 'Current Issues in Art and Design Education: The Future of the Arts in Schools', Volume 10, No. 1, pp. 9–22; Robinson, K. (1992) 'The Arts as a Generic Area of the Curriculum', Volume 11, No. 1, pp. 9–26; Best, D. (1992) 'Generic Arts: An Expedient Myth', Volume 11, No. 1, pp. 27–44; Tweddle, P. (1992) 'Arts Education: the Search for a Third Way for Schools', Volume 11, No. 1, pp. 45–60; Abbs, P.

(1992) 'The Generic Community of the Arts: Its Historic Development and Educational Value', Volume 11, No. 3, pp. 265–286.
5   See, for example, Arthur Efland, Pat Stuhr, Kerry Freedman, Jeff Adams, Robyn Stewart, Graeme Sullivan, Steers and Swift, Duncum, P. (1996) 'From Surat to Snapshots: What the Visual Arts Could Contribute to Education' in *Australian Art Education* Volume 19, No. 2, pp. 36–45, *et al.*
6   Twenty authors contributed to *'Directions', Journal of Art and Design Education* Volume 18, No. 1, 1999, Oxford: Blackwell.
7   I am indebted to Professor John Swift for his constructive comments on a draft of this chapter.

References

Allison, B. (1982) 'Identifying the Core in Art and Design', *Journal of Art and Design Education* Volume 1, No. 1, pp. 59–66, Abingdon: Carfax.

Barrett, M. (1979) *Art Education: A Strategy for Course Design*, London: Heinemann.

Baynes, K. (1985) 'Defining a Design Dimension of the Curriculum', *Journal of Art and Design Education* Volume 4, No. 3, pp. 237–243, Abingdon: Carfax.

Binch, N. (1994) 'The Implications of the National Curriculum Orders for Art', *Journal of Art and Design Education* Volume 13, No. 2, pp. 117–131, Oxford: Blackwell.

DfEE (2000) *The National Curriculum for England*, London: Department for Education and Employment.

Edwards, S., Rogers, R. and Steers, J. (2001) *Survey of Art and Design Resources in Primary and Secondary School*, London: Clore Duffield Foundation.

Eisner, E. (1972) *Educating Artistic Vision*, New York and London: Macmillan.

Eisner, E. (1985) *The Educational Imagination*, New York: Macmillan.

Encyclopaedia Britannica (1998) *Practice and Profession of the Arts: Impact of the Bauhaus*, CD-ROM (keyword 'Bauhaus').

Feldman, E. (1982) 'Varieties of Art Curriculum', *Journal of Art and Design Education* Volume 1, No. 1, pp. 21–46, Abingdon: Carfax.

Gundera, J. and Fyfe, C. (1999) 'Intercultural Visual Literacy and Art History', in Boughton, D. and Mason, R. (eds) *Beyond Multicultural Art Education: International Perspectives* pp. 87–102, Münster, Munich, Berlin and New York: Waxmann.

HMI (2001) *Primary Subject Reports 2000/01: Art and Design*, London: Ofsted.

Hughes, A. (1998) 'Reconceptualising the Art Curriculum', *Journal of Art and Design Education* Volume 17, No. 1, pp. 41–49, Oxford: Blackwell.

Macdonald, S. (1970) *The History and Philosophy of Art Education*, London: University of London Press.

Mason, R. and Iwano, M. (1995) *National Survey of Art and Design and Technology Curricula and Courses at Key Stages 3 and 4 in England and Wales*, London: University of Surrey Roehampton.

National Curriculum Council (1990) 'The Arts 5–16: A Curriculum Framework', Harlow: Oliver & Boyd.

Read, H. (1965) 'Education through Art: A Revolutionary Policy', a lecture given by Sir Herbert Read at an Open Meeting at University College, London, 3 January 1965 (pamphlet published by Society for Education through Art).

Robinson, K. (ed.) (1982) *The Arts in Schools: Principles, Practice and Provision*, London: Calouste Gulbenkian Foundation.

Ross, M. (1995) 'National Curriculum Art and Music', *Journal of Art and Design Education* Volume 14, No. 3, pp. 270–276, Oxford: Blackwell.

Ruskin, J. (1857) *The Elements of Drawing*, London: Smith, Elder & Co.

Sausmarez, M. de (1964) *Basic Design: the Dynamics of Visual Form*, London: Studio Vista.

Schools Council (1977) *Report of the 18 + Art Syllabus Steering Group*, London.

Scruton, R. (2001) 'What Mozart had and Tracey hasn't', *The Sunday Times Magazine* 20 May 2001.

Secondary Examinations Council (1986) *Report of the Working Party: Art and Design Draft Grade Criteria*, London: SEC.

Swift, J. (2000) 'Editorial and Dedication', *Journal of Art and Design Education* Volume 19, No. 1, Oxford: Blackwell.

Swift, J. and Steers, J. (1999) 'A Manifesto for Art in Schools', *Journal of Art and Design Education* Volume 18, No. 1, 1999, pp. 7–14, Oxford: Blackwell.

Taylor, R. (1986) *Educating for Art: Critical Response and Development*, Harlow: Longman.

Thistlewood, D. (ed.) (1992) *Histories of Art and Design Education: Cole to Coldstream*, Harlow: Longman and NSEAD.

United States Department of Education (1970) *National Assessment of Educational Progress – Art Objectives*, Washington, DC.

Wilson, B. (1995) 'In School or in Life? In Self or in Society? Where are the Goals of Art Education Met?' *Proceedings of 1995 InSEA Asian Regional Congress Taiwan, ROC*, pp. 343–362, Chunghua: National Chunghua University of Education.

4   Design and technology

Richard Kimbell

The emergence of design and technology

It is hardly a major claim to assert that 'technology' was the only significant subject innovation in the original version of the National Curriculum. White, in Chapter 1, has already drawn attention to the observation by Aldrich that the list of ten 'subjects' in the original National Curriculum prescription is very similar to that presented in 1904 as a requirement for the new state secondary schools. All those subjects (except 'technology') existed then – and still exist now. Indeed many of them have existed far longer. In 1965 Raymond Williams wrote *The Long Revolution* in which he analysed the roots of our current curriculum. He concluded:

> The fact about our present curriculum is that it was essentially created by the 19th century, following some 18th century models and retaining elements of the medieval curriculum near its centre.
>
> (Williams, 1965, p. 188)

At least the new (1990) National Curriculum included technology, and that was different. In the original formulation, technology comprised design and technology and information technology (IT), but by the time of the 1995 version, these two aspects had been separated out and design and technology had become – in its own right – a National Curriculum subject. This chapter deals with design and technology. It was created in thirty years – an incredibly short time in the context of curriculum change generally – and through the interaction of an extraordinary series of circumstances and players.

In 1960, nothing that resembles design and technology existed in the curriculum. There were lots of craft work (e.g. woodwork, cookery) and some engineering-related studies (technical drawing and engineering workshop theory and practice). While most of the curriculum at that time was built on discrete bodies of *knowledge*, the practical subjects were built on accumulations of *skills* (for cutting, forming and joining a limited range of materials). Equally, while the pedagogy of traditional academic subjects centred on students accumulating 'right answer' propositional *knowledge*, the situation was not very different for practical subjects, where teaching was based on 'right answer' models of expertise-building in *skills*: 'watch the expert – now do it like him/her'. In this way I achieved (in 1966) my A levels in metalwork and technical drawing. The previous year, Raymond Williams had published his book – and if he was aware of the astonishing transformation in the offing (I suspect he was not), I was certainly not.

There were rustlings of discontent in the undergrowth. Crowther (1959) had thrown down a serious challenge. Too many bright sixth-form students were turned off by the dry academic curriculum, and Crowther proposed an 'alternative road' to learning – through practical engagement with tasks. A few short years later Newsom (1963) challenged teachers to create such 'active' learning opportunities for young school leavers. From these two sources grew two Schools Council curriculum research and development projects:

- school technology; linking science to workshop activity for 'bright' (sixth-form) youngsters.
- design and craft education; linking craft to thinking [designing], for young school leavers.

The subsequent emergence of design and technology might be characterised as a continuing tussle between these two schools of thought and their adherents. 'School Technology' was a sort of problem-solving science – with a clear knowledge base (e.g. electronics) but not much in the way of skills. 'Craft and Design' was based on the idea of *thoughtful* making (designing solutions and then making them) – with a clear skill base (e.g. in wood or textiles) but not much required knowledge. Through the 1970s and early 1980s both schools of thought came to see that design (the verb) lay at the heart of things: *designing* technological solutions (such as automatic switching systems for ventilating a greenhouse), or *designing* more crafted objects (e.g. furniture or packaging). In 1985 the title 'Craft, Design and Technology' (CDT) was used to draw things together for the launch of the new GCSE examination system, and by 1989 it was (finally) agreed to drop craft, and *design and technology* became the title. Through this thirty-year evolution process there were (as one might expect) winners and losers in all manner of arguments – and there was much blood on the walls. It was a fast, furious and fascinating evolution process.

Extraordinarily, '*designing*' had become the defining feature of National Curriculum design and technology, which originally had five (then four, then two, and now one) attainment targets. The curriculum for design and technology was (and remains) entirely procedural; describing the process of design and development. Whilst there are categories of knowledge and skills defined in the Programmes of Study (PoS), these have to be seen as resources for action – not as ends in themselves. So the Attainment Target (against which student performance is to be measured) makes no mention of this content, focussing rather on the capabilities that pupils need to demonstrate in deploying that knowledge and skill to solve design problems. So whilst the PoS demanded that students should be taught how 'to join materials in permanent forms', the attainment target did not require that this be assessed. Rather teachers had to assess students' ability 'to review how to make best use of materials, procedures, tools and equipment' or 'to use knowledge of materials, components, tools equipment and processes to change working procedures to overcome obstacles as making proceeds' (DES, 1990). So one thing gets taught – and a different and much more sophisticated thing (youngsters ability to *use* their knowledge and skills in solving problems) gets assessed. This was radical stuff.

There was all kind of mayhem in getting design and technology up and running in schools, not least because the good practice on which the National Curriculum had been drafted existed in very few schools (the vast majority were still some way back in the evolution). Every change in the Order since then (the 1995 and 2000 Orders – not to mention the unofficial rewrites in 1992 and 1994) were all concerned with making it simpler for teachers to implement. In the process of doing this we have lost quite a lot of the vision. But equally, over the last twelve years, the majority of teachers and schools have caught up with the idea *and* the practice, so design and technology is far more established across the country. However, Ofsted reports that performance still remains patchy – more patchy than for any other subject. The best practice is phenom-enal and the worst is horrid. Given the transformations in the subject in the thirty years leading up to the 1990 National Curriculum, we should not be surprised by this.

One of the major changes in the 2000 Statutory Order was the inclusion of an explicit statement about the distinctive value of studying design and technology. It is, I believe, an excellent encapsulation of the vision that has driven the evolution of the subject as I have described it over those thirty (now forty) years.

> Design and technology prepares pupils
> . . . to intervene creatively to improve the quality of life.
> . . . to become autonomous and creative problem solvers.
> . . . to combine practical skills with an understanding of aesthetics, social and environmental issues and industrial practices.
> . . . to reflect on and evaluate present and past design and technology, its uses and effects.
> Through design and technology, all pupils can become discriminating and informed users, and can become innovators.
>
> (DfEE/QCA, 1999, p. 7)

This developing story of design and technology raises several issues that are central to the debates in this book. Specifically I am concerned with the issue of how (or to what extent) design and technology as characterised in this vision-statement above supports the achievement of the National Curriculum aims outlined in Chapter 1. We saw that these aims now embrace a frighteningly complex and difficult set of issues, concerning values; teamwork; problem solving; communication; learning to learn; creativity, and knowledge management. Is design and technology cut out for this challenging task? And if so how?

The 'skills' of designing

In a recent research study for the Design Council (Kimbell *et al.*, 1997), we were invited to examine the notion of *design decision-making*, and how it is different (if at all) from 'ordinary' decision-making. We worked for a year with a group of headteachers, and we began the year by asking them to provide a detailed case study of a significant decision they had made in their school in the last six months. What was the decision about? How was it arrived at? What have been its consequences? Among the examples they provided were a change to the corridor/stairway system (introducing a one-way flow); a change to the meals provision; a change to playground security arrangements; a change to the Key Stage 3 curriculum structure. All were major changes involving significant upheavals. Working in collaborative groups we invited the headteachers to analyse their decision-making processes, looking for similarities and differences; strengths and weaknesses in their processes of decision-making.

The second phase of the project then required them to look at design decision-making. We attached them to a group of design students engaged in a six-week design project. They worked alongside the students from start to finish noting how the students made their design decisions. In seminar sessions away from the students the head-teachers were asked to reflect on how the design decision-making was taking place, and on how it was similar to or different from their 'ordinary' (non design) decision-making.

The culmination of this second phase of the project was fascinating, as intelligent, thoughtful, non-designers applied their minds to the question 'what's special about design decision-making?' There was, of course, much overlap between design and non-design decision-making in these case studies, but there were also differences. Some of the qualities that exist on the periphery of 'ordinary' decision-making were much more central to design decision-making – and vice versa. Nonetheless, a list emerged of what were universally agreed (by the head-teacher group) to be the *'operational strategies'* that inform design decision-making. These are presented below, and I have elaborated the descriptions by reference to the design literature.

Unpacking wicked tasks

The design literature is full of accounts of the complexity and 'wickedness' of design tasks. This wickedness derives from the fact that design tasks do not have right answers or set procedures. They are typically multi-dimensional involving users in contexts – and both need clarifying, so designers have to unpack this messiness to clarify what (and who) is involved. Moreover, this process is not merely a starting strategy, but is rather a progressive one, so the designer is continually and progressively unpacking the task to identify its constituent elements and their significance.

'Playing' with reality

There is an expanding body of evidence that links designing to ideas of playfulness. Kathy Sylva for example, has researched extensively the value of structured play with very young children (Sylva *et al.*, 1976), and Papanek (1972) talks of design as 'goal-directed play'. The significance of this playfulness is that it allows imagination to operate without too tight a framework of constraints.

> The concept of 'what might be' – being able to move in perception and thought away from the concrete given of 'what is' to 'what was, what could have been, what one could try for, what might happen' and ultimately to the purest realms of fantasy – is a touchstone of that miracle of human experience, the imagination.
>
> (Singer and Singer, 1990, p. 241)

Optimising values (thinking as others)

Design is about 'improvement'. And the concept of improvement is essentially value-laden. Good design practice therefore seeks to identify the stakeholders in any task and to make their values explicit from the outset.

When designing a school security system, for example, the stakeholders might include teachers, parents, pupils, governors, support staff and the community police officer. It is inconceivable that the members of these groups would share a single set of values concerning school security. They do not, and never will. Accordingly most of the dispute about whether a new design is an 'improvement', will in reality be a dispute about values; about what is to count as a 'good' solution. Designers need to be able to see the task through others' eyes — getting inside the values and priorities of all the stakeholders. Forcing these values to become explicit is a critical step.

Modelling possible futures

Part of the problem of dealing with 'the new' is that it is very difficult to make the necessary judgements about it if we cannot first create a realistic simulation of what it is going to be like. Designers therefore continually model their concepts of the future to enable them to experience it vicariously and thereby make informed judgements about it. The closer this vicarious experience can simulate the ultimate reality, the better we will be able to judge its impact in a new reality.

The value of modelling relates to the issue of risk in the new and innovative, since modelling exposes the *consequences* of decision-making. Risks can (and invariably need to) be taken in the *thinking* and *development* that eventually emerge as an outcome. But processes of modelling allow the designer to mitigate and offset the risk by testing out its consequences *in advance* of coming to a conclusion.

Managing complexity

Design tasks are typically multidimensional and messy, and they often take place over an extended period of time. This places complex management demands on designers: managing (and optimising) time, cost, materials, production processes, technical performance and much more in ways that enable them to complete their task. At the end they typically have to bring together all the strands of thought and development into a single holistic solution. They need to be holistic integrative thinkers — whilst managing the messy and often contradictory strands of thought within a project.

It is not surprising that 'the project' has become the dominant pedagogic strategy in design. And much of the learning centres on the management of the activity: developing a plan and a schedule; checking and amending it at regular intervals; trying to iron out factors over which one has less control and maximising those over which one has control. In short, designers have to learn to manage complexity.

Task-related knowledge

Since the demands in any task may vary considerably, designers need to develop robust, self-confident strategies for informing their designing by acquiring appropriate resources of knowledge and skill. This is widely acknowledged even in the examination rubrics that dominate school-based assessment in design and technology.

In the late 1970s, the emerging A level syllabuses in design and technology boldly and explicitly made this point and refused to pack their syllabuses with fixed bodies of knowledge. They then ran foul of the university admissions system which was unused to such a flexible and active approach to knowledge and refused to acknowledge design and technology as an appropriate university entrance qualification. In the end, to illuminate the issue, a study was undertaken by the Council for National Academic

Awards (CNAA) in association with the Standing Conference on University Entrance (SCUE). In a landmark report, they commented as follows:

> When embarking upon a new design, the package of knowledge and skills necessary for the success of the venture will emerge as the design progresses, and so the need to acquire knowledge and skills (and sometimes extend the boundary of knowledge and devise new skills) becomes a clear requirement for the designer.
>
> (CNAA/SCUE, 1985, p. 7)

Subsequently, in 1981, the Department of Education and Science produced its booklet *Understanding Design and Technology*, in which the very same view of knowledge was adopted.

> The designer does not need to know all about everything so much as to know what to find out, what form the knowledge should take, and what depth of knowledge is required for a particular purpose.
>
> (DES, 1981, p. 12)

This is not an exhaustive list of the strategies that designers employ. Nor is it a list that applies exclusively to designing. But these strategies do lie at the heart of the subject design and technology as it exists in the National Curriculum:

1   unpacking wicked tasks.
2   'playing' with reality.
3   optimising values (thinking *as* someone else).
4   modelling possible futures.
5   managing complexity.
6   task-related knowledge.

I would argue that these qualities are more *evident in* design and technology than they are in other subjects, and more *developed through* design and technology than through other subjects. Taken together, they amount to a manifesto for design and technology as a curriculum activity.

The challenge of a knowledge economy

One of the key features of these qualities that are developed through design and technology is that they are not free-standing. They co-exist and interact in important ways that tend to transform them into more than the sum of their parts. In the process of managing complex tasks, we require students to derive task-related knowledge, and clarify the value stances of the stakeholders, and be playful with ideas for the 'new', and model the consequences of their decisions. And this interaction – particularly concerning task-related knowledge in the management of wicked tasks – results in design and technology breaking the boundaries of conventional academic life. In 1959 C.P. Snow analysed what he saw as the two cultures that divided intellectual life in Britain: the world of the sciences and the world of the arts: 'there seems to be no place where the two cultures meet. . . . Thirty years ago the cultures had ceased to speak to each other.' He went on to make the observation that:

the only way out of all this . . . is of course by rethinking our education . . . nearly everyone will agree that our school education is too specialised.

(Snow, 1959, p. 26)

Whilst Snow's other complaint about British education – its unremitting élitism – has been tackled with conviction in the intervening years, his central concern about its disciplinary apartheid has received only lukewarm attention.

Part of the discomfort that has been experienced by design and technology over the last thirty years arises from its awkward insistence on being neither a specialist art nor a specialist science. It is deliberately and actively interdisciplinary. The 'design' sub-label leans towards the arts, and the 'technology' towards the sciences. But neither will do as a natural home. It is a restive, itinerant, non-discipline.

In the context of a knowledge economy this is increasingly recognised as a strength rather than a weakness. When analysing the 'skills challenge' of such an economy, Seltzer and Bentley observe that companies are more likely to recruit for adaptability and fresh ideas – away from 'subject' skills and competencies and towards 'soft skills' such as communication, teamwork and problem solving.

> innovation increasingly relies on the interface between different kinds of knowledge, for example the combination of new information technologies with a new accounting system, or of design and technical skills in creating new websites . . . value is realised when different bodies of knowledge are brought together. Interdisciplinary skills are more and more valuable to individuals and organisations . . . interdisciplinary knowledge means far more than just specialisation in more than one subject. It requires the ability to understand the *interface* between different areas of knowledge and to apply insights from one to the other.
>
> (Seltzer and Bentley, 1999, p. 34)

Seltzer and Bentley go further and argue that this view of the demands of the knowledge economy requires a shift from a model of curriculum based on formal *content* (however divided into subjects) towards a more fluid definition based on *practice*. They argue that this would involve learning structured around projects, based on identifying and solving problems, in a range of contexts in which students transfer knowledge across different domains, using portfolio models of presentation and assessment.

This is precisely the model of learning through which design and technology operates. Its products are not to be seen as the artefacts that youngsters produce, be that novel furniture, computer mouses, hats or control systems. The real products of design and technology are empowered youngsters, capable of taking projects from inception to delivery, creatively intervening to improve the made world, entrepreneurially managing their resources, capably integrating knowledge across multiple domains, sensitively optimising the values of those concerned, and confidently working alone and in teams.

Yet if this is the outcome of 'best practice' in design and technology, this vision of the subject is itself the outcome of the frenetic curriculum development years from Crowther and Newsom up to the launch of the National Curriculum in 1990. And given that such frantic curriculum development was bound to have a 'leading edge' and a 'trailing edge' of implementation, it is a fair question to ask; 'what was the relationship between this emerging vision of design and technology and the Statutory Order for design and technology in 1990?'

Design and technology and the National Curriculum

There is no doubt that the Statutory Order for design and technology was drafted on the basis of best practice in a few centres of excellence – mostly in secondary schools. Accordingly, for many teachers – particularly primary teachers – design and technology appeared first on their horizon because of the National Curriculum. Before 1990 they may well have been unaware of its existence. Not surprisingly, therefore, the reactions to it were varied – some teachers felt alarmed and threatened by it, and some were excited and liberated by it. But given that it had evolved through so many different guises so rapidly and so very recently (it even looked different from the GCSE version of 1985–1986), it would not be surprising if many of its constructs and complexities were unclear and untested.

It is only fair to report that a good deal of unexciting, and/or ill-conceived work was evident in the early days of the National Curriculum. The difficulties arose from a number of sources. First, there was the problem I outline above (p. 46) about the apparent mismatch between the Programmes of Study and the Attainment Targets, that appeared to demand that teachers teach one thing but assess something different. Second, there were problems in coralling five formerly separate subjects (but principally home economics and CDT) into a coherent whole. Third, the Programmes of Study themselves were far too involved, with specifications of what *materials* to teach; what *contexts* tasks should be set in; and what kinds of *outcomes* were required. This strand in particular was very intrusive on teachers' autonomy in developing their curricula.

Overlaid across all these problems was the speed of evolution through which design and technology had emerged, the authoritarian manner of the implementation of the National Curriculum in 1990, and its original ludicrous assessment regime. Taken together, these undermined teachers' confidence in their own ability to make sound judgements about curriculum and assessment. Ironically, the leading edge teachers on whom the development of design and technology had depended felt constrained, whilst many others (not at the leading edge) were running scared. For a detailed analysis of these issues see Kimbell 1997, especially Chapters 4 and 5.

The fact was that, prior to the National Curriculum Statutory Order, there had not been time for design and technology to 'bed down' into a clear consensus amongst teachers about what it was like, what it was for, and how to teach it. There were some leading-edge LEAs where practice was (in my opinion) generally excellent, and others where it definitely was not. Owing to the pace of development and the major differences between its emerging form and anything else in the curriculum, at the time when the National Curriculum Order was written, there was no single clear view of design and technology that would amount to a 'paradigm' within which teachers' practice could be reliably located. We were in a phase of development that Kuhn (1962) would have described as 'pre-paradigmatic', with many practitioners working on the same thing from different perspectives, writing books for wide and diverse audiences, but without the precise targeting that arises once a paradigm has coalesced.

So, in many ways, the National Curriculum Statutory Order for design and technology *defined* the paradigm. The Order was not so much *reflecting* the common practice and experience of teachers (as did most of the subject Statutory Orders). Rather, it emerged as a *prescription* for what such practice might (and even should) *become*. As a practising teacher at the time, Hope, ironically, read it with despair:

Design and technology (as every child's entitlement) was launched on the unsuspecting British educational public without a clear definition of what the subject was. Essential underlying questions had not been addressed: What was its rationale, its knowledge base, its underlying philosophy? What were its meta-skills to be? What were their contributory skills and knowledge? How do the cognitive and haptic build together into the education of the skilled design & technologist? What is design capability? The only part of the document which seemed applicable to lessons across all the disparate subject areas that huddled under the design and technology umbrella was *The Design Process* (identify needs – generate solutions – evaluate results). For many teachers this is still what design and technology is about, despite the passage of time and changes in the wording of the National Curriculum documents.

It became obvious to me, reading journals and conference proceedings after the introduction of the National Curriculum, that research into how children learn had transformed itself into how children could best be taught the National Curriculum. I remember walking down the path to my classroom thinking to myself, 'research is dead then.' This seemed especially true in design and technology. Prior to the National Curriculum there was little research into how small children designed things that they made. After its introduction, books and articles appeared to instruct teachers how to teach them to do so. The National Curriculum became the benchmark against which to measure capability and progress towards being good at design and technology.

(Hope, 2002, pp. 92–93)

I think that, at the time of wandering down the path to her classroom, Hope was overestimating the power of the Statutory Order to control what teachers do. And part of the reason for that in the specific context of design and technology is that the National Curriculum paradigm had emerged as an entirely *procedural* construct. It tells us (teachers) that we have to teach students to identify tasks, and develop design solutions. But it doesn't say *what* tasks we should set – or what would count as a good solution. That is for teachers to decide. Of course, QCA – with the help of the Design and Technology Association (DATA) – has produced a national scheme of work that teachers can adopt if they feel the need to, but it is merely guidance, and not statutory. Accordingly if I (in my classroom) want to get students working on tasks that are large scale and architectural – while you (in your class) work on animatronic puppets, then that's fine. The flavour of the design and technology in your class will be different from that in mine. But that's OK, it's allowed. And the result of this is that the Order has proved to be – in some important ways – transparent.

In design and technology, confident teachers, who do not 'play safe' by following the QCA schemes of work, expose something of themselves (their own views and interests about design) through the work that they initiate with students. It is not so much a case of the emperor with no clothes, as the emperor with clothes that are (at least somewhat) translucent. Barlex describes this situation in the following terms:

consider the position of design and technology in the curriculum as if it were a brand, in competition with the other brands i.e. other school subjects, in the educational market place. . . . I choose for my example Absolut Vodka. The branding here is highly innovative in that the product itself is almost invisible – the blank bottle shaped space provides a window in which the advertiser can place content that will appeal to particular audiences. In *Harper's* the content is intellectual; in *Wired* it is futuristic; in *Spin* alternative; in *Out* it is loud and proud; with 'Absolut Centrefold' in *Playboy*. Here the product is like a chameleon taking on, not colours from its surroundings, but areas of interest and associated values that will appeal to particular market sectors … gay men, fashion conscious women, young techno males, straight men and those interested in politics.

(Barlex, 2002, pp. 6–7)

Barlex's point develops from the issue I raised earlier about design and technology being essentially cross-disciplinary; neither a specialist art nor a specialist science. He takes up this point in the context of his 'branding' analogy:

Subjects are expected to have boundaries by which they are clearly defined, inside which sit their bodies of knowledge, tests of truth and accepted techniques – just as a brand defines itself so that it is recognisable and differentiated. So I see design and technology as a brand to be analogous to Absolut Vodka. It can take up a variety of positions along an art-science spectrum. Indeed pupils will adopt many different positions along such a spectrum as they move through a single designing and making project. It can appeal to a wide variety of learning styles. It can generate educational outcomes in many different domains. [*It might appear comforting if*] the design and technology brand had some of the features recognisable in other brands – clearer boundaries, especially defined and testable knowledge. Yet I believe the subject needs to be true to its core values. To look to become more like other subjects would be to sell out on what we have to offer our pupils.

(Barlex, 2002, pp. 6–7, *my insertion in italics*)

So we might summarise the position of design and technology in the National Curriculum as being a newly created brand, dominantly characterised as a procedural activity focussed on bringing about change in the made world. It is not a 'subject' in the normal sense of that world. And it is susceptible (like Absolut Vodka) to a receiving audience customising it through their own value systems and priorities.

There is a further feature of the National Curriculum construct that needs to be acknowledged: assessment. It can be argued that the whole edifice of the National Curriculum was based on the priority of assessment, but here too – as I shall attempt to illustrate – design and technology breaks the conventional boundaries of the academic world.

The challenge of assessment

In grappling with the implementation of design and technology, one of the many challenges for teachers was to deal with the apparent dislocation of the Programmes of Study (PoS) from the Attainment Targets (ATs). The former deal with 'that which must be taught', whilst the latter deal with 'what will be assessed'. In most subjects there was a 1:1 correspondence between these two. You *teach* quadratic equations (or whatever), and you then *test* that youngsters can do them. Not so in design and technology!

There was a specification of knowledge and skills to be taught (e.g. about materials), but in the ATs pupils were not assessed on whether or not they knew about these areas of knowledge. Rather they were assessed against a measure of their capability to *make use of* that knowledge and skill in tackling real designing and making tasks. The ATs therefore focussed on the *process* and not on the knowledge and skills.

> We have argued that because knowledge is a resource to be *used*, a means to an end, it should not be the prime characteristic of attainment targets for design & technology.
>
> (DES/WO, 1988, para. 2.19)

Since the aim was the development of technological capability, it was the *tackling of tasks* that became the focus for assessment and hence the 'stuff' of attainment targets. The Working Group even went so far as to say that the approach to assessment should 'ideally' be based 'on the systematic observation of pupils' work throughout a design & technology task from recognition of the need to appraisal of the product' (DES/WO, 1988, para. 1.30).

It was inevitable therefore that project-based coursework would become the central plank of assessment; and this is how it has emerged. 'Performance' is the measure, not knowledge, or dislocated sets of skills. Can you complete a task and derive a satisfactory outcome? And can you do it in a rigorous, thoughtful and imaginative way?

Design and technology is the only subject in the National Curriculum whose Attainment Target is defined entirely procedurally, describing (at various levels) the ability of students to identify, grapple with, and resolve design tasks. This is another element of the mix that makes design and technology different.

The 'fit' to National Curriculum aims

As we have seen from Chapter 1, the aims of the National Curriculum are no longer expressed in terms of the certainties of high status disciplinary knowledge. The language now is explicitly embracing the difficult territory of values; teamwork; problem solving; communication; learning to learn; creativity and knowledge management. The 'fit' of these generic aims to the key qualities of design and technology (outlined above) is obvious. I have no illusions about the political significance attached to the subject, particularly when set against high status disciplines. Indeed the recent Government White Paper *Excellence and Opportunity from 14–19* (January 2003) has removed statutory support for all subjects (including design and technology) other than English, maths and science. I am not surprised by this decision – attempting as it does to pigeon-hole design and technology as a 'vocational subject'. As I have tried to illustrate in this chapter, however, this is a seriously mistaken position, since it is the best current manifestation of the aims espoused in the National Curriculum as a curriculum for *all* youngsters.

This current political twist is an illustration of the challenge raised by the emergence of design and technology. The attempt to label subjects as vocational or otherwise is a tacit admission of the rightness of 'subjects' as organising features of the curriculum. Yet the new aims imply the need to rethink the old certainties of a subject-based curriculum. The requirements of a *National* Curriculum (from 5–16) that appropriately prepares students for life and work in a knowledge economy have blurred the edges of these subject-certainties, but not sufficiently (it seems) for politicians to revise their historic adherence to traditional subjects – only some of which they see as vocational. These two positions seem to me to be incompatible.

So yes, there is no doubt that design and technology does match up very well to the new aims of the National Curriculum. But this is not because it has been shaped and manipulated in order to fit it to those aims. Rather it is because the aims of the National Curriculum have moved towards the territory that design and technology has been carving out for itself in the last forty years. Twelve years ago – at the launch of the National Curriculum – design and technology was seen as a cuckoo that had somehow forced its way into the conventional curriculum nest. It was an uncomfortable misfit that kept raising difficult conceptual and pedagogic problems.

But increasingly it is exactly these problems (values; teamwork and problem solving) that have come to be seen as the heartland of the curriculum debate. So by an amazing twist of fate, we are no longer the cuckoo, but rather the 'model subject' for the new curriculum. In 2000, after the publication of the latest version of the National Curriculum, David Hargreaves – the Chief Executive of the Qualifications and Curriculum Authority – addressed a conference at the Institute of Education in London University. In his talk he explicitly dealt with the transformation that was required in the curriculum and that he saw so well exemplified in design and technology.

> Design and technology is moving from the periphery of the school curriculum to its heart, as a model of the combination of knowledge and skills that will be at a premium in the knowledge economy, and it is from this best practice that other subjects can learn about effective teaching and learning.
>
> (Hargreaves, 2000, published in Design Council 2001, p. 25)

I couldn't have put it better myself.

References

Barlex, D. (2002) 'Questioning the Design Paradigm', in Norman, E. (ed.) *The Proceedings of the DATA International Research Conference* (pp. 1–11), Wellesbourne: The Design and Technology Association.

CNAA/SCUE Council for National Academic Awards/Standing Conference on University Entrance (1985) *A Level Design & Technology: the Identification of a Core Syllabus*, a report by P.M. Threlfall on behalf of CNAA.

Crowther, W. (1959) '*15–18' A report of the Central Advisory Council for Education (London)*, London: Routledge & Kegan Paul.

Department for Education and Employment (DfEE)/Qualifications and Curriculum Authority (QCA) (1999) *The National Curriculum Handbook for Teachers in England*, London: HMSO 1999.

Department of Education and Science (DES) (1981) *Understanding Design and Technology*, London: HMSO.

Department for Education and Science (DES) (1990) *Technology in the National Curriculum*, London: HMSO.

Department for Education and Skills (DfES) (2003) *Excellence and Opportunity from 14–19*, London: HMSO (White Paper).

Design Council (2001) 'Towards Education for Innovation', in *Changing Behaviours*, London: Design Council.

Hargreaves, D. (2000) *Towards Education for Innovation*, a public lecture presented at the Institute of Education, London University, 22 November 2000.

Hope, G. (2002) 'Questioning the design and technology paradigm', in Norman, E. (ed.) *Pro-

ceedings of the DATA International Research Conference, Wellesbourne: The Design and Technology Association.

Kimbell, R. (1997) *Assessing Technology: International Trends in Curriculum and Assessment*, Buckingham: Open University Press.

Kimbell, R., Mahony, P., Miller, S. and Saxton, J. (1997) *Decisions by Design*, London: Design Council.

Kuhn, T.S. (1962) *The Structure of Scientific Revolutions*, Chicago: The University of Chicago Press.

Newsom, J. (Chairman) (1963) *'Half our Future' A report of the Central Advisory Council for Education (London)*, London: HMSO.

Papanek, V. (1972) *Design for the Real World: Human Ecology and Social Change*, New York: Pantheon Press.

Seltzer, K. and Bentley, T. (1999) *The Creative Age: Knowledge and Skills for the New Economy*, London: DEMOS.

Singer, D.G. and Singer, J.L. (1990) *The House of Make Believe*, Cambridge, Mass: Harvard University Press.

Snow, C.P. (1959) *The Two Cultures*, Cambridge: Cambridge University Press.

Sylva, K., Bruner, J.S. and Genova, P. (1976) 'The role of play in the problem-solving of children 3–5 years old', in Bruner, J.S., Jolly, A. and Sylva, K. (eds) *Play, its Role in Development and Evolution*, New York: Penguin.

Williams, R. (1965) *The Long Revolution*, Harmondsworth: Penguin.

5 English

Bethan Marshall

English as a school subject is about the art of language. That is its unique contribution and why it should remain central to the curriculum. The purpose of this chapter is to unravel this seemingly bland statement; to understand why it is potentially highly controversial and why, in the end, it is the only justification for continuing to have a discrete subject called English for the duration of compulsory schooling.

The only way of coming to grips with the current state of affairs is by understanding the past. This is because English has not neatly progressed from one set of views to another but has been marked by competing traditions that have jostled and vied with each other for prominence over the past two hundred or so years. These views have always, to a greater or lesser extent, co-existed, overlapped and mutated over time. That is what makes them so hard to track. Similar perspectives manifest themselves in subtly different ways in different periods.

But any attempt to define what we want from school English has, to have any credence at all, to acknowledge the provenance of its position and take cognisance of the arguments and philosophies that it is adopting and rejecting. Indeed almost anyone trying to present a rationale for English begins by setting out the alternative positions.

In his influential *Growth Through English*, first published in 1967, John Dixon (1975) identified three views of the subject, which he called 'cultural heritage', 'skills' and 'personal growth'. The 1975 Bullock Report also identifies 'personal growth' and 'skills' along with 'English as an instrument of social change' (DES, 1975, para. 1.3). Professor Brian Cox and his working party who created the first version of National Curriculum for English, identified five 'views of English teaching: personal growth, cross curricular, adult needs, cultural heritage and cultural analysis' (DES and WO, 1989, para. 2.20–2.27).

What these accounts fail to do is present an historical perspective. As we shall see below, views on the teaching of English have become almost inseparable from broader views about the purpose of education and a vision of the good society. The teaching of English has often been almost synonymous with a template for utopian reform. That is why cool and level-headed neutrality about the subject is so hard to achieve. Question someone's position about the teaching of phonics and you are potentially challenging the very core of their beliefs.

Moreover it is part of the job of those most intimately involved in the controversy to be adept at capturing the nuances of any given phrase or statement. By way of illustrating the impact this has on the debate, and as a way into the history lesson that is to follow, it is worth picking apart the statement that began this chapter.

To begin with, I omitted any reference to the media and ICT. This will immediately alienate certain sectors of the English teaching community. Next, I use the word 'language', not 'literacy' or 'communication'. This indicates that I am steering away from words which may be construed as either utilitarian, or, read another way, potentially radical: I explore the background to this below. The word 'art', as we shall see, is also problematic. For some it is élitist, for others it means salvation. And so I could go on. What I leave out or put in carries the weight of two hundred years of controversy. So let us begin to examine the different positions on English teaching in more detail.

A brief history of English

Liberal arts

We start with Matthew Arnold, sometime critic and poet, who has always been held responsible for English as a school subject. Arnold's conception of school English arose in opposition to the one he found in his job as a school inspector. So while we will be examining his position, we are by default exploring the view with which he disagreed and which took around seventy years to lose its dominance.

Matthew Arnold was in almost at the start of Her Majesty's Inspectorate. He had been inspecting schools for almost ten years before the system changed in 1862 and he was required to implement what became known as the Revised Code. This was the result of the Newcastle Commission, which was looking for cost-effective elementary education. Robert Lowe, the minister responsible for education, set up a system of payment by results. Inspections took the form of an annual visit in which children were put through their paces. Broadly speaking, the better the marks, the more the money.

For Arnold, this regime undermined the purpose of education. Writing in 1869, he complained 'All test examinations . . . may be said to narrow reading upon a certain given point, and to make it mechanical' (Arnold, 1979, p. 95). He felt that the inspections had become governed by 'a narrowing system of test examinations' when there were 'organisations wanting to be guided by us into the best ways of learning and teaching' (ibid., p. 95). He went on to warn of the dangers of teaching to the test when the stakes were high, for the school grant depended on pupils' success in the test.

> It tends to make instruction mechanical and to set a bar to duly extending it . . . [and] must inevitably concentrate the teachers' attention on producing this minimum and not simply on the good instruction of the school. The danger to be guarded against is the mistake of assuming these two – the producing of the minimum successfully and the good instruction of the school – as if they were identical.
>
> (Ibid., p. 95)

The relevance of these extracts to the debate about the English Curriculum lies in the language he uses. He believed that over-testing makes education 'mechanical'. It is the use of this word that connects his view of the purpose of schooling to wider arguments in Victorian Britain about the nature of a good society.

Published in the same year as these education reports, *Culture and Anarchy* is Arnold's attempt to both define and change the world in which he finds himself. He writes:

> Faith in machinery is, I said, our besetting danger; often in machinery most absurdly disproportioned to the end which this machinery, if it is to do any good at all, is to serve; but always in machinery, as if it had a value in and for itself.
>
> (Arnold, 1948, p. 48)

Such an observation echoes both Thomas Carlyle's *Signs of the Times* and Dickens's *Hard Times*. Written in 1854, Dickens's novel uses, amongst other vehicles, the education system to rail against the destructive nature of what he views as the pervasiveness of a utilitarian philosophy. He opposes Choakumchild's and Gradgrind's world of 'facts, facts, facts' to the realm of the imagination as represented by the circus child Cissy.

Arnold (1979, p. 97) similarly believed that 'whatever introduces any sort of creative activity to relieve the passive reception of knowledge is valuable'. He felt that subjects should be taught in a 'less mechanical and more interesting manner [to] call forth pleasurable activity' (ibid., p. 98). Central to this aim was the teaching of literature and in particular poetry, both its creation and its reception.

But this was not simply to prevent the ravages of the machine age by encouraging a spot of imaginative writing. In an era characterised by a crisis in faith – Arnold's own poem *On Dover Beach* being a defining manifestation of this – literature became the new source of spirituality. Art was the food of the soul. For Arnold the classics were still the most obvious source of such sustenance but for the population at large, who did not have the time or wherewithal for such study, English provided the most accessible substitute.

Arnold never challenged what might be construed as the inherent élitism of such an argument. Moreover, his thesis, most clearly articulated in *Culture and Anarchy*, was dependent on the notion that the population at large was potentially a frightening, unruly mass. Some twenty years before, Paris had once again erupted in a fervour of revolutionary sentiment. Literature could civilise the mob. Yet because he so passionately believed in the redemptive properties of the arts, he was the first to argue for what might loosely be termed an entitlement view of the curriculum, based on the necessity of providing life-changing experiences for the child. For this reason it is possible to detect a progressive strand within Arnold's educational philosophy.

This same strand, and the tension within this position, is evident in the heirs of his legacy. It was the Newbolt Report of 1921 (DCBE, 1921) that established the place of English at the heart of the school curriculum. But it is the contribution of one of its chief authors, George Sampson, that makes the tension in the Arnoldian inheritance clearest. After the ravages of the first world war education was to provide the key to national recovery and unity.

In his book *English for the English*, also published in 1921, Sampson writes: 'There is no class in the country that does not need a full education in English. Possibly a common basis for education might do much to mitigate the class antagonism' (Sampson, 1952, p. 44). He goes on to add, 'If we want that class antagonism to be mitigated, we must abandon our system of class education and find some sort of education common to all schools of all classes,' and concludes, 'The one common basis for a common culture is a common tongue' (ibid., p. 45).

This apparently egalitarian aim has to be set against his view that the masses were to be feared. Writing against the backdrop of the Russian Revolution, Sampson observed 'Deny to working class children any common share in the immaterial and presently they will grow into the men who demand with menaces a communism of the material'

(Sampson, 1952, p. xv). It was English, to use Arnold's phrase, that was to bring 'sweetness and light' and soothe their turbulent souls.

Hence the predominant view of English as a 'fine art' in the Newbolt Report. The writers of the report argue that the teaching of English

> In its full sense connotes not merely acquaintance with a certain number of terms, or the power of spelling these terms correctly and arranging them without gross mistakes. It connotes the discovery of the world by the first and most direct way open to us, and the discovery of ourselves in our native environment ... For the writing of English is essentially an art, and the effect of English literature, in education, is the effect of art upon the development of the human character.
>
> (DCBE, 1921, Ch. 1, para. 14, p. 20)

What is significant about the report and about Sampson's work is their antagonism to the utilitarian. This took the form of opposition to the examination of literature teaching and claimed, as Sampson put it, 'that ... the purpose of education [is] not to prepare children *for* their occupations, but to prepare children *against* their occupations' (Sampson, 1952, p. 11).

All this is evident in the work of F.R. Leavis, who took up the mantle of Arnold. Newbolt believed that a new, special breed of teacher would be required to deliver the English curriculum. Leavis saw it as his job to provide this. His reign at Cambridge transformed the study of English, and some of the most influential players in the English school curriculum of the twentieth century were his disciples.

What emerges most clearly from Leavis is the meritocratic strand within the liberal arts position. It connects the way in which he sought to define a pecking order of literary merit with a view of society that wished to ensure that the best should not be held back. Significantly, *Hard Times* was an essential text in Leavis's *Great Tradition*. It exemplified the struggle against the utilitarian and celebrated the indomitable spirit of the imagination.

It also highlights, once more, the complex relationship that those espousing a liberal arts view have with the common man and woman. As individuals, ordinary folk are replete with human potential and entitled to equality of opportunity. It is only as a mass that they become troublesome. Interestingly, and again reflecting his day, Leavis's anxiety about the masses has a slightly different spin. He fears mass culture and its power to indoctrinate. A reason for teaching English becomes to inoculate everyone against the power of mass culture, in part by encouraging literary discernment.

Such a view survives to the present day in writers who reflect elements of the Leavisite position in their work. Richard Hoggart comments:

> The level of literacy we now accept for the bulk of the population, of literacy unrelated to the way language is misused in this kind of society, ensures that literacy becomes simply a way of further subordinating great numbers of people. We make them literate enough to be conned by the mass persuaders ... the second slogan has to be 'Critical Literacy for All'. Critical Literacy means ... teaching about the difficulties, challenges and benefits of living in an open society which aims to be a true democracy.
>
> (Hoggart, 1998, p. 60)

The working party, headed by Brian Cox, which produced the first National Curriculum for English in 1990 (DES and WO, 1990) belongs to this same liberal arts position. At Cambridge towards the end of Leavis's heyday, Cox writes of the legacy of Arnold in his autobiography:

> Behind all these arguments about resources and organisation lies the question of how far we retain the faith of Matthew Arnold in the civilising power of the Humanities. My life-long enthusiasm for teaching literature testifies to my own commitment. I still hold to the words that I wrote in 1968 at the end of our editorial for the tenth anniversary of *Critical Quarterly*: 'Great literature helps to keep alive our most subtle and delicate feelings, our capacity for wonder, and our faith in human individuality'.
>
> (Cox, 1992, p. 268)

As we shall see, the dominance of this view in official manifestations ended with this document, but it is worth noting that it has made discussion of English problematic because of its apparent élitism. The next position that we will examine, while in part predating Arnold, becomes, as it develops, a potential way of combating this.

Critical dissent

This perspective is less acknowledged but has contributed to English being seen as a subversive subject and its proponents as 'cultural guerrillas' (Phillips, 1994). The term 'critical dissent' (Marshall, 2000) is designed to reflect two different but not unrelated traditions: radical dissent and critical literacy. On the surface these two have little in common, being separated by time, focus and theology. Neither do they immediately have anything to do with English teaching in this country. But they have more than tangentially influenced its development.

Though now both highly secularised, critical literacy and dissent originate from disputes within the Roman Catholic and Anglican Churches respectively. The former is of much more recent origin, the latter dating back to the Act of Uniformity of 1662, which insisted on conformity to the Church of England.

If we begin with dissent, we find that although by the end of that century so-called 'dissenters' from the Act were allowed to worship as they pleased, they were ostracised from privileged mainstream society until well into the nineteenth century. Yet their influence was considerable, if not central, both in this country and arguably even more so in the United States where many of them fled. As Christopher Hitchens comments in his essay on Thomas Paine, a one time Unitarian minister and in some ways one of the chief architects of the United States:

> Paine belongs to that strain of oratory, pamphleteering and prose that runs through Milton, Bunyan, Burns and Blake and which nourished what the common folk like to call the Liberty Tree. This stream as chartered by E.P. Thompson and others often flows underground for long periods. In England it disappeared for a long time.
>
> (Hitchens, 1988, p. 16)

His list, while eclectic, is interesting and pertinent to this chapter in that he unites the two strands that have so influenced a certain type of English curriculum and teacher

– the link between literature and language on the one hand and a democratic, sometimes radical vision of society on the other.

The connection between such views and education is less tenuous than it may seem. One of the most significant legacies of the dissenters' separation from the establishment was that parents either would not or could not educate their children in any of the major public schools. As a result a network of so-called dissenting academies sprang up. Well-known literary figures of the early nineteenth century were educated in these establishments, including Keats and Hazlitt. Mary Wollstonecraft, while not a dissenter herself, set up a school with help from the Newington Green Dissenters, a group which included the prominent dissenter Richard Price. One of her early publications on education was printed by the dissenting publisher John Johnson.

These institutions, while religious in origin, were based on a precept that education was a source of social good. This came from a belief that people, while sinful, were rational. Learning to think and reason was integral to their view of education. In his biography of Keats, Motion describes the philosophy of Keats's school, which avoided the teaching of the classics, as 'distinctly progressive' (Motion, 1998, p. 22). Commenting on other dissenting academies, he adds that they were 'defiantly forward looking . . . they explored rational teaching methods that emphasised the value of doubt and questioning' (ibid., p. 24). Moreover the dissenters' particular take on the idea that all are equal in the sight of God meant that they also believed in social equality and justice. This led in turn to support for the common man, a belief in his rights as a citizen and by association the English vernacular. Language was power.

Well before Newbolt, therefore, they saw the importance of making English rather than Latin the main vehicle for developing language and, through language, independent thought. One of the chief exponents was William Enfield, a Presbyterian minister who taught at the Warrington Academy, where another radical thinker of the day, Joseph Priestley, also worked.

In 1774 Enfield published what might be seen as one of the first English text books for use in schools – *The Speaker: or miscellaneous pieces selected from the best English writers, and disposed under the proper heads, with a view to facilitate the improvement of youth in reading and speaking.* As the lengthy title suggests, this was essentially an anthology of writing, unusually for the time, organised under generic headings such as Narrative Pieces, Didactic Pieces, Argumentative Pieces etc. Again, as the title makes clear, the aim was both to improve the elocution of pupils as well as to extend their thinking through encounters with good writing. Enfield did not confine his efforts to producing text books and was a regular contributor to the *Monthly Magazine* under the pseudonym 'The Enquirer'. One of his essays 'The Enquirer On Verse and Poetry' (Enfield, 1796) is said to have influenced Wordsworth's 'Preface to the Lyrical Ballads' which also celebrated the vernacular tongue.

The egalitarian streak within the Warrington Academy did not fully extend to girls but the daughter of another member of staff, John Aiken, did attend and was inspired to produce a similar anthology for girls. Anna Laetitia Bacbauld published *The Female Speaker* in 1816. Some years earlier Wollstonecraft had also published *The Female Reader*. In her Preface she explains her debt to Enfield and while much of her justification for the volume may seem slightly conservative or modest for such a proto-feminist, nevertheless the link between thought, literature and its role in education is evident. For her, thinking is more important than perfect elocution which 'may teach young people what to say; but will probably prevent them ever learning to think' (Wollstonecraft, 2003). For Wollstonecraft education was the key to empowerment.

In Hazlitt, and others like him, the dissenting tradition became secularised. The son of a Unitarian minister, Hazlitt in his writing established a view of criticism and art as politically engaged. As the poet Tom Paulin, who has attempted to revive this tradition from what he sees as a century of neglect, writes, the 'idea of free-floating impartiality would have been incomprehensible to ... Hazlitt' (Paulin, 1998, p. 69). He attributes the change in our view of criticism to Arnold, who, as we have seen, has dominated school English. In Paulin's project of re-establishing Hazlitt's view of criticism he defines its position thus:

> This would involve recognising that all critical writing is essentially polemical, but at the same time stripping away many of the negative qualities which are so often associated with the term 'polemic'. The disinterested imagination takes a position, but is not entrenched, obdurate or rigid; rather it is based on an active flexible way of knowing that it is essentially dialogic. It doesn't talk to itself.
>
> (Ibid.)

We will discuss the impact of this description later, but for now we will examine critical literacy. This is less focussed on the politics of art but shares the belief that language, and in particular literacy, are intimately connected. Its origins lie within the Roman Catholic Church, in particular a movement known as Liberation Theology. Once again, its exponents were motivated by a belief that education should be a vehicle of ensuring a God-given right to equality rather than a mechanism for social division. Central to this endeavour was literacy. As Paolo Freire, whose seminal *Pedagogy of the Oppressed* made him one of the leading figures in this movement, explained:

> Literacy becomes a meaningful construct to the degree that it is viewed as a set of practices and functions to either empower or disempower people. In the larger sense, literacy must be analysed according to whether it promotes democratic and emancipatory changes.
>
> (Freire and Macedo, 1987, p. 41)

The notion of critical literacy, more rapidly, perhaps, than dissent, soon lost its theological roots and became a way of deconstructing or reading the society in which we live:

> Critical literacy responds to the cultural capital of a specific group or class and looks to ways in which it can be confirmed, and also at the ways in which the dominant society disconfirms students by either ignoring or denigrating the knowledge and experiences that characterise their everyday lives. The unit of analysis is social and the key concern is not individual interests but with the individual and collective empowerment.
>
> (Aronowitz and Giroux, cited in Ball *et al.*, 1990, p. 61)

As we have seen, those with a less overtly radical agenda, such as Richard Hoggart, use the term 'critical literacy' to describe a form of literacy that goes well beyond the basics. We will go on and consider its continuing, powerful influence later in this chapter.

Conservatives

Such subversive talk causes alarm in our final group. *The Daily Mail* columnist Melanie Phillips sums up such fears:

> English, after all is the subject at the heart of our definition of our national cultural identity. Since English teachers are the chief custodians of that identity we should not be surprised to find that revolutionaries intent on using the subject to transform society have gained a powerful foothold, attempting to redefine the very meaning of reading itself.
>
> (Phillips, 1997, p. 69)

It is over this battleground that most of the recent skirmishes over the English curriculum have taken place. As Phillips' remark suggests, her anxieties are born from the perceived threat to a particular hegemonic view of society and Englishness. The antecedents of her position are to be found in the work of T.S. Eliot. In *Notes Towards a Definition of Culture* he wrote:

> There is the question of what culture is, and the question whether it is anything we can control or deliberately influence. These questions confront us whenever we devise a theory, or frame a policy, of education.
>
> (Eliot, 1975, p. 294)

His use of the word 'control' is in itself significant. It connotes a view of society as needing control through schooling rather than liberation through education. He expands this idea in the same essay when he warns of the dangers of cultural disintegration and looks to education as a way of shoring up the crumbling citadel. Moreover for Eliot, the definition of culture was inextricably linked with a particular view of Englishness:

> It includes all the characteristics and interests of the people: Derby Day, Henley regatta, Cowes, the twelfth of August, a cup final day, the dog races, the pin table, the dart board, Wensleydale cheese, boiled cabbage cut into sections, beetroot in vinegar, nineteenth century Gothic churches and the music of Elgar. The reader can make up his own list.
>
> (Eliot, 1975, p. 298)

Edward Said spells out the sub-text of such an approach: 'In time, culture comes to be associated, often aggressively, with the nation or the state; this differentiates "us" from "them", almost always with some degree of xenophobia' (Said, 1993, p. xiii). In this context, any attempt to define what literature might be studied becomes less an attempt to establish a list based on literary merit, as Leavis had attempted, than a means of asserting the cultural dominance of one group over another.

Not all agree with this interpretation, however. Former chief executive of the Qualifications and Curriculum Authority Nicholas Tate, who, like Leavis, comes from a liberal arts perspective, used Eliot's list in an attempt to reopen the debate about Britishness and citizenship. In 1996 he called for an inclusive culture which feeds a notion of citizenship:

We have ended up with the rather odd situation where people can be deeply sympathetic to other people's cultural traditions but disdainful towards their own. We fail to distinguish between 'national identity' and 'nationalism' and have virtually altogether abandoned the word patriotism. We fail to grasp that ideas are multiple, complex and fluid. It is perfectly possible to feel a strong sense of British identity alongside identity as a Jew, as a European, or even as a 'citizen of the planet'. It is equally possible to have a sense of British, or English identity which is inclusive and which gives the majority culture its due while respecting minority cultures.

(Tate, 1996)

What he goes on to argue for is a cultural pluralism with a sense of civic identity at its core. This, he believes, will create 'a sense of dignity and self esteem' (ibid.). Yet the speech is an exercise in failure, not because of what it attempts to achieve, but because of its inability to conceive of a tradition other than that in which Eliot worked.

The dilemma facing Tate is that a multicultural relativism cannot meet his objective. Eliot's aggressive antisemitism would, for example, have to be allowed as being a legitimate part of what it is to be 'us', 'we'. For, as Gauri Viswanathan argues, even if we take the more relativistic stance of multiculturalism within Eliot's tradition and

broaden the curriculum to include the literature of other cultures . . . the relative tolerance of [this] position does not negate the possibility that even the most inclusionary curriculum can itself be part of the process of control.

(Viswanathan, 1989, p. 167)

In other words it may still be 'an instrument of hegemonic activity' (ibid., p. 167).

The notion of things going from bad to worse is echoed in the standards debate. Almost from the beginning of public education in this country there has been a relentless stream of reports bewailing declining levels of literacy. In 1912, for example, a head teacher wrote to *The Times* complaining that 'Reading Standards are falling because parents no longer read to their children and too much time is spent listening to the gramophone' (cited in Cox, 1995, p. 37). In the same year the English Association wrote that, 'It is a plain fact that the average girl or boy is unable to write English with a clearness or fluency or any degree of grammatical accuracy' (ibid., p. 37).

The Newbolt Report of 1921 commented that 'the teaching of English in present day schools produces a very limited command of the English language' (DCBE, 1921, Ch. 3, para. 77, p. 72). In the same report all but a few employers complained that they had found difficulty in 'obtaining employees who can speak and write English clearly and correctly' (ibid., Ch. 3, para. 77, p. 72).

Seven years later little had changed. The Spens Report of 1928 wrote 'It is a common and grave criticism that many pupils pass through grammar school without acquiring the capacity to express themselves in English' (cited in Cox, 1995, p. 38). The Norwood Report of 1943 claimed to have received 'strong evidence of the poor quality of English of Secondary School pupils . . . the evidence is such as to leave no doubt in our minds that we are confronted by a serious failure of secondary schools' (ibid., p. 38).

What is significant about the standards debate is the way that, by a sleight of hand, or curious elision, standards of written and spoken English are used as a moral gauge. This fear of the moral consequences of falling standards was given its clearest articulation under the Conservative government in the 1980s. It was Norman Tebbit who remarked in an interview in 1985:

> If you allow standards to slip to the stage where good English is no better than bad English, where people can turn up filthy and nobody takes any notice of them at school – just as well as turning up clean – all those things tend to cause people to have no standards at all, and once you lose your standards then there's no imperative to stay out of crime.
>
> (Tebbit, cited in Graddol *et al.*, 1991, p. 52)

Such a view was given credence not only by Tory ministers. John Rae, the former head teacher of Westminster School, while making the link less crudely causal, also saw a connection between the permissive society and progressive teaching. In 1982 he wrote in *The Observer*:

> The overthrow of grammar coincided with the acceptance of the equivalent of creative writing in social behaviour. As nice points of grammar were mockingly dismissed as pedantic and irrelevant, so was punctiliousness in such matters as honesty, responsibility, property, gratitude, apology and so on.
>
> (Rae, cited ibid., p. 52)

With such a view grammatical rules become societal laws. Any suggestion that the rules might be redefined or abandoned becomes a threat to civil order. It was this view of the English curriculum that was embodied in David Pascall's 1993 version of the English curriculum for England and Wales (DfE and WO, 1993) which was bitterly contested by English teachers. Indeed it might be argued that the reason for revising Cox's original version of the curriculum was precisely to ensure that this conservative vision of the English curriculum found its way into statute (see Marshall, 2000).

As we have seen, the idea of a canon of literature is highly controversial, quite apart from any professional debate about who gets to choose the texts children study. In order to avoid this controversy Brian Cox refused to include a list of prescribed authors. Yet Pascall, for reasons akin to Eliot's, introduced just such a canon of predominantly white, male writers to be studied. In addition his group changed Cox's 'knowledge about language' strand into the acquisition of standard English. Although it never made its way into statute, it formed the basis of the 1995 English curriculum produced under Ron Dearing (DfEE, 1995). The canon remained, barely amended, and the standard English section was only partially softened to a section entitled 'Standard English and Language Study' (ibid.).

New Labour's take on standards is different but no less rigidly defined. For them, apparently, a functionalist, economic rather than a moral imperative has driven their definition of what constitutes English. As David Blunkett, then Secretary of State for Education, wrote at the beginning of the national literacy strategy, 'All our children deserve to leave school equipped to enter a fulfilling adult life. If children do not master the basic skills of literacy and numeracy they will be seriously disadvantaged later' (DfEE, 1998). There is a distinctly utilitarian flavour to the words 'equipped' 'skills' and 'basics' that detracts from the apparent desire for 'fulfilment'.

It was this view that led New Labour to introduce the non-statutory National Literacy Strategy (NLS) (DfEE, 1998) for the primary sector and the Key Stage 3 framework for English (DfEE, 2001). While the latest National Curriculum for English (DfEE, 1999) has the force of law behind it, in reality it has far less significance. So inextricably is the canon now linked with the standards debate that, despite rumours that it would be dropped from the National Curriculum in 2000, it still remains.

Yet despite the overt economic and functionalist arguments for the literacy strategy, David Blunkett, who oversaw its introduction, echoes the sentiments of Rae and Tebbit in his justification of New Labour's approach. He wrote in the *Daily Mail* 'I still encounter those in the education world who would prefer the quiet life of the past, where education was "progressive"', adding 'that it ends the ill disciplined "anything goes" philosophy which did so much damage to a generation' (Blunkett, 1999).

Again, the language is emotive. Teaching grammar will restore order to the chaos brought about by child-centred teaching. But New Labour's approach, which emphasises skills and competencies and itemises in lists the technical terminology to be acquired in each year from five to fourteen, has echoes of another philosophy – the utilitarian approach so opposed by Matthew Arnold. Children's writers such as David Almond (1999) and Philip Pullman (2002) have railed against the cramping of the imagination produced by the strategy in terms very similar to writers of over a century ago. Their chief objection appears to be the mechanistic, Gradgrindian nature of New Labour's view of English.

The present debates and future directions

In essence, the current manifestation of the English curriculum in the literacy framework attempts to atomise and itemise knowledge as if what is learnt in English were akin to historical dates or the periodic table. It insists that children become familiar with an array of arbitrary technical terminology, which it lists in a detailed programme and then tests at regular intervals throughout the child's career.

Part of the difficulty with approaching English in this atomistic way, apart from any philosophical qualms, is that the purpose of doing so becomes vague. Rob the teaching of English of the wood and pupils and teachers alike become lost in a myriad of trees, the individual significance of which becomes increasingly unclear the more you look.

Why do nine year olds need to be able to identify the passive voice? Should eight year olds spend hours teasing out the differences between a metaphor and simile only to repeat the process for the next three years? Why must twelve year olds be tested on the use of the semi-colon in a novel? Sit at the back of yet another class identifying anything from the use of assonance to the generic features of the horror story and the reason for any activity becomes increasingly unclear. If learning outcomes are prescribed too closely, you begin to wonder what the point of it all is or what place English has in the curriculum.

Fast capitalism and multi-modality

Not all critics of this approach, however, do so on the grounds that it will suffocate the imagination, bore the children to death or simply end up being a pile of rubble made up of named parts with no observable purpose. There is a growing trend to use the economic imperative of so-called 'fast capitalism' against the current model of English imposed in schools.

Gunther Kress (1995, 1997) argues, for example, that the model of literacy apparently endorsed by the NLS will not fit pupils for the economy of the future. Part of his contention is that traditional 'schooled literacy' does not pay sufficient attention to the demands of new technologies. But his argument is, more significantly, dependent on the notion that the new economies, built on 'fast capitalism', demand adaptable and flexible workers. He writes:

> The question I am posing is simply this: in relation to the economic and social futures such as these, what is the English curriculum doing? . . . If jobs are moveable with the speed of global fiscal markets, then certain requirements of a fundamental kind follow the kind of person whom we are preparing for that world. Somehow they will have to be prepared not just to cope, but to control their circumstances.
>
> (Kress, 1995, p. 18)

His view finds favour with economists and financiers. Alan Greenspan, the US Federal Reserve Board Chairman, comments:

> Skill has taken on a much broader meaning than it had only a decade ago. Today's workers must be prepared along many dimensions – not only with technical know-how but also with the ability to create, analyse and transform information and with the capacity to interact effectively with others. Moreover, they must recognise that the skills they develop today will likely not last a lifetime.
>
> (Greenspan, 2000)

The difficulty with the Literacy Strategy is that it encourages the view that there is a fixed body of knowledge which, once mastered, will suffice for ever. In addition Greenspan's argument stresses the need for collaboration and creativity, facets of learning under-represented in the NLS and the Key Stage 3 framework's charts and lists.

This need to develop creativity is picked up by the economist Diane Coyle. She writes, 'Modernising Britain is about improving basic literacy and numeracy but it is also about encouraging the imagination and creativity that will form the key resources in the most successful economies' (Coyle, 1998). She has also commented that

> Although literacy and numeracy are essential of course – making it tricky to argue with the official Gradgrinds focused on achieving higher standards in this small area of necessary skill set – the real need is a robust need to think independently.
>
> (Coyle, 2001, p. 48)

Her words find an echo in another comment by Alan Greenspan: 'The broader the context that an inquiring mind brings to a problem, the greater will be the potential for creative insights that, in the end, contribute to a more productive economy' (Greenspan, 1999). He looks to arts education to furnish such thinking:

> Viewing a great painting or listening to a profoundly moving piano concerto produces a sense of intellectual joy that is satisfying in and of itself. But arguably, it also enhances and reinforces the conceptual processes so essential to innovation.
>
> (Ibid.)

As the only compulsory arts subject in the curriculum throughout a child's schooling, English appears ideally placed to help create independent, imaginative thinkers. We will return to this justification later. For now it is worth digressing to consider an element within the English curriculum not yet been covered in our trawl through the subject's history – the visual media and ICT.

It is pivotal to Kress's argument that the current model of English teaching does not fit pupils for the twenty-first century economy. This goes beyond the usual cries for visual literacy. Indeed to circumscribe his argument by the terms 'media' or 'ICT' is to limit the scope of what he is arguing for. In *Before Writing* (1997) he asks us to accept that traditional forms of print literacy, since enshrined in the NLS and Key Stage 3 framework, are being replaced by a much more multi-modal future. As people increasingly turn to electronic forms of information sources, reading becomes more overtly interactive: presentation shifts between words, pictures and moving image, all interacting to create meaning in a non-linear form. Essentially Kress demands that to accommodate these trends we need to redefine the basics.

Such a view has become almost mainstream amongst the English teaching chattering classes. Glance at many a recent edition of the journal *English in Education*, where the future of English is regularly thrashed out, and it is evident that Kress's perspective has taken a foothold. One edition is called 'Electronic English' (Andrews, 1997) and includes articles entitled 'Navigating Cyberspace: Vision, Textuality and the World Wide Web' (Stannard, 1997); 'Reading on Screen: Exploring Issues in Reading for Information with CD ROMs' (Darby *et al.*, 1997). Another edition boasts such titles as 'Hypermedia as a Medium for Textual Resistance' (Barrell and Hammett, 1999); 'Digiteens: Media Literacies and Digital Technologies in the Secondary Classroom' (Burn and Reed, 1999). The list goes on.

Indeed the authors of an editorial called 'The Future of English' take Kress as their starting point. They write that there needs to be a

> recognition of the developing and extending contexts in which English needs to be redefined, including multiculturalism, globalisation and 'the changing landscape of communication', in which new technologies, sound, the visual and the body itself are taking on new significance [Kress, 1995, pp. 94–95].
>
> (Cliff Hodges, Moss and Shreeve, 2000, p. 2)

This view is often coupled with a desire to encourage a particular view of critical literacy that is connected to our earlier definition but has been so developed as to appear de-racinated. To understand this view of critical literacy, without descending into the complexities of post-modernist literary theory, it is enough to know that debates which have raged over what constitutes appropriate subjects for study in university English departments have settled, uneasily, around the unassuming word 'text'. This has allowed people to study anything from the back of a cereal packet via soap operas to *Hamlet* and everything in between, but the unit of analysis has become increasingly linguistic in its focus. In education departments the emphasis has been to discover so-called discourse features of any given text with a view to either teaching them or critiquing them. The editorial quoted above is illuminating. Citing Lankshear, a leading proponent of critical literacy, it argues that this, combined with Kress's model

> demonstrates . . . how particular reading strategies can expose who and what controls meaning; the significance of various local, national, and global perspectives to the meanings which are found in texts; the value of readers making use of under-

standing which come from outside the curriculum subject of English; and the relevance to reading of the communication systems which texts are placed in.

(Ibid., p. 2)

Once more English is a lever for changing the world. The curious thing is, however, that for all its radical fervour, the realisation of such practices in the classroom, with the heavy emphasis on discourse and linguistic analysis, can end up as dry and prescriptive as anything offered by current government strategies. As an approach it has left little room for the aesthetic and experiential. There are, however, reasons for this.

Language as art

One of them is that both the notions of multi-modality and critical literacy appear to be democratic in their approach. This is why they have gained such popularity amongst some English teachers. As we have seen, the difficulty with situating English within an arts paradigm is that, because of the history of the subject, a liberal arts view can be construed as problematic. Again, as we have noted, this is because English either becomes too individualistic and meritocratic or is too focussed on high culture – or worse, because it becomes a mechanism for perpetuating a notion of Englishness with which the teachers in question fundamentally disagree.

Yet it is a mistake to denude English of the aesthetic. Peter Abbs has long argued fiercely against those, who, in his words, over-emphasise the socio-linguistic dimension of English. He is equally adamant that he does not want it to revolve around the Leavisite tradition of literary criticism either. He finds both approaches overly analytical. Instead, Abbs wants to see 'English not as a literary-critical discipline, but as a literary-expressive discipline within the wider epistemic community of the arts' (Abbs, 1982, p. 33). But even Abbs, who wants to encourage pupils to write creatively rather than pick over the bones of language, and to see the artistry in the process, is problematic to those who would wish to give English a more radical agenda. The difficulty with his position is that he fails to address, in any of his writing, the social dimension.

The question remains, then: how to address the need for an inclusive, democratic, as opposed to meritocratic, vision of society within an arts paradigm? For it is within the arts that English must ultimately find its justification for inclusion in the curriculum. If English becomes simply a subset of communication skills or a radical version of citizenship, it can be delivered across the curriculum. It may be needed in the primary sector, but once the basics have been delivered there is little need to extend it throughout compulsory schooling as a discrete subject.

It is here that the legacy of dissent – the notion that art and politics are inseparable – may be of service. Commenting on his own experience of English lessons as a way of carving out a sense of what the domain of English might look like in the future, Peter Medway writes:

English is supposed to be about language, and at one level it really is. Those who enjoy English will say they have developed a feel for words, get satisfaction out of deploying them well and appreciate the language of the speakers and writers they admire. But for me at school, and I know for many others, it wasn't only, or perhaps mainly, because it was about language that English was so congenial. What counted was its being about life. We got our lessons about life from the books we read in English and from our English teachers who, more than others, shared with us their own takes on the world, on relationships, existential dilemmas, moral conflicts, what made people tick.

(Medway, 2003: 5)

Medway's description of the thinking prompted by English lessons has something in common with the aims of those early dissenting academies. It is an acknowledgement that grappling with the mechanics of language, either in one's own writing or in the writing of others, is essentially about the creation of meaning; about having something to say and finding the most powerful way to articulate it. It is about shaping the world in words. And this is an aesthetic endeavour. The job of the English teacher is to build the repertoire of pupils through exposure and practice, to enable them to engage in that process as readers and writers. Again, as Medway observes:

What you come out of an English course with is not – or the important part is not – knowledge that you can write out in a test. Rather, you come out able to do a variety of different things, having developed the linguistic muscles and brain-word co-ordination to generate a wide range of subtle and complex performances.

(Ibid.)

He might have added that English is also a place where fantasy and imagined worlds also exist, that books are a place of escape from reality. Such an observation could and should be extended to the moving image media. Indeed, in accordance with Kress's multi-modal future, English teachers have long been integrating adaptations of literary texts in an almost seamless manner (cf. Parker, 1999 and Oldham, 1999). Moreover, the study of film and television programmes, with their predominantly narrative structure and their own grammar, create similar opportunities to those described by Medway. What is significant is less the technology than the capacity of that technology to create those imagined worlds.

Yet to isolate this process from the world itself, to assume some lofty, critical neutrality or purely individualistic pleasure would be a nonsense. Tom Paulin's demand that we re-discover Hazlitt's 'engaged disinterestedness' is a timely solution. Texts arise from and are created by social and political contexts. Writers intend to challenge, subvert and explore the world in which they live. It is engagement with the big ideas and the possibility of finding a voice in the noise of post-modernity that will empower pupils when they leave behind the school gate. This is the future of English.

References

Abbs, P. (1982) *English Within the Arts: A Radical Alternative for English and the Arts in the Curriculum*, London: Hodder & Stoughton.

Almond, D. (1999) 'Leave time for the imagination', The *Independent*, July 15.

Andrews, A. (1997) 'Electronic English', *English in Education* 31(2).

Arnold, M. (1948) *Culture and Anarchy*, Dover Wilson, J. (ed.), Cambridge: Cambridge University Press.

Arnold, M. (1979) *Selected Poetry and Prose*, Thompson, D. (ed.), London: Heinemann.

Ball, S.J., Kenny, A. and Gardiner, D. (1990) 'Literacy Policy and the Teaching of English', in Goodson, I. and Medway, P. (eds) *Bringing English to Order*, London: Falmer.

Barrell, B.R.C. and Hammett, R.F. (1999) 'Hypermedia as a Medium for Textual Resistance', *English in Education* 33(3).

Blunkett, D. (1999) 'Commentary: Moaners Who are Cheating your Children', *Daily Mail*, July 19.

Burns, A. and Reed, K. (1999) 'Digiteens: Media Literacies and Digital Technologies in the Secondary Classroom', *English in Education* 33(3).

Cliff Hodges, G., Moss, J. and Shreeve, A. (2000) 'The Future of English', *English in Education* 34(1).

Cox, B. (1992) *The Great Betrayal: Memoirs of a Life in Education*, London: Hodder & Stoughton.

Cox, B. (1995) *Cox on the Battle for the English Curriculum*, London: Hodder & Stoughton.

Coyle, D. (1998) *The Weightless World*, Oxford: Capstone Press.

Coyle, D. (2001) 'How Not to Educate the Information Workforce', *Critical Quarterly* 43(1).

Darby, R., Dawes, L., Dennison, A., Gallagher, C., Loomes, W., Reid, H. and Stanton, J. (1997) 'Reading on Screen: Exploring Issues in Reading for Information with CD ROMs', *English in Education* 31(2).

DCBE [Departmental Committee of the Board of Education] (1921) *The Teaching of English in England* [The Newbolt Report], London: HMSO.

DES (1975) *A Language for Life* [The Bullock Report], London: HMSO.

DES and WO (1989) *English for Ages 5–16* [The Cox Report], London: HMSO.

DES and WO (1990) *English in the National Curriculum*, London: HMSO.

DfE and WO (1993) *English for Ages 5–16* [Pascall Curriculum], London: HMSO.

DfEE (1998) *The National Literacy Strategy*, London: HMSO.

DfEE (1999) *English: The National Curriculum for England*, London: HMSO.

DfEE (2001) *Framework for Teaching English: Years 7, 8 and 9*, London: HMSO.

DfEE and WO (1995) *English in the National Curriculum*, London: HMSO.

Dickens, C. (1980) *Hard Times*, Harmondsworth: Penguin.

Dixon, J. (1975) *Growth Through English*, Oxford: Oxford University Press.

Eliot, T.S. (1975) 'Notes Towards a Definition of Culture', in Kermode, F. (ed.) *Selected Prose of TS Eliot*, London: Faber & Faber.

Enfield, W. (1796) 'The Enquirer on Verse and Poetry', *Monthly Magazine* 2(6).

Freire, P. (1998) *Pedagogy of the Oppressed*, London: Continuum.

Freire, P. and Macedo, D. (1987) *Literacy: Reading the Word and the World*, London: Routledge.

Graddol, D., Maybin J., Mercer, N. and Swann, J. (eds) (1991) *Talk and Learning 5–16: An Inservice Pack on Oracy for Teachers*, Milton Keynes: Open University Press.

Greenspan, A. (1999, 19 Oct.) http://www.bog.frb.fed.us./BoardDocs/Speeches.

Greenspan, A. (2000, 22 March) http://www.bog.frb.fed.us./BoardDocs/Speeches.

Hitchens, C. (1988) *Prepared for the Worst: Selected Essays and Minority Reports*, London: Chatto & Windus.

Hoggart, R. (1998) 'Critical Literacy and Creative Reading', in Cox, B. (ed.) *Literacy Is Not Enough: Essays on the Importance of Reading*, Manchester: Manchester University Press.

Kress, G. (1995) *Writing the Future: English and the Making of a Culture of Innovation*, Sheffield: NATE Papers in Education.

Kress, G. (1997) *Before Writing*, London: Routledge.

Marshall, B. (2000) *English Teachers – the Unofficial Guide: Researching the Philosophies of English Teachers*, London: RoutledgeFalmer.

Medway, P. (2003) 'English method', *English and Media Magazine* 47: 4–7.

Motion, A. (1998) *Keats*, London: Faber & Faber.

Oldham, J. (1999) 'The Book of the Film: Enhancing Print Literacy at KS3', *English in Education* 33 (1).

Parker, D. (1999) 'You've Read the Book, Now Make the Film: Moving Image media, print literacy and narrative', *English in Education* 33(1).

Paulin, T. (1998) *The Day Star of Liberty*, London: Faber & Faber.

Phillips, M. (1994) 'Education's Guerrillas Prepare for War', The *Guardian,* 3 January.

Phillips, M. (1997) *All Must have Prizes*, London: Little, Brown & Co.

Pullman, P. (2002) *Perverse, All Monstrous and Prodigious Things*, Sheffield: NATE Publications.

Said, E. (1993) *Culture and Imperialism*, London: Chatto & Windus.

Sampson, G. (1952) *English for the English*, Cambridge: Cambridge University Press.

Stannard, R. (1997) 'Navigating Cyberspace: Vision, Textuality and the World Wide Web', *English in Education* 31(2).

Tate, N. (June, 1996) *Why Learn?*, London: Association of Teachers and Lecturers.

Viswanathan, G. (1989) *Masks of Conquests: Literary Study and British Rule in India*, London: Faber & Faber.

Wollstonecraft, M. (2003, Jan. 15) web address: http://www.duke.usask.ca/−vargo/barbould/related_texts/wollstonecraft.html.

6 Geography

David Lambert

Introduction: finding and keeping a place in the sun

Geography occupies an uncertain place in the school curriculum. In part, this may be because of the long-standing difficulty geographers have in articulating what it is they do and how geography can be justified as a subject on the curriculum. It would be difficult to get a coherent and stable picture of the subject by asking a group of geography teachers to describe the main purpose of the subject. Debates about the subject are common-place among university teachers and undergraduates to the extent that it seems geographers have a persistent identity crisis. This point may explain to some extent the relative difficulty that seems to exist in establishing geography effectively, particularly in primary schools where specialists in geography are rare. To non-specialists it is not at all clear how to interpret the geography curriculum beyond the fairly obvious building blocks of the subject, such as descriptions of the physical environment, interest in places and the use of maps and atlases.

'Geography has an identity crisis' is so pervasive a theme that organisations such as the Geographical Association (GA) invest considerable energy in helping teachers state the case for geography in an increasingly competitive and congested curriculum. This has resulted in both strengths (in that the subject is endlessly contested and there are few taken for granted or given positions) and some profound weaknesses. It is a relatively recently established academic discipline at university and those who believe in its 'importance' in the school curriculum (not least in supplying a stream of fresh undergraduates) have been rather more keen to defend its hard-won school curriculum 'place in the sun' (against even newer competitors such as business or media studies) than to grapple honestly with its educational role.

To illustrate the point, I find some geography teachers are seriously challenged by even the hint of a suggestion that the widely held notion of 'geographical' skills may in fact be flawed. Clinging to the claim that the subject can supply young people with such allegedly unique attributes is partly a reaction to the public image of geography as the stuffy gazetteer of 'capes and bays'. However, even though there are skills which geographers use expertly, there is nothing intrinsically 'geographical' about reading, writing, listening, talking, or even reading or drawing a map. Resistance to voicing such a thought arises because it seems to deny the right of the subject to exist in its own right, which would certainly weaken geography's position in the curriculum turf wars. But *do* geographers read maps differently from historians or mathematicians, or landscapes differently from artists? They may come to different conclusions, but this is not because they apply a special set of skills but because the *purpose* of their 'reading' is different. And this is what is difficult to articulate – the purpose of geography in education. Hence when the question is posed, what does it mean to think about something 'geographically'? I think geography teachers are far less clear about this than they could be, which serves to confirm to a knowing public that geography is more a burden on the memory than a light in the mind.

One characteristic of geography, or more precisely geography educators, is their comparative insecurity within the academic firmament. This is a result of the identity crisis I have begun to discuss but it is currently fuelled by declining numbers of students taking up the subject at both GCSE and A level.[1] Thus, there is a tendency for the geographer in me to say 'ouch' when I read John White's association of geography and remembering things (see above p. 7). This link seems to echo the popular view of geography being rather tedious and dull, being concerned simply to list oceans, mountains and countries: the irony here is that the one time school geography is sure to hit the headlines is when some survey or other (they come around frequently) shows that schools are unsuccessful even in this modest aim! Note for example the front page of the *Daily Mirror* (21 November 2002), which screamed 'Where is Iraq?' in order to draw attention to its report that six out of seven Americans cannot find Iraq in a children's atlas. It concluded that 'George Bush is on the brink of invading Iraq – but most Americans have no idea where the country is' (p. 5). Would the population of Britain (in whose schools geography *is* taught, unlike in most States in the USA) fare any better? Possibly, for Britain is closer to Iraq. But the National Geographic Society survey, which formed the basis of the *Mirror's* anxieties, was an international one and showed eye-catching 'geographical ignorance' in Britain too. It seems that either places are not taught very effectively, or young people cannot (or do not want to) remember them.

However, so keen have geography teachers been to shed their corduroy image of reciting capes and bays with pupils it is sometimes difficult to persuade beginning teachers to use such basic tools as atlases at all in their classroom, lest they betray signs of an anorak-obsession with place names, or are labelled 'boring' by their pupils. This is unfortunate and in my view akin to trying to teach English without recourse to dictionaries. Perhaps geography is caught between a rock and a hard place in this respect. For geography is not simply concerned with the basic 'vocabulary' of the world – i.e. the 'facts' recorded in the atlas – but its 'grammar' too. The latter involves pupils in understanding how the world 'works', and therefore needs to turn to cultural, economic, environmental, physical, political and social processes. Geography teachers often teach with a passion and the source of this is commonly to get students (and other readers of maps) to begin to see the stories behind the map: put another way, if the data on the map provides the nouns and adjectives, then it is geographical study that provides the verbs. One without the others makes no sense, but it is quite possible that an over-zealous pursuit of principle, or process, may well become careless of the basic vocabulary of the subject – the points, lines and spaces recorded in the atlas, most of which have a name.

When the National Curriculum Order for geography passed through the House of Commons in 1991, the then Secretary of State, Kenneth Clarke, observed rather proudly that the content had been put back into geography, an antidote to what he perceived to have been an overemphasis on values enquiries and debates in geography classrooms (DES, 1991). In other words, geography was defined, and laid out, as a content rich subject. Notwithstanding claims such as those in my previous paragraph, geography was identified as just another component of 'cultural literacy' (Dowgill and

Lambert, 1992; Hirsch, 1988), a form of 'general knowledge' that a national education system should be expected to impart to its future citizens. This may have added to the suspicion that geography was seen to be lightweight, easy, for the less able and a break from the real business of school to prepare young people for their future economic lives through the National Curriculum core subjects.

To begin with, the mere presence of geography on the list of National Curriculum subjects was taken by geographers in education to be a major victory. At the beginning of the 1980s, when government made its first moves to regulate and ultimately specify the school curriculum, geography did not seem to figure at all. The usual insecurity, undoubtedly aided by a basic instinct for survival, encouraged many movers and shakers in the subject and especially those in the vibrant Geographical Association, to believe that there was a real risk of a National Curriculum emerging with geography notable only by its absence. By the time of the Education Reform Act of 1988, geography's place had been assured. In large measure this was due to highly successful lobbying activities by the GA (Rawling, 2001). Thus, just as the geography teaching 'establish-ment' had seen off earlier threats of rural studies, world studies and environmental studies through the curriculum free-for-all of the 1960s and 1970s (Goodson, 1983), geography became a foundation subject along with all the paraphernalia that denoted its new status, including (at first) the promise of SATs.

To summarise, the priority for geography, a relative newcomer as an academic discipline, has always been to secure its place in the school curriculum. I argue that in order to achieve its place in the list of National Curriculum subjects, certain kinds of debates concerning geography in education were shelved, notably those to do with what characterised geographical thinking, or the geographical mind. Instead, geography teachers, through the organs of the leading subject association, the GA, played politics with the politicians who made the deeply political judgement to 'put the content back into geography'. The outcome was that by the beginning of the 1990s, school geo-graphy seemed secure throughout the years of compulsory schooling, perhaps for the first time. This security was illusory and remarkably short lived as King (1989) warned at the time, albeit in rather aggressive terms:

> although some form of geography is guaranteed to appear in the National Curricu-lum, the fight for geography as a separate and distinct subject is yet to be con-cluded. One battle has been won, but the war is not yet over.
>
> (Ibid., p. 135)

Geography loses its way?

The original National Curriculum Order was very difficult to use, especially in primary schools. Without aims and the barest minimum of a rationale it had the appearance merely of a list of contents. With over 180 'statements of attainment' spread across five 'attainment targets' these contents were supremely difficult for teachers *to arrange*, mainly because the selection process (a primary purpose of curriculum planning) had been so well hidden from view. The drive of teachers to use a loved subject to fulfil educational aims and purposes, the passion mentioned in the previous section, was replaced with an urgent need to simply make sense of the 'rules of engagement'. Essen-tially, the teacher merely had to accept what the pupils needed to be taught and find a way to 'deliver' it. Why teach geography? Because it was there!

There were several attempts to support the implementation of the geography National Curriculum through the preparation of Key Stage 3 textbooks, including one by this author (Lambert, 1991). By far the most commercially successful was *Key Geography* (Waugh and Bushell, 1991) which was put together by the simple expedient of cutting up the statements of attainment and arranging them not by the application of themes, key ideas or any other curriculum planning device, but by grouping them into roughly equal piles to fit the requisite number of double page spreads for a three book series. This was in some respects a highly successful strategy, in that it undoubtedly helped many teachers, especially non-specialists, fulfil their statutory obligations. But these circumstances left significant damage not only to the case for defending geography in its newly won statutory place in the curriculum (as we shall see below), but also to the capacity of subject specialist teachers to provide meaningful educational experiences for pupils.

Grappling with an impossible National Curriculum Order, geography teachers in fact relinquished curriculum planning and development at the school level to textbook writers − and the Waugh series in particular which achieved in excess of 60 per cent market share (Lambert, 1999). Even though the National Curriculum was revised in 1995, and again in 2000, into a much more coherent form, a damaging hangover from 1991 continued for at least ten years. In primary Key Stages, the geography Order was actually suspended, possibly to the relief of many teachers, to be reinstated in 2000; but again long lasting damage to the idea of a broad and balanced curriculum had been done in that the 'humanities' were understood to be expendable. It has been argued that there are now signs of change (Rawling, 2001), with renewed interest in school based curriculum renewal, but until this happens the long shadow of the original National Curriculum remains. The hangover has the following characteristics:

- control over what is taught is perceived to come from outside the specialist teaching community;
- it is presumed that school geography has to 'cover' in approximate balance the full range of what is geography − the human, the physical, the environmental, the regional;
- it is taken as given that geography is essentially 'content rich' − an empirical account of the earth's features, or mimesis;
- despite lip service paid to techniques to promote 'enquiry learning', geography fundamentally fulfils the requirements of an 'answer culture.'

I can turn to personal anecdote to illustrate the impact of this hangover, with some confidence that it will ring bells and sound true to other geography educationists. When my daughter dropped geography at the end of year 9 (in 1997) I was naturally interested why. When she finally left school in 2002 I asked her to look back and reflect on this question. She wrote,

> 'What's the point?' was my reaction to taking geography at GCSE level when the idea was suggested to me at options time. As far as I could see, there were far more interesting things to be learnt than how the odd rock formation came about, or where various volcanoes were. It all seemed so, well, fragmented and for that reason I chose history instead: there was, after all, a story in history!

Interestingly, when it came to the next options moment, after her GCSEs, she returned to geography, taking the A level examination:

> Geography, it turned out, was an interesting subject, partly because it is constantly changing. Those rock formations that I had hastily pushed aside were actually quite important to understand and the volcanoes I had never thought much about before caused havoc in the lives of those people that lived at their bases. Geography is an incredibly broad subject encasing social, political, environmental and economic aspects of what is happening in the world today. It has taught me to understand that we can be affected by events all over the world; for example, El Niño doesn't just affect the weather off the coast of Peru, but it has in the past caused freak weather in most continents. Of course geography is not just about weather. During the A-Level course I also learnt about development and disparity in Los Angeles (the 'ecology of fear'), about wilderness areas and the threats towards them and (maybe most importantly) about poverty, how it comes about and how people try to deal with it.

I think Jessica finally saw the point of studying geography and, at A level at least, the subject appeared to excite her interest and commitment. But her criticism of her Key Stage 3 experience is highly significant. It chimes with the falling popularity of GCSE geography nationally (Westaway and Rawling, 2001) and may even evoke the issues that lie behind reports from Ofsted that the quality of teaching in KS3 geography is problematic (Ofsted, 1999). What Jessica appeared to have experienced was a series of disconnected ('fragmented') bits, which she found difficult to knit together or link in a way that gave her a sense of travelling or moving forward. There did not seem to be much point to learning geography. Geography in its National Curriculum formulation, with all that content returned to it, did not seem relevant to Jessica. I do not blame the textbook writers and I certainly do not blame the teachers – Jessica learned her geography in a successful and lively department. I refer back to the four characteristics of the post-1991 'hangover' listed above (p. 78).

Taking the first two from my list, the perceived need for teachers to 'cover' a kind of authorised version, or subset, of the subject discipline called 'school geography', has led to the ultimate curriculum death wish, namely the belief that what is to be taught is largely uncontentious and can be passed on from a central authority. Ivor Goodson noted this some time ago: 'The curriculum is avowedly and manifestly a social construction. Why, then, is this central social construct treated as such a timeless given...?' (Goodson, 1992, p. 66). It tends to be treated like this in a world in which we talk of 'delivering' the curriculum and teachers are often understandably reluctant to deviate from what they imagine is the given line for fear of criticism from Ofsted and others. The curriculum experience becomes 'stuck' and increasingly disengaged from both the wider discipline and the *lived* experience of the teacher and students. It is hard to overemphasise this point. Why isn't the Middle East taught in school? (if it were, it is likely that more students would remember where Iraq is located). Why is migration reduced to generalised 'push and pull' models? (which appear to distance or even dehumanise the process). How can we teach a 'reverence for rivers'? It is not that any of these *should* be taught, nor that any particular element of the National Curriculum Order *should not* be taught. It is simply that the teacher needs to be empowered to exercise some choice in the matter so to gear his or her teaching to a particular time and place, his or her own interests and specialisms and the motivations of the students.

The second two characteristics from my list take us from the curriculum to matters of pedagogy. Ever since the 1970s and the sophisticated curriculum development work in geography from the Schools Council (Geography for the Young School Leaver [GYSL]; The Bristol Project; Geography 16–19), it has become the received wisdom that 'enquiry classrooms' promote good teaching and learning. One of the significant unresolved tensions of the National Curriculum working group for geography was the role of enquiry in geography. Perhaps the debate at the time was too polarised leading to somewhat arcane questions, such as: how does enquiry in geography differ from investigation in science? Unless a substantial difference could be shown the conclusion was that science should 'cover it', leaving geography to its content. As we have seen geography acquired a lot of content, which meant that teachers wanting to engage in enquiry with students had precious little time to do so. Enquiry in teaching and learning geography is still not well understood (however see Roberts, 2003) and has, at its worst, become reduced to asking a 'key question', providing some data and steering students to the summary/conclusion. Open questions with less than clear cut solutions are not easy to find, leading to my contention that geography teaching, against the better judgement of most practitioners, supports an answer culture rather than, say, a culture of argument (Myerson and Rydin, 1996) which may better prepare students for the complex and uncertain world of risk they are growing up to meet.

Rekindling a sense of direction

Curriculum plans are assumed, to a greater or lesser extent, to be guided by an overriding principle of '*fitness for purpose*'. Thus, the plan may require teachers to think about *how* the teaching and learning takes place as well as *what* is relevant, worthwhile and motivating to learn; but the background question should be invoked regularly – *for what purpose do we plan this or that sequence of lessons?* In other words, we may establish what we would like pupils to learn, and the way we would prefer them to learn it, but *why* do we want pupils to learn these things, in these ways? Sometimes answers to these questions are not very clear. Worse still, in some cases it appears that such questions are not examined seriously by the planners at all, leaving the curriculum (and teachers interpreting the curriculum at the level of classroom experience) open to all manner of hidden influences, and free to be blown this way and that by the slipstream of any passing bandwagon.

I fear that this is the outcome of school geography having lost (for the moment) its direction. Thus, the *Sunday Telegraph* (25 November 2002) reported some 'research' that yielded the headline 'Children "being brainwashed" by new green geography lessons'. This is a familiar attack on 'geography', confusing several arguments which together amount to a rejection of any attempt to tackle contemporary debates and challenges with students. On the one hand it wants geography to 'develop critical thinking' but on the other contends that 'replacing knowledge' with trying to understand the competing values that underpin environmental issues is an act of dumbing down. The article goes on to quote 'a parent' as being:

> 'appalled' to discover that one of her sons in the early years of secondary school could talk about 'renewable energy resources' and 'population issues' but could not point to Egypt or even Africa on a map.

I draw attention to this article simply to demonstrate the need to recognise that some level of professional control of the curriculum, even that with a strong and confident sense of moral purpose, is still likely to be constrained by outside influence. To emphasise my point, the Campaign for Real Education in the same article asserts that

> the QCA and the GA are obsessed with political correctness . . . We have had terrible difficulties with the history being taught in state schools and now geography is a real problem too.

Why teach geography? Not because 'it is there', for no subject has an automatic right to be there. It is possible that attacks by those who have 'terrible difficulties' with the human sciences may do for geography altogether in an age which seems to emphasise economic and vocational utility above everything else. If there is anything worth fighting for it needs to be at a level of sophistication to dispatch those who accuse geography of indoctrination the moment they perceive it takes pupils beyond 'the facts'.

For some time now influential curriculum developers in geography have established that 'geography' is not to be mistaken for an end in itself. Why study geography? – not because it is there, but because it is a means to serve educational ends. We can think of Frances Slater's *Learning Through Geography* (1982), Michael Naish coining the phrase 'geography as a medium of education' and more recently David Leat's *Thinking Through Geography* (1998): all denote a healthy approach to the notion of a curriculum, in which 'geography' is likened to a resource for learning, or a vehicle. Thus, the place of geography in the whole curriculum can be justified in terms of the subject's enormous potential as an educational resource.

One of the benefits of rational curriculum planning has been the clear enunciation of which of the 'elements of learning' (grouped under knowledge, understanding, skills and values) can be addressed through the various subjects, and one of geography's great strengths lies in the range and combinations of knowledge, understandings, skills and values that it has the potential to cover. Geography straddles the arts and the sciences, uses skills from across the whole spectrum and is concerned with real-world decision making involving people and their humanly constructed and physical environments. In short it can show the value of holistic thinking. What is more, it is topical and can engage with the future. It recognises that contemporary concepts such as 'sustainability' and 'globalisation' are slippery, catch-all terms that mask enormously complex and urgent disputes about all our futures. And finally, the subject provides viewpoints about place and spatial relations that, through the operation of political processes resulting from the state's occupation of territory, provide learners with a means of grasping issues to do with identity and citizenship (Lambert and Machon, 2001).

In providing the above glimpse of the potential richness of geography as a resource for learning, I do not wish my task to be mistaken for merely promoting or even defending 'geography' per se, as intrinsically good or worthwhile. *Some* geography in schools may not be worth defending, but in any case this is not the point. The point is much more to do with the profoundly important question about the kind of curriculum we want; that is, a curriculum fit for what purpose? Of course, there are (possibly conflicting) purposes laid down by the state and/or its agencies, examination organisations, and other 'interests', all of which are beyond the capacity of individual teachers to influence directly. To argue for a piece of the curriculum action to be called geography is fine, but in the end little more than an empty and self-serving gesture, unless it is accompanied by a thoroughly convincing case for what educational purpose it serves. In my view it is teachers, not awarding bodies or curriculum agencies, who need to be able to make this case. The position of geography in the curriculum is only meaningful if we can be confident that the box called geography is filled in a way that contributes to the curriculum we want. As Eleanor Rawling's call for school based curriculum development (1996, 2001) makes plain, there are 'levels' of curriculum development, including, crucially, at the level of the classroom – where the action is. It is in the classroom that 'curriculum' may become indistinguishable from 'pedagogy' (Moore, 2001). What guides teachers' curriculum/pedagogic decisions therefore is a matter of great importance. They must be driven by a concern that they be fit for purpose. If teachers are not framed by a sense of moral purpose – if *they* cannot 'see the point' – the curriculum experience of pupils is inevitably compromised.

However, before pursuing this point in more detail it is worth acknowledging that there are some dangers in pursuing this line of argument *too* assiduously. The purpose, or value, of doing geography may indeed lie in the subject matter itself. I am certainly prepared to accept that there are cases where this is true, and would urge curriculum managers and geography teachers not to undervalue the intrinsic power of geography. The legitimate 'point' of geography lessons, for example, may be to ensure that pupils are exposed to scenes they have never seen before, to experience at first hand (through fieldwork) or indirectly (through mediated images) some amazing scenery, some extra-ordinary weather or the power of rushing water whether in a river valley or against the sea defences on the coast. To gaze at alpine peaks and to imagine what forces have been involved in their creation is a way to take pupils outside themselves. Geography can provide spiritual opportunities and experiences.

The role and purpose of teachers

The distinctive aspect of a *teacher's* sense of purpose is that it is dominated by matters to do with children's learning. The state and other infrastructural interests such as awarding bodies and subject associations are usually less interested in individuals and more interested in society wide matters or even issues of efficiency and commercial success. Many commentators have argued most strongly that the school represents the state's key apparatus for maintaining stability, fulfilling a conservative function of guaranteeing quiescence (see Moore, 2001 for a general discussion). Subject associations such as the Geographical Association, representing teachers in schools may be presumed also to be profoundly conservative partly through their role to 'defend' the interest of the subject (but as we have seen in the previous section they have also been accused of being bastions of left wing political correctness too).

But many geography teachers are motivated by an essentially 'child-centred' ideal. They are commonly committed to developing in their pupils independent and enquiring minds, together with positive dispositions to issues that society at large sometimes finds difficult, such as respecting diversity, tolerating the different (and the difficult), supporting the disadvantaged and so on. Pupils are presented with the means to see alternative viewpoints, encouraged to question naturalised 'facts' and challenge common-sense or 'hegemonic' views. In order to achieve such goals, pupils need to be actively involved – meaning intellectually engaged – which is why we might pigeon-hole such concerns as matters of pedagogy. But the whole authentic learning experience, including both content and process, needs to be engineered so that it makes a difference to individuals and is not just 'plastered on'. In geography we may be able to live up to the implications of such bold notions when we are confident enough to take seriously the personal geographies of pupils and to work with and from their geographical imaginations. But this is difficult in a world where it has become a naturalised pedagogic 'fact' that it is always good practice to be clear and precise about the learning outcomes of the lesson and to share these with the pupils at the start.

Real, authentic 'experience' is not something that is simply done to us, but something we take part in and construct, often in the company of others. A great many teachers and curriculum theorists would argue that such an approach – broadly what Edwards and Kelly (1998, p. 1) describe as 'education as development through experience' – can be equated with notions of an open society which values the democratic ideal. John Dewey is often cited in this respect, but also Basil Bernstein envisaged the emergence of a more diverse, yet open society and a shift

> 'from pedagogy which . . . was concerned with the learning of standard operations . . . to a pedagogy which emphasises the exploration of principles; from schools which emphasise the teacher as solution-giver to schools which emphasise the teacher as problem poser or creator' and 'to more personalised forms of control where teachers and taught confront each other as individuals'.
>
> (op. cit., cited in Edwards and Kelly, 1998, p. 4)

Bernstein's anticipation was somewhat premature, for few would recognise over 30 years later that much progress towards his vision has been made. And yet, the *purpose* behind a teacher's actions, planning and implementing a lesson or sequence of lessons, can still be linked to such ideals, even if the ostensible role of school in society is not. Teachers can change pupils through the experiences they provide. They are not employed to change society and few would see this as their role, but they do have a responsibility to 'make a difference' with the individuals they teach. It is difficult to imagine any understanding of 'effective' curriculum planning and development that did not have this in mind.

Thus, merely conducting a 'pedagogic adventure' with pupils is not enough to change (or is that 'challenge'?) them, for appropriate materials (content) will also have to be selected. This is why it is important to have highly trained specialists in secondary schools. For example, the published curriculum may require pupils to study 'the changing face of British industry'. The steel industry may be a recommended example or case study – there is after all much historical as well as current geographical information that is readily available through textbooks and other sources. However, the geographically trained mind can see it is the *scale* at which we study the material (and teachers are free to choose the emphasis) that crucially affects what we study and what we learn (see, for example, Taylor, 1993, pp. 40–48). Most of the industry is now owned by a Dutch trans-national (Corus). The industry contracted rapidly through Britain's periods of de-industrialisation of the 1980s and 1990s and Corus announced plans in 2001 for further 'rationalisation', largely through the closure of a plant in South Wales. Whether the industry is studied on a global scale (the 'reality' scale of international capital, in which case certain 'inevitable' economic realities may explain the closure – and others around the world), the national scale (the scale of 'ideology', in which case the role of government may be examined, for example as to whether the industry should be strategically protected by subsidy) or on a local scale (the scale of 'experience', in which case the dramatic impact of closure on people's lives – and not just former steel workers – would come to the fore) governs to a significant degree the kind of data we need pupils to interact with and the kinds of questions that may be posed, not only by the teachers but by the pupils themselves. In this way, content and pedagogy closely inter-relate and closely influence learning outcomes.

Studying matters such as economic (and political, environmental, social or cultural) change in real places, in a way that shows the significance of (the human construct) scale, is a supreme educational contribution of geography. As a friend of mine (someone who regrets giving up the study of geography at school) said recently, geography is 'a prerequisite for watching *Newsnight* intelligently.' I understood this to mean that geography taught well can help people make sense of the world.

Conclusions

School geography is perhaps in a confused condition. It is often said to be 'popular', but at the same time 'lacklustre'. Although the space for innovation has returned after the National Curriculum hiatus in the early 1990s, in reality the school subject appears 'stuck'. There is uncertainty about whether we can reasonably talk about a geography curriculum 'entitlement' and we have yet to see what a Humanities College with geography as the lead subject may look like in practice. Some in the school geography community now appear fearful of the competitive environment in which 'predators', such a media studies, citizenship, business education and psychology, may swallow perfectly good students! All these are familiar and in some ways recurring problems, and unless geography educationists turn again to wider theoretical perspectives of the curriculum as a whole, rather than accept the existing subject frame as an enduring given, I feel curriculum developers in geography will for ever be locked into ultimately senseless curriculum 'turf wars'. To use Rawling's (2001) phrase, if geography educationists end up trying to defend their 'subject tribe', this will almost certainly happen at the expense of considering the needs of learners.

I think that organisations such as subject associations can, without any sense of betrayal to their (subscription paying) 'subject communities', begin to work with each other when it makes sense to do so. In what has been dubbed the post comprehensive era, they may support different local solutions to the classic curriculum dilemma (of 'quarts into pint pots'). Geography may become, or remain, a strong and successful single subject in some schools, a contributor to science in another, a member of the arts and humanities faculty in another, a key organiser and contributor to citizenship in another. . . . My view is that this can happen only when the purpose of geography (and what it means to 'think geographically') is understood and the curriculum is developed as a whole – in a way that involves people with specialist subject perspectives including those who understand the value of a geographical mind. This has implications for teacher education and training, for levels of subject specialist expertise of teachers becomes more important in this model. Again, there is a clear role for subject specialist associations in this configuration.

I am for expert, scholarly geography teaching in schools. As we have seen, a strongly subject focussed curriculum in England has not been entirely successful in providing this. The more we are concerned to define the specifications of school geography –

particularly in terms of the holy grail of pupil subject 'entitlement' – the more we may run the risk of selling pupils short. As Edwards and Kelly (1998) explain: 'The term entitlement is a moral term; it encapsulates the notion of rights. And, in a democratic context, the rights any individual has are intended to benefit him/her rather than society at large. Thus, the right to an 'entitlement curriculum' is a right to a form of education deliberately designed to promote the development of each individual' (p. xii). The thought of a '*geography* entitlement,' therefore, makes no sense – though I am confident that in geography there is a rich, disciplined resource to draw on to help fulfil what is the pupils' entitlement. This entitlement, to return to Edwards and Kelly, means: 'offering genuine educational experiences to young people. In order to be genuine, these experiences must be their own and must relate in some direct way to the development of their own thinking, their own attitudes, their own values' (p. xv).

To put this crudely, the argument posited here is that *education* is the only entitlement, as a single entity. Edwards and Kelly advocate an adjectival curriculum based on the 'areas of experience' (DES, 1977) identified by Her Majesty's Inspectors, and this implies an end to 'geography' as an entitlement. For me, the logical outcome of this thinking requires such a reconceptualisation of curriculum organisation that it becomes impractical – and certainly takes us beyond the scope of this chapter. However, the case is persuasive enough for geographers to be less precious about the borderlands of the school subject. Effective curriculum development is not concerned with protecting geography as if it were an endangered species, but primarily and relentlessly interested in how to interest and motivate young people and how to enrich their knowledge and skills for dealing with a risky and uncertain world. To be sure, thinking geographically has a lot to offer in this project. Those with a geographical bent of mind are likely to feel relatively well prepared for what they encounter.

Acknowledgement

I thank Mary Biddulph of Nottingham University for her helpful comments on an earlier draft of this chapter. The remaining weaknesses are, however, all mine.

Note

1   This is not the place for a full analysis. It is worth noting however that the figures show geography at A level dropping two places from seventh to ninth in the ranking of most popular A level subjects, being replaced by art and design and psychology. Whilst the geography candidature continued to fall during 2001–2002, drama, computing, media studies, psychology, music and religious studies all gained.

References

DES (1977) *The Curriculum 11–16*, London: HMSO.
DES (1991) *Geography in the National Curriculum (England)*, London: Department of Education and Science/HMSO.
Dowgill, P. and Lambert, D. (1992) 'Cultural Literacy and School Geography', *Geography*, 77, 2, pp. 143–152.
Edwards, G. and Kelly, A.V. (eds) (1998) *Experience and Education: Towards an Alternative National Curriculum*, London: Paul Chapman Publishing (a Sage Company).
Goodson, I. (1983) *Social Subjects and Curriculum Change*, London: Croom Helm.

Goodson, I. (1992) 'On Curriculum Form: Notes Towards a Theory of Curriculum', *Sociology of Education*, 65, 1, pp. 66–75.

Hirsch, E. (1988) *Cultural Literacy: What Every American Needs to Know*, NY: Vintage Books.

King, R. (1989) 'Geography in the School Curriculum: a Battle Won But Not Yet Over', *Area*, 21, 2, pp. 117–136.

Lambert, D. (1991) *Jigsaw Pieces, The Cambridge Geography Project*, Cambridge: Cambridge University Press.

Lambert, D. (1999) 'Exploring the Use of Textbooks in Key Stage 3 Classrooms', in *The Curriculum Journal*, 10, 1, pp. 85–105.

Lambert, D. and Machon, P. (2001) *Citizenship Through Secondary Geography*, London: RoutledgeFalmer.

Leat, D. (1998) *Thinking Through Geography*, Cambridge: Chris Kington Publishing.

Myerson, G. and Rydin, Y. (1996) *The Language of Environment: a New Rhetoric*, London: UCL Press.

Moore, A. (2001) *Curriculum and Pedagogy*, Teaching and Learning Series, London: RoutledgeFalmer.

Ofsted (1999) *Standards in the Secondary School Curriculum 1997–1998*, London: HMSO.

Rawling, E. (1996) 'The Impact of the National Curriculum on School-Based Curriculum Development in Secondary Geography', in Kent, A., Lambert, D., Naish, M. and Slater, F. (eds) (1996) *Geography in Education: Viewpoints on Teaching and Learning*, Cambridge: Cambridge University Press.

Rawling, E. (2001) *Changing the Subject: the Impact of National Policy on School Geography 1980–2000*, Sheffield: GA.

Roberts, M. (2003) *Learning Through Enquiry: Making Sense of Geography in the Key Stage 3 Classroom*, Sheffield: Geographical Association.

Slater, F. (1982) *Learning Through Geography*, London: Heinemann.

Taylor, P. (1993) *Political Geography*, Harlow: Longman, Third Edition.

Waugh, D. and Bushell, T. (1991) *Key Geography*, London: Stanley Thornes.

Westaway, J. and Rawling, E. (2001) 'The Rise and Falls of Geography', *Teaching Geography*, 26, 3, pp. 108–110.

7   History

Terry Haydn

There are those who feel comfortable about teaching history, as long as it remains firmly about the past.

(Gallagher, 2002)

What is history supposed to do for young people?

In a recent monitoring exercise, the Qualifications and Curriculum Authority (QCA) argued that 'it is important that the history curricula taught in schools reflect the changing world and are relevant, motivating and appropriate to pupils' (QCA, 2001). How well do current arrangements fulfil these aspirations?

The History Working Group which formulated the original National Curriculum for history drew up a list of nine purposes of school history, which embraced both traditional justifications – giving pupils a sense of identity and an understanding of their cultural roots and shared inheritances – and elements which had come to prominence in more recent years – introducing pupils to the distinctive methodology of historians, and 'preparing pupils for adult life by imparting a critically sharpened intelligence with which to make sense of current affairs' (DES, 1990: 1–2).

The 1999 revision of the National Curriculum for history reiterated several of these purposes, and noted that pupils should be able to 'research, sift through evidence and argue for their point of view – skills that are prized in adult life.' There was explicit reference to the use of history to develop intellectual autonomy: 'What they learn can influence their decisions about personal choices, attitudes and values. In history, pupils find evidence, weigh it up and reach their own conclusions' (DfEE/QCA, 1999: 148).

In addition to this rationale for history, the overall aims and values of the National Curriculum stipulated that all subjects should develop 'enjoyment of and commitment to learning', and 'build on pupils' strengths, interests and experiences and develop their confidence in their capacity to learn and work independently and collaboratively.' The general aims of the National Curriculum also put significant emphasis on the development of critical intelligence, intellectual autonomy, and active citizenship – school leavers are to be equipped to 'think creatively and critically, to solve problems and to make a difference for the better … to make informed judgements and independent decisions' (DfEE/QCA, 1999: 11).

History was also to be a major vehicle for citizenship education in the UK (Mac-Gregor, 1995; QCA, 1998; DfEE, 1999), in terms of developing pupils' political literacy, enquiry and communication skills, and 'in particular, the ability to critically evaluate evidence and analyse interpretations ... to reflect on issues and take part in discussions' (DfEE, 1999: 183).

The current position of history in schools

Recent Ofsted inspections reveal that at Key Stage 4 history is regarded as the best taught subject. University applications to study history in 2001 increased by 8 per cent. In spite of teacher shortages in many school subjects, history continues to attract a plentiful supply of high-calibre graduates. General interest outside schools, in terms of audiences for history programmes in the media, and sales of history magazines, is buoyant, with audiences for many history programmes on television outstripping those for popular soap operas. History was recently described in the national press as 'the new rock and roll' (*Guardian*, 2 September 2002).

Against this, after the 1995 review of the National Curriculum, history up to the age of sixteen is no longer compulsory; it has to fight for its place in the post-14 option system, and is under pressure from what Lambert (see Chapter 6) terms the 'predators' of business studies, psychology, citizenship and media studies. This has led to a decrease in the number of pupils studying the subject at examination level at 16 and 18 (Husbands, 2001: 41).

Perhaps even more disconcerting is the number of pupils who have, in recent years, regarded school history as 'useless and boring'. A 1968 Schools Council survey revealed that only 29 per cent of pupils thought that history was useful, and only 40 per cent found it interesting. A similar study in 1983 found that 53 per cent of pupils thought that the subject was useful, and 61 per cent found it interesting (see Aldrich, 1987). More recently, Adey and Biddulph surveyed a sample of over 1,400 Year 9 pupils, and found that 68 per cent of them said that 'overall', they had enjoyed the subject at Key Stage 3, but only 42 per cent of the pupils surveyed thought it would be useful. A particular concern was that 'only a handful' of the 1,400 pupils could give cogent reasons for studying the subject: 'Their understanding of the relative "usefulness" of history and geography to their future is limited to direct and naïve reference to forms of employment. Their understanding of the wider contribution each can make to their future lives is disappointingly uninformed' (Adey and Biddulph, 2001: 439).

This points to a particular problem for the teaching of history. Whereas many pupils are aware of the importance attached to maths and English (whether they enjoy the subjects or not), many of them 'can't see the point' of doing history.

One of the most common causes of poor history teaching by trainee teachers is that they have not thought through clearly the purposes of school history, and do not have a sound grasp of the full breadth of benefits that young people can derive from the study of the past. After teaching a lesson about the Battle of Sedgemoor, one of my former history PGCE students wrote in his evaluation of the lesson (honestly but worryingly), 'I have no idea why I am teaching this.' If the grown-ups aren't clear about why we inflict history on young children, what hope is there that the pupils will make sense of it?

The case for history in schools needs to be based on more than a concern for 'market share' of examination entries and curriculum time. One of the fundamental challenges over the next decade, if history is to 'reflect the changing world' and be 'relevant, motivating and appropriate to pupils' is to find ways to convince pupils of its relevance and usefulness in their lives outside the classroom, and after they leave school.

There needs to be a clear and well-articulated vision of the full range of ways in which the study of the past can be rendered relevant to the needs of young people. This is not made easier by the fact that there is no consensus on the purposes of school history, and that some of the views put forward take little account of the nature of the pupils, and the sort of lives they will lead.

The shaping of history in schools

If one is to attempt a diagnosis of the health, vitality and relevance of school history in Britain at the start of the twenty-first century, it is helpful to look at the influences which have shaped its current form – not least to understand the tenacious influence of traditional (or what might even be called 'Victorian') views on its teaching.

As Tosh (1984) and Aldrich and Dean (1991) have pointed out, for much of the time that history has been a part of the school curriculum, the justification for making young people study it was moral and civic. The Board of Education's 1927 *Handbook of suggestions for teachers* concluded that history in schools was 'pre-eminently an instrument of moral training' (Board of Education, 1927: 114). An indication of this can be discerned from an earlier version of the Handbook: 'The lives of great men and women, carefully selected from all stations of life, will furnish the most impressive examples of obedience, loyalty, courage, strenuous effort, serviceableness, indeed all the qualities which make for good citizenship' (Board of Education, 1905: 6).

This positive rendering of the national past, focussing on Britain's success in empire, industry and institutions was to be an enduring one. As recently as 1994, Secretary of State for Education John Patten reinforced the traditional case for history in schools, stating that 'all children must understand such key concepts as empire, monarch, crown, nobility, peasantry', arguing that 'public education systems contribute to a willingness of persons to define themselves as citizens, to make personal sacrifices for the community and to accept the legitimate decisions of public officials' (quoted in Porter, 1994).

The idea of a historical education being essentially one of 'cultural transmission' remained very strong in the eyes of many politicians and policymakers. There were still many people in influential positions who felt that the primary purpose of history in schools was to persuade pupils that, in the words of Paul Johnson (*Daily Mail*, 30 April 1994), 'To be born British is to win first prize in the lottery of life.'

As the French historian Theodore Zeldin (1993) has pointed out, there are elements of nostalgia in this portrayal of the national past, exemplified by MP John Stokes' lament (1990): 'Why cannot we go back to the good old days when we learnt by heart the names of the kings and queens of England, the feats of our warriors and our battles and the glorious deeds of our past?'

Meanwhile in schools, the last quarter of the twentieth century saw the emergence of a different rationale for school history, which reflected a change of thinking about what qualities 'good citizens' needed to have, and the ways in which history might contribute to these. There was a move towards taking into account the vocational needs of pupils, their interests, and their disposition towards learning. The transmission of a comprehensive historical 'canon' was seen as less important than the ability to learn new skills and understandings in the context of the perceived need for flexible, adaptable learners living in a modern information society. There was a move away from history teaching for the transmission of values, and towards education for intellectual autonomy. There was a move towards making the curriculum more 'relevant' to pupils who it was felt were increasingly disaffected and disengaged from the traditional 'grammar-school' curriculum (see for instance, Elliott, 1991; MacDonald, 2000).

Thus, in some, but not all, schools from the 1970s onwards, there was a move towards a more critical and detached approach to the national past, which put more emphasis on history as a *form* of knowledge, with its own particular disciplinary procedures and methods. It was seen as a way of reversing the decline of history as a school subject, and of responding to the negative reactions of many pupils to it. These moves by history teachers to explore a 'new' approach to school history, provoked a hostile and defensive counter-reaction from many politicians, tabloid newspapers and right-wing think-tanks (McKiernan, 1993; Crawford, 1995).

The National Curriculum for history which emerged in the 1990s was an uneasy mix of old and new traditions of history teaching. Throughout the debate, there was a heavy emphasis on curriculum content, sustaining the idea that the main thing that young people got out of school history was a body of knowledge about the past. The Chief Executive of the School Curriculum and Assessment Authority (SCAA), Dr Nicholas Tate (a political appointee), stressed the importance of history's role in providing young people with a sense of national identity, urging that pupils be taught about British heroes, and stressing the primacy of cultural transmission as the main purpose of school history (Tate, 1995). There were however, several elements of 'new' history which were incorporated into the National Curriculum, such as the requirement to assess the significance of events, people and changes, to understand and evaluate differing interpretations and representations of the past, and to develop skills of enquiry.

Although 'new' history made mistakes and had its problems, overall it has been the baleful influence of the defenders of 'Victorian' ideas about school history (and about learning) which has limited the extent to which the subject 'reflects the changing world and is relevant, motivating and appropriate to pupils.'

History for ordinary children

A key weakness in the process of formulating and revising the National Curriculum was the lack of thought given to the nature of the pupils who would experience this curriculum. A sense of 'audience' was conspicuously absent from the process of curriculum design.

The professional expertise and experience of teachers and their first hand knowledge of the nature of the pupils they taught did not significantly contribute to the deliberations on what form a historical education for those pupils should take (Aldrich, 1991; Phillips, 1998). Researchers who had devoted years to understanding pupils' thinking in history, ascertaining how pupils learn, and thinking through exactly what it means 'to get better at history', were ignored or marginalised. At times, decisions were taken by politicians and policy makers whose knowledge of ordinary schools and pupils, and of teaching and learning processes was extremely limited. The slim polemics of right-wing think-tanks, the influence of 'knowledge panic', tabloid headlines, and the nostalgic prejudices of grammar-school and privately educated politicians counted for more than professional expertise. It was a case of the blind leading the sighted.

In the words of Hollindale (1995), 'the story is one of systematic rejection of the experts, disregard of facts, indulgence of prejudice, nostalgia and instinct.' This 'top-down' model of curriculum making, combined with the influence of 'forces of conservatism' and out of touch (but influential) anti-liberal élites (Quicke, 1989; Crawford, 1995) resulted in several barriers to the effective teaching of history.[1]

Weaknesses of current arrangements

Failure to take into account the nature of pupils and their attitudes towards learning

Many policy makers were (and are) out of touch with the realities of teaching 'ordinary children' in comprehensive schools. In addition to pupils with very little written or spoken English, and those with very low general cognitive ability, there are pupils whose attitude to school and to learning is literally beyond the comprehension of many politicians, academics and policymakers.

Those who disparaged the idea of 'relevance' in the curriculum (see for example, Lawlor, 1989) generally worked at some distance from the world of comprehensive schools and their pupils. Learning was seen by some academics as a simple matter of transmission; the historian Norman Stone urged that children should have the national culture 'rammed down their throats' (quoted in Crawford, 1995), as if the average pupil was an unresisting and absorbent *tabula rasa*, and learning was something that could be just stuffed into pupils (it is the same misapprehension that leads some politicians to think of ICT as an unproblematic educational miracle). There was a tendency to be dismissive about learning theory, exemplified by Sheila Lawlor's claim (1989: 67) that there is no useful role for pupil talk in the classroom:

> Why should greater emphasis be put on pupils discussing amongst themselves and with the teacher? It is not clear. There is no reason to imagine that pupils learn from talking. Indeed, they may not want to talk. They may have nothing to say.

Those who work in comprehensive schools are aware that not all pupils come to school with the intention or desire to learn. They are not all committed scholars, but many of them are 'biddable' to the idea of learning if they believe there is some point to it. The degree to which pupils will engage with the whole project of education in school subjects is to a large extent related to their views on their interest, utility and relevance (see, for instance, Mansilla, 2001; Zamorski and Haydn, 2002). In the words of Sue Hallam (1996), 'They must want to learn; if you lose that, you lose everything.' Pupils need to be able to answer the question, 'Why are we doing this?', a point noted by HMI (1985: 12), 'Skills are unlikely to be acquired, let alone effectively applied, unless they are related to content that has some inherent interest and appears to relate to the lives of the pupils.'

The corrosive influence of 'coverage' and 'the canon'

The debate on the National Curriculum for history was dominated by ideas about 'what all children should know', defined primarily in terms of substantive historical content. Once you start from this base, it is difficult to decide which monarchs, revolutions, inventions and battles should be omitted, and the history curriculum comes across to teachers as primarily a mass of content to be covered. One critique of the first revision of the history curriculum objected to the omission of pre-Roman British history, and argued that 'most of the thousand or so years from 55 BC to the eleventh century will have to be taught at the rate of about 50 minutes a century' (McGovern, 1994: 3). This 'coverage' mentality flies in the face of much recent research about effective teaching and learning.

Research and inspection findings suggest that this struggle to cover content means that pupils often have at best a limited understanding of political and historical concepts, and struggle to develop coherent overviews of development over time, or make meaningful connections between the past and the present (Ofsted, 1995, 1997; Kerr *et al.*, 2002). This means that for many pupils, history comes over as a lot of unconnected dates and facts, and makes no real sense to them. In the words of Sam Wineburg (1997: 257), they often fail to make 'the crucial step between knowing X, and using X to think about Y'.

The problem of content has been exacerbated by the prevailing influence of old-fashioned ideas about a historical 'canon', exemplified by Robert Conquest's contribution to the influential 'Black Papers' on education:

> An educated man must have a certain minimum of general knowledge. Even if he knows very little about science and cannot add or subtract, he must have heard of Mendel and Kepler. Even if he is tone deaf, he must know something about Debussy and Verdi; even if he is a pure sociologist he must be aware of Circe and the Minotaur, of Kant and Montaigne, of Titus Oates and Tiberius Gracchus.
>
> (Conquest, 1969)

Suggested topics for the National Curriculum for history in the interim report included the Bible in Welsh, St Hilda of Whitby, Milton, Netsuke and New England Vernacular architecture. If the proponents of these topics were ever to go near an inner-city comprehensive school and hold 9Z's attention with this subject matter, one suspects that it would primarily be because the pupils regarded them as creatures from another world, which in a sense, they are.

Many pupils are quietly and passively disaffected and disengaged from learning (Oakley, 2002). Most of those who think that school history is 'useless and boring' will not ask the teacher, 'What has this got to do with my life?' but they probably ask themselves this question, as they 'play truant in mind'. There ought to be a better answer than, 'because it's part of the canon.'

Cordoning off the past from the present

Compared to many other countries, pupils in the UK learn very little about the recent history of their own country. There have been attempts to try and break down the 'Iron Curtain' between history and the present, such as the Humanities Curriculum Project (see Stenhouse, 1975), where pupils were actively encouraged to analyse historical events in the context of current issues and problems, but more commonly, study of British history ended at World War Two *at the latest* (Patrick, 1988). A 1988 survey conducted by the University of Essex found that 80 per cent of 15 and 16 year olds in Britain believed that they never got the chance to discuss major political developments in class, or issues affecting their own communities (*Times Educational Supplement*, 10 April 1988).

Although politicians have expressed concerns about the limited political literacy of young people (see for example, Patten, 1994; Blunkett, 1999), there have been reservations about using school history to address these limitations. Such was the distrust of teachers and 'The Educational Establishment' that at one point, Secretary of State for Education Kenneth Clarke ordered that any study of political history should stop short at 20 years before the present day (Graham, 1993). The decision came in the wake of a series of right-wing pamphlets (Beattie, 1987; Deuchar, 1987; Kedourie, 1988), criticising what was seen as the 'politicisation' of school history, as it moved away from its traditional 'Whiggish' mode. Part of Clarke's rationale for this rule was that there should be a clear delineation between history and current affairs (not that current affairs was to feature elsewhere in the National Curriculum). Although the '20 years rule' was quietly discarded when the National Curriculum was revised in 1995 (DfE, 1995) the same revision also brought about the abandonment of suggestions for including the study of twentieth century British history as part of school history.

Given that one of the stated purposes of the teaching of history is that it should enable young people to understand the present in the light of the past (DfEE, 1999: 148), this hiatus seems a strange one. In terms of 'telling a story' about the history of the country they are growing up in, it is like 'pulling up the drawbridge.' Ingenuous attempts to 'de-politicise' history, to separate the past from the present, and to rip the last chapter out of the story of the nation's past, do not make it easier for history teachers to persuade pupils of the importance and relevance of history to their lives.

As the 1952 report of the Ministry of Education noted:

> The divorce between current affairs and history, so that they are regarded as two different subjects, gravely weakens both. It accentuates the natural tendency of children to regard history as something remote and irrelevant instead of something which has formed the world around them and which is continuously being formed by that world. And, it accentuates equally the tendency to look at contemporary questions as though they had no context in time, no parallels or precedents.
>
> (Ministry of Education, 1952: 32)

Only if it is accepted that the past should be 'joined up' to the present, and that school history should address contemporary political issues will we escape from 'the Curriculum of the Dead' (Ball, 1993) which has limited the political education of young people in the United Kingdom, and in many cases, limited the extent to which they see history in particular, and education in general, as relevant to their lives.

History as 'just telling them what happened'

Another important characteristic of traditional history teaching in the United Kingdom, was that history was essentially a 'received subject'. Richard Aldrich (1989) pointed out that it was seen as the task of the university historian to determine the historical record, and the job of school teacher, to receive such wisdom and convey it in simplified form to school pupils.

This form of history teaching was described by the novelist Penelope Lively in *Moon Tiger* (1988: 14–15), where a dying historian recalls a history class on Mary Queen of Scots:

I put up my hand. 'Please Miss, did the Catholics think Elizabeth right to cut off her head?' 'No Claudia, I don't expect they did.' 'Please, do Catholic people think so now?' Miss Lavenham took a breath. 'Well Claudia', she said kindly, 'I suppose some of them might not. People do sometimes disagree. But there is no need for you to worry about that. Just put down what is on the board.'

One of the key breakthroughs, in terms of fashioning a more relevant history curriculum has been the move away from just 'telling them what happened'. The incorporation of 'interpretations' into the National Curriculum for history, stipulating that pupils should be taught 'how and why historical events, people, situations and changes have been interpreted in different ways' (DfEE/QCA, 1999: 20) gives history the opportunity to make a major contribution to the general aims of the National Curriculum, and to the citizenship curriculum, in terms of developing pupils' ability to think critically, to make informed judgements, and to become intellectually autonomous.

Part of school history now requires pupils to assess the validity of differing claims about the past, to critique interpretations and understand why it is the nature of accounts to differ, to detect flaws and elisions in arguments, gaps in evidence, and awareness of the extent to which they have been presented with all the evidence available. This is an area where understanding history as a form of knowledge helps pupils to learn to process information intelligently, within academic canons of reliability, explanation and justification (Husbands, 1996). This canon – acquaintance with the procedures and principles which historians use to try to establish the validity of claims – will be more helpful to them in their adult lives than the 'curriculum of the dead' found in the quotation from Conquest above (p. 92).

But as in other facets of school history, there has been some resistance to this move away from traditional history teaching. Lawlor (1989) argued that 'pupils might be confused by being given different versions, and might be better off to master the facts', and Tate (1995) was critical of the move towards 'interpretations', maintaining that school history should be concerned with 'the transmission of an established view of the past'.

This is history with the thinking taken out. Not only does it reduce it to 'unhistorical political mythologising' (Lee, 1994: 43) – the fiction that all historians agree about what happened in the past: it leaves pupils without an intellectually rigorous understanding of what history is, that it is a construct, it has been 'put together' by someone. As Lee and Ashby (2001: 200) point out:

> Many stories are told, and they may contradict, compete with or complement one another, but this means that students should be equipped to deal with such relationships, not that any old story will do. . . . Students who understand sources as *information* are helpless when confronted by contradictory sources.

Writing curriculum specifications in official documents is obviously no guarantee that these will be delivered in practice, and inspection and research findings suggest that the teaching of interpretations has been a problematic area of history teaching over the past decade (Ofsted, 1995; McAleavy, 2000; Culpin, 2002). The teaching of interpretations is comparatively new to the history curriculum, and there is a need to disseminate good practice. There may still be some history classrooms where pupils are told what happened and instructed to 'just put down what is on the board.'

The balance between sources and stories

The move away from historical narrative and towards the use of sources may have brought about gains in terms of pupils' understanding of the principles of procedure of historians, but these were sometimes at the expense of coherence and orientation. The extent of this deconstruction of the past meant that history often came across to pupils as a succession of dismembered gobbets. Often, not enough time was spent putting the pieces of the past together, providing an overview, and explaining the relationship between sources and 'stories'. This coincided with the flight from the essay as an assessment instrument, which might have served as a counterpoise to this 'atomising' of the past. It was thus possible for pupils to get full marks on a GCSE exam question on World War Two, without necessarily knowing who won, or who was on whose side. This lurch away from history as a coherent narrative was noted by HMI:

> Much is made of teachers focusing on the development of historical skills at the expense of what should be their proper concern; the imparting of historical content. Too often discussion has been too strident and ill-informed. But there are issues about getting the balance right; about ensuring that pupils have a secure grasp of events, without being over-loaded; that they are able to use the knowledge they have; and that they do not spend time on mechanical tasks rehearsing formulaic responses to snippets from sources.
>
> (Hamer, 1997)

Not all history departments have worked out a proper balance between sources and stories, ways of explaining the connections between them, and linking 'depth' to 'overview'.

The impact of assessment on teaching methods

There is increasing research evidence to suggest that current mechanisms for assessment in schools do more harm than good (see, for instance, Wilian, 2001; Torrance, 2002). They so obviously lead to testing what is easy or possible to test, rather than what is important and useful. Discussion, argument, debate, collaborative work – many of the activities which might support delivery of the general aims of the National Curriculum and the citizenship curriculum, tend to be underused because they will not directly contribute to success in exam performance.

Distrust of teacher assessment has meant that pupils are assessed almost entirely in terms of written work, which limits the ways in which pupils' progression can be assessed. The pressures to 'teach to the test' influence teaching methods, and distort the balance between written and non-written activities. Two recent surveys of pupils' attitudes to school history show that excessive use of written tasks is one of the main things that puts pupils off the subject (Adey and Biddulph, 2001; Zamorski and Haydn, 2002).

Numerous recent surveys have reported that excessive paperwork and bureaucracy – much of it relating to assessment issues – is having a negative impact on teacher recruitment and retention, and on teacher morale (see, for instance, Spear *et al.*, 2000; Smithers and Robinson, 2001) *The Times Educational Supplement* recently reported that one primary headteacher had weighed all that he had been sent by the DfES for a month; it came to 38 kilos. This is another important area where policymakers need to listen carefully to what teachers say. Political vanity has perhaps led them to be overly concerned with subjects where there are international tests of comparative perform-ance, and insufficiently mindful of the negative consequences and unintended outcomes of the assessment and testing regime.

The marginalising of non-core subjects

One of the most common complaints of practising history teachers is the impossibility of 'doing justice' to the subject in the time available. In the recent monitoring of cur-riculum arrangements for history, this was cited as the biggest single factor limiting the quality and value of history as a school subject (Cooper and Haydn, 2002). This problem has been compounded by the government's decision to focus intensively on the 'core' subjects of maths, science and English, and the pressure on the school timetable of subjects such as citizenship, ICT, and PSHE. This has meant that the time allocated to history at Key Stage 3 has been reduced, often to a single period of the week (a fate which used to be confined largely to music and religious education). As Ian Dawson (2002) has noted, 'Many teachers have less than an hour a week to cover British History from 1066 to 1900 by the end of year 8 – in just 2 years . . . This leads to either shallow coverage of everything, which makes it difficult to engage pupils' enthusiasm, or coverage of some topics in depth and others in overview, which means that some events have to be covered cursorily.' Not only do these time constraints lead to over-simplification, drastic cuts and superficiality, they do not allow time for teachers to explore the connections across time, and to the present that help pupils to develop a meaningful 'mental-map' of the past which give coherence to the study of history.

In some schools, 'targets' have focussed almost exclusively on performance in core subjects and this has inevitably shaped pupils' perceptions of the importance of non-core subjects. High stakes testing has also tempted some heads of history to repeat or at least overlap GCSE and post-16 exam syllabuses, so as to allow more time for the development of exam technique. This has exacerbated recent trends towards narrowing the breadth of history that pupils study in school.

Ways forward for history in schools

Strengthening and empowering the history teaching community

The general aims of the National Curriculum state that the school curriculum should 'develop enjoyment of and commitment to learning' and 'build on pupils' strengths, interests and experiences' (DfEE/QCA, 1999: 11) but there was little evidence of this in the construction of the history curriculum. The dead hand of 'the canon', 'coverage' mentality, and Clarke's attempt to cordon off the present from the past made it more difficult to teach the subject in a way that made sense to pupils. The revisions to the original model have been helpful, but more than anything, it is the initiative, imagin-ation and insight of history teachers as a professional community that have helped to sustain and develop the vitality and usefulness of the subject (see, for instance, Husbands and Pendry, 2000).

The circulation of *Teaching History*, the main professional journal for history teachers, has risen to over 3,000 over the last four years. It has probably been the single most influential factor in improving the quality of history teaching in the UK in recent years, together with the annual conferences of the Historical Association and the Schools History Project. It has disseminated innovative practice and sustained the morale of the history teaching community in the face of the decimation of LEA history advisors and teachers' centres, and the almost complete collapse of in-service training for history teachers (Cooper and Haydn, 2002).

There is an urgent need to go back to trusting and investing in teachers. At least some of the millions currently spent on inspection and testing arrangements should be redirected to improving financial support for departments and subject coordinators, so that they can buy *Teaching History*, go to conferences, buy data projectors, meet up with each other to share good practice, and take some time out to go on short term secondments.

Reviewing and reforming assessment and testing arrangements

There needs to be an urgent review of both the GCSE examination and the 'levels' system for Key Stages 1–3. The latter system has never commanded the full confidence of history teachers, and does not provide a comprehensive and reliable model for progression in the subject. As Torrance (2002) has suggested, the development of a wide range of assessment instruments, including a greater emphasis on teacher assessment, would probably do more than anything to promote assessment for learning, and enable teachers to escape from the straitjacket of written tasks. ICT now makes it much easier to share such materials, and useless or inappropriate instruments would simply wither into irrelevance, whilst page-ranking technology would make it easy to find out which exercises, tasks and instruments were being used widely by departments. Any losses in 'accountability' would be more than compensated for by reductions in pupil disaffection and disengagement from learning, and improvements in teacher morale.

The current assessment and testing arrangements are probably the single largest barrier to making significant progress towards realising the general aims of the National Curriculum. Even if 'levels' go up at various points, this will not mean that standards are improving, it will just mean that people are getting better at working the system (see Torrance, 2002).

Focussing on the idea of 'historical perspectives' and linking the past to the present

Another important consideration in persuading pupils that the study of the past is of relevance to their lives is to clarify the relationship between historical knowledge and the present. There are many definitions of history, but Aldrich's is particularly helpful to the history teacher. 'History is about human activity with particular reference to the whole dimension of time – past, present and future' (Aldrich, 1997: 3). It is important to be explicit about the idea of historical perspectives as one of the ways of understanding how things are today, and how they might be in the future. Is there any present-day problem or question where it might not be possible to gain further insight by considering what has gone before? There is still too often a reluctance to 'open up' historical issues, and make connections from the past to the present. As Husbands (1996: 34) notes:

Learning about the concept of kingship (*or whatever*) frequently involves two sets of simultaneous learning: learning about power and its distribution in past societies, and learning about power and its distribution in modern society. The former cannot be given real meaning until pupils have some more contemporary knowledge against which to calibrate their historical understandings.

If we want politically literate citizens, they will need to integrate their political understandings of the past with present-day political issues and problems. Without this, even events as important as the Holocaust can come across to pupils as something that happened a long time ago, that has nothing much to do with their lives. Study of The Chartists can be done 'in isolation', or as something which leads into the issue of how methods of extra-parliamentary opposition have developed in the twentieth century, and up to the present day. Many trainee history teachers initially dislike teaching the industrial revolution, until they realise that if 'opened up', it can help to develop in pupils an understanding of many of the concepts, issues and controversies which will have a profound influence on their working lives. We have to accept that history teaching is inextricably political in nature, and make a virtue out of this, rather than attempting (like Kenneth Clarke) to bowdlerise the history curriculum, rendering it harmless but irrelevant.

One of the biggest mistakes is to teach history as if it is just about the past. The more connections that are made across time, and to the present, the more relevant, useful and engaging the subject will be.

Developing and improving the teaching of interpretations, significance and enquiry

The incorporation of these three elements to the National Curriculum for history has provided a very helpful framework for making the purposes of school history more transparent to pupils. As Martin Hunt (2000) points out, the inclusion of 'significance' draws out the 'So what?' question and gets pupils to consider the importance of aspects of the past in an intellectually rigorous way. The study of interpretations and significance helps to make the point that controversy and argument surround most aspects of the past, not just topics such as slavery and the Holocaust.

The arguments that arise out of studying issues of significance and interpretation help bring history to life (the recent 'Great Britons' television debate is one example of this). Examining competing claims about the past, and making comparisons between the past and the present are ways of making history powerful, rigorous, relevant and interesting to pupils. Getting pupils to engage with these arguments orally and collaboratively, in debate and discussion as well as in writing, is one of the ways in which history can further many of the overall aims of the school curriculum. One of the determinants of the quality of history teaching, and the extent to which it can motivate, engage and challenge pupils, is the skill with which historical issues, events and protagonists can be 'problematised', in the areas of significance and interpretation.

If intellectual autonomy is an aim of the school curriculum, 'enquiry' also becomes a key element of history teaching. If pupils have acquired the skills of intelligent enquiry, they are not just able to examine the historical record, but also the contemporary one which unfolds in newspapers, on television, and on the Internet.

There is now a substantial body of literature on these aspects of history teaching (particularly in recent issues of *Teaching History*), but there are still classrooms where these elements are underused.

Being explicit about the use of history to develop pupils' information literacy

David Birch (2002) has warned that advances in technology mean that in the relatively near future, 'it will be impossible to trust any picture, movie or soundbite'; already, there is unease about film and television portrayal of history, 'at a time when young people have such an inability to distinguish between truth and fiction' (Beevor, 2002).

If we are going to spend time in history classrooms talking about reliability, inference, corroboration, utility and so on, we should be explicit about the uses to which these terms can be put in everyday life. If we spend time looking at Tudor portraits, we should also get pupils to look at newspaper images, Internet sites and extracts from television programmes. There are no school subjects better placed than history to get pupils to learn not to accept all they are told at face value – that the Internet is not the ultimate repository of trustworthy information, that people, organisations and governments do not always tell 'the whole truth', and that the media do not always report their sources of information in a neutral and transparent manner. Given the importance of information or 'media' literacy in contemporary society, history teaching should be more 'upfront' about addressing it. This again requires it to encompass the present as well as the past.

Conclusions

There is encouraging evidence to suggest that fewer pupils consider history to be 'boring and useless' than some years ago, but there are still many who are uncertain about exactly what they gain by studying history. 'Developing an enjoyment of, and commitment to learning' through the study of the past is as important as any other objective for the future of history as a school subject. In an era of 'targets', 'levels', and 'hints and tips' to enhance exam performance, it is easier to lose sight of some of the broader objectives of school history. Jeffrey Richards, formerly Reader in history at Lancaster University reminds us of some of these:

> My own subject, history, teaches many useful skills – information handling, problem solving, the public presentation of arguments and assessments. But that should be secondary to the broader objectives of discovering how we were, and how we got to where we are. It is not my aim to turn out tunnel-visioned computer operators concerned only about where their next Porsche is coming from. I seek to awaken in my students an open minded broad visioned humanity, informed by a love of learning, a love of ideas, a love of books, a love of argument and debate.
>
> (The *Independent*, 8 April 1989)

Current pressures mean that the last few items on Richards' list are sometimes neglected. One of the ways forward is to accept that coverage has to be reduced. It is not possible or desirable to teach about all the kings and queens, heroes and inventions: it leads to superficial and ineffective teaching. As one commentator recently remarked in a working group reviewing current arrangements for history, 'Too many times . . .

we're doing it because it's written in the National Curriculum. What teachers do in history lessons should be significant and it should be interesting. If it is not both, it is not worth doing' (Anon.).

If you have a school curriculum based on subject disciplines, it is all the more important to keep an open approach to what issues might be helpful to pupils' overall academic, personal and social development. There are times when history lessons might profitably venture into aspects of philosophy, sociology, ethics, psychology, or the history of art. History should be a mind-opening subject, not a socialising one. It should also look for opportunities to develop pupils' general educational and social skills through the use of collaborative work, discussion and debate. At the moment, the assessment and testing regime does not encourage this.

One of the most radical changes to school history over the past thirty years has been the move from being almost exclusively about developing pupils' understanding of the past as a body of knowledge, to being also concerned with pupils' grasp of history as a form of knowledge.[2] On the whole, this change of emphasis has been helpful in enabling history to be taught in a way that makes sense to pupils. To use a computing analogy, most history teachers now accept and understand that progression is not just a matter of filling up pupils' hard disk space, but of developing them as more powerful and effective information processors. It is now generally accepted that there is more to getting better at history than simply 'knowing more stuff'.

This has not, however, been cost-free in terms of the amount of time available for developing pupils' grasp of the substance of history (Slater, 1989; Starkey, 2002). One of the key challenges for history teachers is how to keep breadth and coherence, whilst also developing pupils' grasp of history as a form of knowledge, in the limited curriculum time available. One possible way forward is in the use of new technology to make it possible for pupils to spend as much time exploring history outside the classroom as in school (see Slatta, 2001), but in this country at the moment ICT structures are not always sufficiently developed to make this possible.

The general aims of the National Curriculum suggest that policymakers *are* concerned that the school curriculum should reflect the changing world and be relevant, motivating and appropriate to pupils. The attributes which they wish the curriculum to develop in pupils are radically different from those expounded by the Board of Education at the start of the twentieth century. Most history teachers who read the overall aims and values would be broadly in sympathy with them, but would shake their heads at the dissonance between these statements and the current arrangements and systems for trying to realise them. Only if teachers have much more freedom to influence delivery and assessment will this gulf between theory and practice be significantly reduced (again, the current assessment and testing regime is a major impediment to this).

It is ironic that history seems in danger of being marginalised as a school subject at a time when it has never been more essential in terms of preparation for adult life. It has never been harder for people to find out exactly what is happening, and to 'get at the truth' in a society which has become increasingly adroit at concealing and distorting it. In the words of Norman Longworth (1981: 19),

> It does require some little imagination to realise what the consequences will be of not educating our children to sort out the differences between essential and nonessential information, raw fact, prejudice, half-truth and untruth, so that they know when they are being manipulated, by whom, and for what purpose.

History can be taught in a way which develops pupils' knowledge and understanding of the substantive past *and* helps them to handle information intelligently. It has been inelegantly described by Postman and Weingartner as a 'crap-detecting' subject (quoted in MacBeath, 1998). It is difficult to think of another school subject which offers the same potential for the development of this skill, or (in the age of spin doctors, media manipulation, soundbite politics and information overload), any other time in history when it has been a more precious asset for school leavers to possess.

Notes

1 'Forces of conservatism' is not a party political or 'left-right' term in this context, it refers to those who do not seem to see any need to change the purposes of school history from those pertaining in Victorian times, and who see any departure from this model as 'not proper history'. One of the landmark 'texts' on school history was that of Keith Joseph, in his 1984 address to the Historical Association ('Why teach history in schools?', *The Historian*, No. 2, Insert). See also, Oliver Letwin (1989) 'A grounding', in Moon, B., Murphy, P. and Raynor, J. (eds) *Policies for the Curriculum*, London, Hodder & Stoughton: 70–73.
2 Lee and Ashby emphasise that this was not a retreat from the importance of pupils acquiring historical knowledge, 'instead "knowledge" was treated seriously, as something that had to be understood and grounded. It is essential that students know something of the kind of claims made by historians and what those different kinds of claim rest on' (Lee and Ashby, 2001: 200).

References

Adey, K. and Biddulph, M. (2001) 'The influence of pupil perceptions on subject choice at 14+ in geography and history', *Educational Studies*, Vol. 27, No. 4: 439–451.

Aldrich, R. (1987) 'Interesting and useful', *Teaching History*, No. 47: 11–14.

Aldrich, R. (1989) 'Class and gender in the study and teaching of history in England in the twentieth century', *Historical Studies in Education*, Vol. 1, No. 1: 119–135.

Aldrich, R. (1997) *The End of History and the Beginning of Education*, London: Institute of Education, University of London.

Aldrich, R. and Dean, D. (1991) 'The historical dimension', in Aldrich, R. (ed.) *History in the National Curriculum*, London: Kogan Page: 93–113.

Ball, S. (1993) 'Education, Majorism and the curriculum of the dead', *Curriculum Studies*, Vol. 1, No. 2: 195–214.

Beattie, A. (1987) *History in Peril*, London: Centre For Policy Studies.

Beevor, A. (2002) 'Hollywood glamorises Nazis says Beevor', *Times Educational Supplement*, 11 October.

Birch, D. (2002) 'Technology that fakes the truth', *Guardian Online*, 4 July.

Blunkett, D. (1999) *Keynote address to Citizenship Conference*, Institute of Education, University of London, 7 July.

Board of Education (1905) *Suggestions for the Consideration of Teachers and Others Concerned in the Work of Public Elementary Schools*, London: HMSO.

Board of Education (1927) *Handbook of Suggestions for Teachers*, London: HMSO.

Cooper, H. and Haydn, T. (2002) *Monitoring the History Curriculum 3–19: Review of Research and Other Related Evidence*, London: QCA.

Conquest, R. (1969) from Cox, B. and Dyson, A. 'Fight for Education: a Black Paper', in *Critical Quarterly*, quoted in Ballard, M. (ed.) (1970) *New Movements in the Study and Teaching of History*, London: Maurice Temple Smith.

Crawford, K. (1995) 'A history of the right: the battle for control of National Curriculum history 1989–1994', *British Journal of Educational Studies*, Vol. 43, No. 4: 433–456.

Culpin, C. (2002) 'Why we must change history GCSE', *Teaching History*, No. 109: 6–9.

Dawson, I. (2002) Quoted in The *Independent*, 15 November.

DES (1989) *Interim Report of the National Curriculum History Working Group,* London: HMSO.

DES (1990) *National Curriculum History Working Group: Final Report*, London: HMSO.

DfE (1995) *History in the National Curriculum*, London: HMSO.

DfEE/QCA (1999) *The National Curriculum: Handbook for Secondary Teachers in England*, London: DfEE/QCA.

Deuchar, S. (1987) *History and GCSE History*, London: Centre for Policy Studies.

Elliott, J. (1991) *Action Research for Educational Change*, Buckingham: Open University Press.

Gallagher, C. (2002) 'The future of history and the challenge of citizenship', in McCully, A. and O'Neill, C. (eds) *Values in History Teacher Education and Research*, Lancaster, HTEN: 44–53.

Graham, D. (1993) *A Lesson For Us All: the Making of the National Curriculum*, London: Routledge.

Hallam, S. (1996) *Unpublished Lecture on Differentiation*, Institute of Education, University of London, January.

Hamer, J. (1997) 'Ofsted and history in schools', *The Historian*, No. 53: 24–25.

HMI (1985) *History in the Primary and Secondary Years: an HMI View*, London: HMSO.

Hollindale, C. (1995) 'Subversive Texts', *Times Educational Supplement*, 22 September.

Hunt, M. (2000) 'Teaching Historical Significance', in Arthur, J. and Phillips, R. (eds) *Issues in History Teaching*, London: Routledge: 39–53.

Husbands, C. (1996) *What is History Teaching?*, Buckingham: Open University Press.

Husbands, C. and Pendry, A. (2000) 'Research and practice in history teacher education', *Cambridge Journal of Education*, Vol. 30, No. 3: 321–334.

Husbands, C. (2001) 'What's happening in history? Trends in GCSE and "A" level examinations, 1993–2000', *Teaching History*, No. 103: 37–41.

Kedourie, H. (1988) *The Errors and Evils of the New History*, London: Centre for Policy Studies.

Kerr, D., Lines, A., Blenkinsop, S. and Schagen, I. (2002) *England's Results From the IEA International Citizenship Study: What Citizenship and Education Mean to 14 year olds*, Slough: NFER.

Lawlor, S. (1989) 'Correct core', in Moon, B., Murphy, P. and Raynor, J. (eds) *Policies for the Curriculum*, London: Hodder & Stoughton: 58–69.

Lee, P. (1994) 'Historical knowledge and the National Curriculum', in Bourdillon, H. (ed.) *Teaching History*, London: Routledge: 41–52.

Lee, P. and Ashby, R. (2001) 'Progression in historical understanding 7–14', in Seixas, P., Stearns, P. and Wineburg, S. (eds) *Teaching, Knowing and Learning History*, New York: New York University Press: 195–220.

Letwin, O. (1989) 'Grounding comes first', in Moon, B., Murphy, P. and Raynor, J. (eds) *Policies for the Curriculum*, London: Routledge/Open University: 70–73.

Lively, P. (1988) *Moon Tiger*, London: Harmondsworth (quoted in J. Slater, *The Politics of History Teaching: a Humanity Dehumanised*, London: Institute of Education, University of London).

Longworth, N. (1981) 'We're moving into the information society – what shall we teach the children?', *Computer Education*, June: 17–19.

McAleavy, T. (2000) 'Teaching about interpretations', in Arthur, J. and Phillips, R. (eds) *Issues in History Teaching*, London: Routledge: 72–82.

MacBeath, J. (1998) 'Turning the tables', The *Observer*, 22 February.

MacDonald, B. (2000) 'How education became nobody's business', in Altricher, H. and Elliott, J. (eds) *Images of Educational Change*, Buckingham: Open University Press: 20–36.

McGovern, C. (1994) *The SCAA Review of National Curriculum History: A Minority Report*, York: Campaign for Real Education.

MacGregor, J. (1995) Quoted in Davies, I. and John, P. 'Using history to develop citizenship education in the National Curriculum', *Teaching History*, No. 78: 5–7.

McKiernan, D. (1993) 'History in the National Curriculum: imagining the nation at the end of the twentieth century', *Journal of Curriculum Studies*, Vol. 25, No. 1: 33–51.

Mansilla, V. (2001) 'Expecting high standards from inner-city students: challenges and possibilities', in Dickinson, A., Gordon, P. and Lee, P. (eds) *Raising Standards in History Education: International Review of History Education*, London: Woburn Press.

Ministry of Education (1952) *Teaching History, pamphlet No. 23*, London: HMSO.

Oakley, J. (2002) 'RHINOs: a research project about the quietly disaffected', *Pedagogy, Culture and Society*, Vol. 10, No. 2: 193–208.

Ofsted (1995) *Annual Report of Her Majesty's Chief Inspector for Schools*, London: Ofsted.

Ofsted (1997) *Annual Report of Her Majesty's Chief Inspector for Schools*, London: Ofsted.

Patrick, H. (1988) 'The history curriculum: the teaching of history 1985–7', *History Resource*, Vol. 2, No. 1, 9–14.

Patten, J. (1994) Television broadcast, BBC 1, 24 March.

Phillips, R. (1998) *History Teaching, Nationhood and the State: a Study in Educational Politics*, London: Cassell.

Porter, J. (1994) *Joseph Lauwerys Memorial Lecture*, Institute of Education, University of London, 12 May.

QCA (1998) *Education for Citizenship and the Teaching of Democracy in Schools. Final Report of the Advisory Group on Citizenship*, London: QCA.

QCA (2001) Project specification for monitoring of current arrangements for teaching history and geography in schools.

Quicke, J. (1989) 'The New Right and education', in Moon, B., Murphy, P. and Raynor, J. (eds) *Policies for the Curriculum*, London: Hodder & Stoughton: 74–88.

Slater, J. (1989) *The Politics of History Teaching: a Humanity Dehumanised?*, London: Institute of Education.

Slatta, R. (2001) 'Connecting learning goals with technology', *History Computer Review*, Vol. 17, No. 1: 19–30.

Smithers, A. and Robinson, P. (2000) *Attracting Teachers: Past Patterns, Present Policies, Future Prospects*, CEER, Liverpool: Carmichael.

Spear, M., Gould, K. and Lee, B. (2000) *Who Would Be a Teacher?*, Slough: NFER.

Stenhouse, L. (1975) *An Introduction to Curriculum Research and Development*, London: Heinemann.

Stokes, J. (1990) Speech in the House of Commons, quoted in *Sunday Telegraph*, 1 April.

Starkey, D. (2002) Opinion, *BBC History Magazine*, Vol. 3, No. 3: 8.

Tate, N. (1995) *The Role of History in the Formation of National Identity*; speech to the Council of Europe Conference, York, 18 September.

Torrance, H. (2002) 'Can testing really raise educational standards?', Inaugural Professorial Lecture, University of Sussex, 11 June.

Tosh, J. (1984) *The Pursuit of History*, London: Longman.

Wilian, D. (2001) *Level Best? Levels of Attainment in National Curriculum Assessment*, London: ATL.

Wineburg, S. (1997) 'Beyond "breadth and depth": subject matter knowledge and assessment', *Theory into Practice*, Vol. 36, No. 4: 255–261.

Zamorski, B. and Haydn, T. (2002) 'Classroom management and disaffection', *Pedagogy, Culture and Society*, Vol. 10, No. 2: 257–279.

Zeldin, T. (1993) *An Essential History of Europe*, BBC 2, 21 January.

8   Mathematics

Peter Gill

> There can be no doubt that there is general agreement that every child should study mathematics at school; indeed the study of mathematics, together with that of English, is regarded by most people as being essential.

Thus starts the Cockcroft Report (1982), the biggest and most influential review of mathematics teaching ever undertaken in the UK. In the twenty years since that was written few have tried to argue with the sentiment expressed. The subject has a privileged and uncontested position in the curriculum and in most schools takes up more space in the timetable than any subject other than English. Indeed at primary level the introduction of the 'Numeracy Hour' as part of the National Numeracy Strategy has been blamed for forcing other subjects out of the curriculum (Galton and Macbeath, 2002). But why so much emphasis on mathematics? What arguments are there to support such a dominant role?

Justifying school mathematics

Answers to this question can be seen to fall into one of three categories: first, mathematics is useful to the citizen personally, socially and professionally; second, mathematics provides a sound training for the mind; third, mathematics is a worthy study in its own right and as part of our cultural heritage. These appear clearly in the National Curriculum for mathematics 2000, where it states on page 14:

> The importance of mathematics
> Mathematics equips pupils with a uniquely powerful set of tools to understand and change the world. These tools include logical reasoning, problem-solving skills, and the ability to think in abstract ways. Mathematics is important in everyday life, many forms of employment, science and technology, medicine, the economy, the environment and development, and in public decision-making. Different cultures have contributed to the development and application of mathematics. Today, the subject transcends cultural boundaries and its importance is universally recognised. Mathematics is a creative discipline. It can stimulate moments of pleasure and wonder when a pupil solves a problem for the first time, discovers a more elegant solution to that problem, or suddenly sees hidden connections.

Let us consider these three areas of justification.

Mathematics is useful

At first sight this is self-evident. How can anyone live successfully, particularly in this technological era, without a firm grasp of mathematics? If one is to judge by the mathematical abilities of the average citizen, the answer is 'quite well'. But that is too cynical. This chapter is not trying to argue that mathematics is not needed, far from it. But the question is: what mathematics and how much? Clearly a grasp of basic numeracy – i.e. the number system and the four basic functions of addition, subtraction, multiplication and division – is desirable and empowering. And by this we mean not just the skills but the knowledge of when to use them. An often quoted piece of research entitled 'Is it an add, miss?' (Brown, 1981) shows that even a generation ago children often lacked this knowledge. However that level of numeracy is covered in the National Curriculum, as in most curricula, by the end of primary schooling or age eleven. Does this justify the continuing compulsory teaching of the subject at ever higher levels for a further five years? Clearly not.

But, goes the argument, mathematics is needed in the workplace. This is true of *some* workplaces, although with the increasing power of information technology (ironically based on mathematical foundations) the need is less and less. The checkout assistant at the supermarket no longer needs the mathematical skills of shop assistants a decade ago: the automated bar code reader and computer driven till do it all nowadays. Even when mathematical skills are needed it seems that they are developed in an isolated fashion within the environment in which they are needed. Recent research has shown that even in professions such as nursing, investment banking and commercial flying the practitioners use a limited range of skills which are almost entirely situationally located (Hoyles *et al.*, 1998). In other words, the framework in which the skills reside is the framework of the workplace itself not of mathematics.

The needs of higher education are equally regularly quoted. How can you study, say, physics or engineering at university without a firm grasp of mathematics? The answer is that you can't; but as with the nurses, bankers and pilots, the really useful i.e. applicable, mathematics is learned within the physics and engineering classes, not in the maths lectures, even though those lectures are apparently designed to support the other subjects (Gill, 1999a; Gill, 1999b).

Both the above examples (and there are many others) show that the mathematics learned in the mathematics classroom or lecture hall by and large does not transfer to other situations. This is an acknowledged sociological-psychological problem (Lave and Wenger, 1991) but has been ignored in curriculum design. In schools the problem is worse at secondary level because of subject specialisation among teachers and the independence of the subject departments (Orton and Roper, 2000; Paechter, 1995). The National Curriculum for mathematics contains relatively detailed links to other subject documents but they are quite literally marginalised – printed in pale grey ink in the margins alongside the programmes of study.

At Key Stage 3 from 2002, schools have started to look at 'Numeracy Across the Curriculum' as part of the National Key Stage 3 Strategy for mathematics and English but this has no effect on the content of the curriculum: unless cross-curricular elements are examined in National Tests they are unlikely to affect practice in the classroom.

Recently it has become fashionable to talk about 'civic maths' and with the multiplicity of quasi-mathematical formats available on the smallest of PCs, there seems little doubt that some mathematical skills are indeed needed in order to function as a knowledgeable and critical member of society. Actually this is not such a recent idea. In his wonderful but sadly too often forgotten book *Mathematics for the Million*, Lancelot Hogben, using the phrase '*language of size*' to mean mathematics, says 'The modern (citizen) has got to learn the language of size in self defence, because no society is safe in the hands of its clever people' (Hogben, 1936: 15). The advent of citizenship in the National Curriculum would seem to make this a powerful argument.

Mathematics as training for thinking

This aspect of the argument has already been referred to by John White in Chapter 1. It seems clear that an ability to use reasoning in its purest form, as mathematics can legitimately claim to be, will lead to the development of generally useful, transferable thinking and problem solving skills. However, as the previous two paragraphs have indicated, the evidence is the opposite: even the mathematical skills themselves do not transfer, let alone any hypothesised underlying generalised thinking skills. The fact is that there is no evidence whatsoever that the learning of mathematics, or indeed any other subject, leads to an overall increase in thinking skills.

The very existence of generalised thinking skills is still keenly debated and whenever claims are made for courses or techniques specifically to improve them they are always based on psychological arguments which are content-independent. An example of this would be the Cognitive Acceleration in Mathematics Education (CAME) project (Adhami *et al.*, 1999) which simply uses mathematics as a vehicle in a style of teaching based on the theories of Piaget and Vygotsky and was anyway originally developed within the area of *science* education (Adey and Shayer, 1994). Furthermore the evidence of the success of these schemes (which is real enough) is based on written psychological tests and GCSE results across several subjects. The use of success in tests/exams as an indicator of high level general thinking skills is debatable, to say the least.

One can also argue from the evidence of society. If the study of mathematics really did improve thinking skills, one would expect many of the leading members of society (in, say, politics, business, industry or media) to be maths graduates. This is clearly not the case.

Mathematics as a worthy study in its own right and as part of our cultural heritage

This third area of justification for the learning of mathematics includes many arguments which can be used to justify any of the subjects in the National Curriculum or any other curriculum for that matter. Intrinsic arguments are frequently spurious and are devastatingly and entertainingly dealt with in Peddiwell's essay 'The Saber Tooth Curriculum' (Peddiwell, 1939). References to them will also be found in other chapters of this book.

The cultural argument is undeniably powerful in the case of mathematics both in understanding how similar mathematical ideas developed in different cultures, often at very similar times, and in understanding the technological society we live in. I will not attempt to argue with it.

The National Curriculum for mathematics 2000

Structure

The programmes of study for mathematics consist of four areas of study, or attainment targets though at Key Stage 4 there are two separate programmes of study entitled *Foundation* and *Higher*. A pupil will follow only one of these. The attainment targets are entitled Ma1 – Using and applying mathematics; Ma2 – Number and algebra (only Number at Key Stages 1 and 2); Ma3 – Shape, space and measures; Ma4 – Handling data (but not at Key Stage 1). However on opening the curriculum document the reader could be forgiven for thinking that Ma1 does not exist. The programmes of study for each key stage start with Ma2 and a description of Ma1 only appears on page 87 of a ninety-one page document, and even there only as assessment criteria. Let us also deal with Ma1 last.

Ma2 and Ma3 have grown from traditional practice and at the secondary level reflect the old grammar school curricula. They will be familiar to readers from any educational background, although Ma3 has a more modern approach to geometry. Traditionally, the main diet of geometry was constructing shapes using rulers, compasses, set-squares and protractors and in many countries it still is. In the post-2000 National Curriculum construction still has a place but there is much more about *understanding* angles and shapes, using curriculum ideas developed in the late 1960s and onwards in such schemes as the School Mathematics Project (SMP) and the ILEA (Inner London Education Authority)-inspired SMILE (School Mathematics Independent Learning Experience) project.

Ma4 is probably the area where the UK curriculum differs most from the traditional maths curriculum and from overseas curricula. In it pupils are introduced to ideas of representing and interpreting data. It is a grounding for the subject of statistics.

As a measure of how different this is from the not so distant past, it can be noted that PGCE courses for maths teachers are finding that they have to provide remedial statistics courses for their students. This is despite the fact that those students will all be graduates in mathematics or similar disciplines. Statistics is not generally seen by professional (university) mathematicians as being part of mathematics and university departments of mathematics seldom teach or research into it.

Ma1 initially appeared with the first version of the National Curriculum in 1998. It seemed revolutionary but was a logical development from the introduction of coursework at GCSE. The argument is that 'real' mathematical tasks outside of school are always very extended, taking hours, weeks or even years to complete and cannot be represented by the short questions which are the diet of school mathematics lessons and examinations. In addition, real world problems generally use mathematics from several branches of the subject and this attainment target is where such problems may be introduced. In fact the inclusion of this as a separate attainment target in the curriculum was not without its opponents. They argued that such ideas should permeate all parts of the curriculum and not be separated out. The supporters claimed that unless these ideas were stated separately the curriculum would degenerate into the training of isolated mathematical skills that could be assessed in short tests. In previous versions of the National Curriculum the supporters held sway and there was a separate programme of study for Ma1. The 2000 version does not have this and the elements of the old Ma1 are printed at the start of all the other attainment targets. There is, however no chance of Ma1 disappearing completely as long as it is separately assessed and reported.

The curriculum match

So how does the curriculum match the claims made in *The importance of mathematics* trumpeted at the start of the Mathematics NC document and quoted earlier? We have already seen that there is no reason to think that the study of mathematics develops logical reasoning, problem solving skills and the ability to think in abstract ways except perhaps within the mathematics of the classroom itself. Similarly, we have seen that the mathematics taught in school (and beyond) does not transfer to other situations so its usefulness in everyday life is severely limited, apart perhaps from the basic numeracy of Key Stages 1 and 2. Different cultures have indeed contributed to the development and application of mathematics, but this aspect is entirely ignored in the curriculum. Mathematics really can be a creative discipline but there is no room whatever for creativity in the curriculum as delivered in the classroom. The hopes held out by the proponents of Ma1 as a home for creativity have been dashed by the pressures of assessment. The tasks that pupils are set within this attainment target are almost entirely as a preparation for assessed tasks and at Key Stage 4 are simply a preparation for the increasingly stylised and predictable GCSE coursework requirements.

The ability of the mathematics curriculum to deliver 'moments of pleasure and wonder' is for the majority of pupils quite simply zero. On the other hand the ability of school mathematics to deliver fear and loathing has been well documented for many years (see for example Buxton, 1981), and the literature on maths phobia is huge. A pupil, admittedly at AS level, was recently quoted as saying that the mathematics exam she had just sat was the worst eighty minutes of her life (Henry, 2002). It is interesting to note here that the dislike of mathematics exhibited by a large proportion of pupils (and indeed adults) is seldom apparent at primary level. It is at Key Stages 3 and 4 that the rot sets in (Osborne *et al.*, 1997: 41–42): that of course is when algebra starts. It can be argued that success in algebra requires what is often referred to as 'formal operational thinking' (Küchemann, 1981). Yet the proportion of pupils at Key Stage 4 age able to think in this way is less than 30 per cent (Shayer *et al.*, 1976) and the influential CSMS (Concepts in Secondary Mathematics and Science) survey concluded that a similar proportion or less of fifteen year olds could cope with what could be called *real* algebra (Hart, 1981: 115). The Assessment of Performance Unit (APU) surveys of the same era (see e.g. DES, 1985) produced similar findings. It was also these surveys that first gave rise to an appreciation of the 'seven year difference' (Cockcroft, 1982: 100), i.e. the range of mathematical attainment at age eleven is such that the highest achieving pupils are seven years of average attainment ahead of the lowest achieving pupils.

While it is dangerous to design a curriculum based on expectations set by the results of surveys such as CSMS, and APU, the fact is that the amount and complexity of the algebra at Key Stage 3 and in the foundation programme of study (followed by the lower attainers) is much more likely to deter pupils rather than lead to a position where a pupil experiences 'moments of pleasure and wonder'.

Indeed the whole foundation programme of study at Key Stage 4 is problematical. Essentially it is simply a rerun of the Key Stage 3 programme. Now think of the pupils it is aimed at. They have completed more than nine years of study of the subject and are clearly not doing well. It is not going to do anything positive for their attitude to force them to re-live that failure for a further two years.

Influences on the mathematics curriculum

It would appear then that the present curriculum for mathematics does not match the claims made for it. How then did that curriculum arise?

Initially of course there is history and tradition. Mathematics is one of the oldest school subjects and thus has a very long history. As stated earlier, much of the curriculum at Key Stages 3 and 4 has grown out of the grammar school curriculum that preceded it and when GCSE maths examinations are criticised the criticism is frequently that they are not the same as the GCE O-level of thirty or forty years ago. But the O-level was basically a preparation for the A-level which in turn was a preparation for university study. Thus a main traditional influence has been the university mathematicians who actually only represent the interests of a tiny proportion of the population. It is interesting to note that in the National Curriculum document for mathematics on the page opposite the statement on 'the importance of mathematics' there are statements supporting the teaching of mathematics coming from four professors and one lecturer in mathematics. Again, hardly representative. Anyway, why include such statements in a document that is likely only to be read by mathematics teachers who presumably already believe in the importance of their subject?

It can also be argued that commercial requirements demanded clerks with good computational skills. The development of such skills is no longer needed for industry but their presence can still be detected. An up-to-date version of this would demand the development of IT skills and indeed there is mention of such skills throughout the programmes of study. However they do not feature in the attainment targets and because they are not testable by traditional written exams they are almost entirely absent from classroom practice.

The absence of useful elements of IT in the curriculum can also be traced to the attitudes present in the mathematics departments of our older universities where, at undergraduate level teaching anyway, IT is viewed with distrust. In such places the use of modern graphics calculators is frequently banned in the examination room, only standard scientific models being permitted. This is unfortunate for the students who will virtually all have used modern graphics calculators as an integral part of their A-level studies. They find it incomprehensible that they are forced to revert to the technology of their parents' generation.

Commerce, industry and the world of work still have an interest because they largely use the acquisition of a mathematics GCSE (usually at grade C or above) as an entry qualification. Recently even these players have found the curriculum unsatisfactory and many companies set their own maths/numeracy tests. The ultimate example comes in the case of teacher training places. To start on a PGCE course in any subject area a student needs GCSE maths at grade C or better. But to receive the teaching qualification the student has also to pass another government-imposed numeracy test – a clear admission by government that their own school mathematics curriculum is failing.

But there are other more recent influences on the mathematics curriculum and many of them tend to see the study of mathematics as an important part of personal development for the pupils individually and as members of society. Such influences have introduced much more practical mathematics i.e. using other equipment than just compass, ruler, set-square and protractor. The idea of investigational and problem-solving mathematics developed here. This includes longer open-ended tasks for the pupils where there is not necessarily a single, or indeed any, right answer. Games and collaborative exercises feature and there is the potentially subversive view that mathematics can be fun. These influences were behind the introduction of Ma1 *Using and applying mathematics* into the National Curriculum and its near disappearance from the 2000 version could be seen as an indication of their decline. Many of the personnel involved in the work in this area are either practising maths teachers or former maths teachers operating in university departments of education.

These two groups of influences could be labelled 'trainers' and 'educators' (but see (Ernest, 2000: 6) for a more detailed classification) and can be seen in the continued existence of two subject associations for mathematics: the Mathematical Association representing the 'trainers' group and the Association of Teachers of Mathematics representing the 'educators'. This classification should be used warily, however, as many maths teachers are members of both (or neither) association. The existence of two associations, despite desultory attempts at reconciliation, has considerably weakened the influence of mathematics teachers. This can be contrasted with the situation in science where the Association for Science Education (ASE) represents the interests of the widely differing practices of, say, biology and physics teachers, but by being big and speaking with a single voice carries considerable clout at a political level. The existence of science as one of the three 'core' subjects with maths and English in the National Curriculum is evidence of this.

But the curriculum is set by the government and its advisers, so whom do they listen to? To be credible, a government needs to show that it is listening to 'practitioners'. There is nothing necessarily wrong with this but in the case of mathematics the practitioners are represented by university mathematicians and representatives from industry, both from the 'trainers' side of the groupings and generally with little idea of what takes place in classrooms. An extreme case of this can be seen in the 'maths wars' that took place in California in the late 1990s where the final version of the state maths curriculum ended up being written and revised almost entirely by mathematics professors with no knowledge and experience of school mathematics (Becker and Jacob, 2000).

The influence of industry is more mixed, one might even say muddled. Reports of declining standards of numeracy being experienced by recruiters to business and industry are common but as Sir Ron Dearing said in his review of the 16–19 curriculum 'representations by employers about standards in ... the application of number have been a feature of national life for more than a century. It has always seemed that things were better 20 years ago' (Dearing, 1996: 6). On the other hand, in recent surveys of employers, problems with numeracy barely feature (e.g. Pieda, 2000: 17). What does feature highly as problematical in such surveys is teamworking and communication skills. This is acknowledged in the post-16 curriculum where 'Communication' and 'Working with others' are two of the Key Skills. Strangely enough, these aspects did feature in an early draft of the first National Curriculum for mathematics. In consultative report of the Mathematics Working Group (which set up the original National Curriculum) there were attainment targets in Using mathematics, Communication skills and Personal qualities. The latter included five bullet points of which the last was called – somewhat ambiguously – 'independence of thought and action as well as the ability to co-operate within a group'. The National Curriculum Council (NCC) decided to throw it out entirely in spite of considerable support for it in the consultation responses.

Personal qualities disappeared for ever. This target had been very strongly supported by the industry rep on the Working Group and HMI, but the DES and NCC removed it.[1] The Communication target is taking longer to wither away and remains as part of the slowly fading Ma1.

There is also a strange, almost puritanical, push to make mathematics unnecessarily difficult, perhaps because suffering is thought good for the soul. The banning of graphics calculators from university examination halls is matched by their entire removal from certain school examination papers. This is not to argue that mental mathematical skills should be abandoned, far from it. There is little doubt that in the last decade or so the reduction in time spent on such skills has been detrimental to pupils' mathematical skills and understanding. But the argument against calculator use seems more often based on the idea that anything that makes mathematics easier is somehow a 'bad thing'. Even this is not a new idea. Some four hundred years ago Kepler (on whose work Newton based much of his) was chastised by his tutor for using logarithms because 'it is not seemly for a professor of mathematics to be childishly pleased about any shortening of the calculations' (Casper, 1962). This attitude can be seen in the founding of the National Curriculum for mathematics where one of the traditionalist members of the Working Party was described by the chairman as being someone who was a member 'of the school which believed that a thousand long divisions a day are somehow good for the soul, a kind of spiritual experience in their own right' and who saw 'calculators as a manifestation of evil' (Graham, 1996: 143–144). It is perhaps no coincidence that the country which housed the 'maths wars' of California also houses an enormous number of fundamentalist Christians many of whom are trying to force creationism into the science curriculum as a viable alternative to evolution.

But the single biggest factor that has affected the National Curriculum for mathematics since day one has been the assessment regime. Maths teachers have been criticised for many years for 'teaching to the test' (see for instance HMI, 1979: 121) but with the advent of league tables and testing at age 7, 11, and 14 in addition to the traditional 16+, the curriculum has become increasingly test-oriented. And although there is more use of teacher assessment in reporting pupil attainment than was the case before the introduction of the National Curriculum, such assessment is invariably based on externally set tasks and examinations and it is externally set examinations such as GCSE which are reported to the public. Such tasks are bound to be a poor reflection on achievement yet 'It is seriously believed . . . that a three hour written test will serve to establish the level of a pupil . . . It is further believed that this three hour episode will give a more trustworthy result than can be produced by the teachers who have been teaching that pupil for three years. No one with expert knowledge about the reliability and validity of written tests could take such a proposition seriously' (Black, 1992: 9). Although the schemes of work do contain material that cannot be tested by short written exam questions, such aspects are generally ignored in the classroom. This is doubly unfortunate because a problem-solving, open-ended approach to maths teaching, even within the confines of a National Curriculum, can lead to just as good examination results as a test-focussed approach (Boaler, 1997). Ironically, one of the few issues that the 'trainers' and the 'educators' agree on is the malevolent effect of the current National Curriculum Testing regime.

The result of these varying influences has been to produce a curriculum which is piecemeal. One of the beauties of mathematics is its connectedness but this is almost entirely hidden in the desire to produce a curriculum that (a) satisfies in some way the varying demands of the varied influencing parties and (b) can be examined by timed written tests.

The effect of past practice on the present National Curriculum was referred to at the start of this section and it is perhaps worrying that virtually all the criticisms made so far in this chapter predate the National Curriculum. Documents such as 'Mathematics Counts' (Cockcroft, 1982) and 'Aspects of secondary education in England' (HMI, 1979) highlight all these issues yet these reports have repeatedly been ignored by both the governments that issued them and those that have followed.

The general aims and values of the National Curriculum

As John White discusses in Chapter 1, the 2000 version of the National Curriculum is the first to contain overarching aims and values. How well does the mathematics curriculum contribute to the achievement of those aims and how well does it reflect the values?

Aims

Aim 1 is generally about learning and achievement, particularly at a personal level. There is no doubt that mathematics offers wonderful scope for personal achievement, but as expressed in an assessment led curriculum it offers much more scope for failure for the majority of pupils. The problem of 'maths phobia' has already been discussed. And this curriculum, particularly with its concentration on algebra in the later key stages, is likely to produce as many maths phobics as any past curriculum. For too many pupils both past and present the big red X is all they get from maths exercises.

There is also mention of skills including numeracy, literacy and communication technology. Numeracy is certainly important, but most of that is covered in the first two key stages. Literacy probably does not come much into the picture, but communication and communication technology could certainly exist in a mathematics curriculum and indeed are mentioned in the programmes of study, but in practice in too many classrooms driven by the pressure of exams they simply don't feature. The same is true for working collaboratively and thinking creatively.

As far as the development of thinking skills is concerned, this has been dealt with earlier, but it is difficult to see how any subject taught in isolation can hope to develop general skills. One of the main problems with any subject-based curriculum is the development of subject sub-cultures which are ignorant or even dismissive of what happens in other subjects (Paechter, 1995). The development of a pupil's sense of identity through understanding of such issues as cultural heritage would certainly be possible within a mathematics curriculum. However, not in this present one.

Aim 2 is about social values. The phrase 'spiritual, moral, social and cultural development' is a key one and each earns a mention in the introduction to the National Curriculum for mathematics. *Spiritual development*, it suggests, can be promoted by gaining an insight into the infinite. This is nonsense. The mathematical concept of infinity is complex, technical and in many ways illogical. There is no way that the understanding of it can seriously be described as spiritual. In *moral development* it says that pupils should learn to use logical, i.e. mathematical, reasoning in moral decision-making. This is both specious and dangerous and anyway, as we have seen, mathematical thinking does not travel far from the mathematics classroom. *Social development* could indeed be reinforced by mathematics but again, as argued above, there is no place for it in the current examination-driven curriculum. The same goes for *cultural development*. This is certainly possible through mathematics but entirely absent from this curriculum.

Now, of course, no single subject could hope to meet every aspect of these two groups of aims but the current National Curriculum for mathematics meets virtually none. This is despite the fact that a curriculum for mathematics certainly could be written in such a way as to encompass most of the aims.

Values

One of the primary claims for mathematics as a uniquely powerful area of study and means of communication is that it is value-free. Thus a mathematician would see no role in a mathematics curriculum for value issues relating to the self, relationships, society and the environment as listed in the general 'statement of values' in the National Curriculum. And indeed this is what we have in the mathematics curriculum – an entirely value-free document. This shows the influence of the mathematicians rather than the users of mathematics despite the fact that the number of pupils likely to go on to work with mathematics in its value-free manifestation is diminishingly small.

The value-free nature of mathematics (and the same claim is often made for science) is disputable. It relies on an assumption that mathematics somehow exists to be discovered as Plato claimed. Many educationalists (although by no means all teachers) find this a difficult view to square with the current constructivist models of learning that pervade much of the research literature. They are consciously or unconsciously more sympathetic to the philosophical views of Lakatos (1976) for whom the development of mathematics was a human activity and thus fallible.

Alternative approaches

We have seen that the current National Curriculum largely fails to meets the claims made for it in mathematical terms and equally fails to contribute to the wider development of aims and values. This is not to say that such things are entirely absent from classrooms. There is some wonderfully inspiring teaching going on but teachers, whether inspirational or simply mortal, are heavily restricted by the curriculum they are obliged by law to deliver.

Certain changes to the curriculum could be made to improve the match. The all-important topic of risk management (Royal Society, 1992) which is part of Aim 2 would sit comfortably in Ma4 and it would be relatively straightforward to include a social and cultural dimension by introducing elements of the history of mathematics. This has already been tried successfully at A-level where the Nuffield Advanced Mathematics scheme contained units on 'The history of mathematics' and 'Mathematics, music and art' (Nuffield, 1994). That course no longer exists, forced out by government rule changes on the curriculum. But the idea is valid and could be extended to the earlier key stages. Moreover the history element could be linked to philosophy (a compulsory school subject in some countries) with much wider implications. Most people in the UK know of Pythagoras as a result of his widely taught but almost entirely useless theorem about triangles, yet his influence on Western thought was huge through his school of philosophy, although totally ignored in English schools.

But before we go further down the road of curriculum change we must accept that if we add something to an already overloaded curriculum then something else must go, and the trouble is that each element will have its supporters. I have argued that there is too much in the curriculum to support the development of students who can go on to study mathematics at university level. This is true, but we cannot ignore the rights of that minority who do have the abilities and desires to take the subject further, don't forget the seven year gap. The removal of algebra, as I have suggested, would do much to change the attitude to maths of many secondary pupils but surely that would disadvantage the academic minority. In fact it may well not. In a survey of teachers (Brown, 1995) at a time when it was possible to attain a high grade at GCSE maths without touching algebra, it was found that the teachers of A-level mathematics who took on such students didn't find it a significant problem. A similar argument could be made for abandoning teaching the adding and subtracting of fractions before A-level (Dobson, 1997), and I could go on.

However, this is just playing with details: more radical solutions are necessary. For a start, we need to get away from an exam-driven curriculum. Pupils in the UK are tested more than in virtually any other country. Testing distorts the curriculum, it drives classroom practice, it takes up huge amounts of time and it costs a fortune. The cost of National Curriculum testing (including GCSE) across all subjects in the academic year 2000–2001 was over £129 million! I am not suggesting that pupils' progress should not be monitored and reported, but that it can be done much more efficiently and reliably by increasing the use of teachers' professional judgements, as is done in other countries, and reducing the amount of external testing.

We also need to look at the amount of time spent teaching mathematics. I have already said that the compulsory numeracy hour has been blamed for driving other activities out of the primary classroom. An hour is a large part of a primary school pupil's day. Is it worth it for an exercise which seems mostly designed to increase the UK's league table position in international comparisons rather than improve their mathematics?

At secondary level the existence of the Foundation programme of study for Key Stage 4 as a rerun of Key Stage 3 is an admission that the curriculum has failed the pupils forced to follow it. Why not let them opt out? If they need mathematics later they can opt back in post-16 or more likely, as has been described earlier, learn the mathematics necessary for a context in that context (or more likely as part of their NVQ). We know that happens anyway. Why not accept it and allow the students to spend their time more usefully at Key Stage 4?

However, any changes, whether tinkering with the curriculum or something bolder, will need to be accompanied by extensive professional support for teachers and a restructuring of teacher training (sic) courses. Most maths graduates are inevitably inclined to the 'trainers' group, even those who choose to become teachers (Woodrow, 2001) and are likely to find the inclusion of personal and societal aspects in their maths teaching difficult. Similarly, practising teachers will need help in such unfamiliar waters (Levinson, 2001). This will all cost money but that can easily be found by reducing the huge costly burden of repeated external examinations.

Conclusion

Those of us who have been privileged to teach mathematics in the classroom know that it really does have the potential to be inspiring for pupils at a personal level and empowering for them at a social level.

When introduced in 1988, the National Curriculum for mathematics was in many ways a leap forward, taking the subject away from the traditional grammar-school influenced curriculum that had preceded it. The introduction of such things as data handling and extended investigational work was opening and liberating. Since then, outside pressures, particularly those of external testing, have turned the curriculum into something that satisfies nobody.

The current curriculum for mathematics fails to meet the claims made for it in mathematical terms and also fails to contribute to the overall ethos of the National Curriculum contained in the *Aims and values*. Nothing less than a complete overhaul is necessary if it is to serve our pupils and the society they, and we, live in.

Note

1   I am grateful to Professor Margaret Brown, who was a member of the Mathematics Working Group, for this information.

Further reading

Why Learn Maths? (Bramall and White, 2000) takes further many of the issues raised in this chapter.

The Mathematical Experience (Davis and Hersh, 1980) examines in a series of essays what mathematics is and what mathematicians do.

Experiencing School Mathematics (Boaler, 1997) is an award-winning book describing exactly what takes place in secondary school mathematics classrooms.

References

Adey, P. and Shayer, M. (1994) *Really Raising Standards: Cognitive Intervention and Academic Achievement*, London: Routledge.

Adhami, M., Johnson, D. and Shayer, M. (1999) *Thinking Maths*, London: Heinemann Educational.

Becker, J.P. and Jacob, J. (2000) 'The Politics of California School Mathematics: The Anti-Reform of 1997–1999', *Phi Delta Kappa*, 81(7), 529–537.

Black, P. (1992) 'Introduction', in Black, P. *et al. Education: Putting the Record Straight*, Stafford: Network Educational Press.

Boaler, J. (1997) *Experiencing School Mathematics*, Buckingham: Open University Press.

Bramall, S. and White, J. (eds) (2000) *Why Learn Maths?*, London: Institute of Education.

Brown, M. (1981) 'Is it an Add, Miss?' Part 3. *Mathematics in School*, 10(1), 26–28.

Brown, M. (1995) *The Step between GCSE and A-level in Mathematics*. Report prepared for SCAA.

Buxton, L. (1981) *Do You Panic About Maths?: Coping with Maths Anxiety*, London: Heinemann Educational.

Casper, M. (1962) *Kepler 1571–1630* (E. Doris Hellman, trans.), New York: Collier Books.

Cockcroft, W. (1982) *Mathematics Counts: Report of the Committee of Inquiry into the Teaching of Mathematics in Schools*, London: HMSO.

Davis, P. and Hersh, R. (1980) *The Mathematical Experience*, London: Penguin Books.

Dearing, R. (1996) *Review of Qualifications for 16–19 Year Olds: Summary*, London: SCAA.

DES (1985) *New Perspectives on the Mathematics Curriculum*, London: Department for Education and Science.

Dobson, K. (1997) 'Advanced Fractions, or Use It or Lose It', *Physics Education*, 32(5), 295.

Ernest, P. (2000) 'Why Teach Mathematics', in Bramall, S. and White, J. (eds) *Why Learn Maths?*, London: Institute of Education, University of London.

Galton, M. and Macbeath, J. (2002) *A Life in Teaching: the Impact of Change on Primary Teachers' Working Lives*, London: National Union of Teachers.

Gill, P. (1999a) 'Aspects of Undergraduate Engineering Students' Understanding of Mathematics', *International Journal of Mathematical Education in Science and Technology*, 30(4), 557–563.

Gill, P. (1999b) 'The Physics/Maths Problem Again', *Physics Education*, 34(2), 83–87.

Graham, D. (1996) *The Education Racket: Who Cares about the Children?*, Glasgow: Neil Wilson.

Hart, K. (ed.) (1981) *Children's Understanding of Mathematics 11–16*, London: John Murray.

Henry, J. (2002) 'If maths equals tedium, what's the solution?' *Times Educational Supplement*, 18 October, pp. 24–25.

HMI (1979) *Aspects of Secondary Education*, London: HMSO.

Hogben, L. (1936) *Mathematics for the Million*, London: George Allen & Unwin.

Hoyles, C., Noss, R. and Pozzi, S. (1998) 'Mathematising in Practice', in Hoyles, C., Morgan, C. and Woodhouse, G. (eds) *Mathematics Education for the Twenty-First Century*, London: Falmer Press.

Küchemann, D. (1981) 'Cognitive Demand of Secondary School Mathematics', *Educational Studies in Mathematics*, 12, 301–316.

Lakatos, I. (ed.) (1976) *Proofs and Refutations: The Logic of Mathematical Discovery*, Cambridge: Cambridge University Press.

Lave, J. and Wenger, E. (1991) *Situated Learning: Legitimate Peripheral Participation*, Cambridge: Cambridge University Press.

Levinson, R. (2001) 'Should Controversial Issues in Science be Taught Through the Humanities?' *School Science Review*, 82(300), 97–102.

Nuffield Foundation (1994) *Nuffield Advanced Mathematics*, Harlow: Longman Group UK Ltd.

Orton, T. and Roper, T. (2000) 'Science and Mathematics: A Relationship in Need of Counselling?' *Studies in Science Education*, 35, 123–154.

Osborne, J., Black, P., Boaler, J., Brown, M., Driver, R., Murray, R. and Simon, S. (1997) *Attitudes to Science, Mathematics and Technology: A Review of Research*, London: King's College.

Paechter, C. (1995) *Crossing Subject Boundaries: The Micropolitics of Curriculum Innovation*, London: HMSO.

Peddiwell, J. (1939) *The Saber-Tooth Curriculum and Other Essays*, New York: McGraw-Hill.

Pieda, D. (2000) *The Graduate Labour Market in London: Graduates and Employers*, London: Focus Central London.

Royal Society (1992) *Risk: Analysis, Perception and Management*, London: The Royal Society.

Shayer, M., Küchemann, D.E. and Wylam, H. (1976) 'The Distribution of Piagetian Stages of Thinking in British Middle and Secondary School Children', *British Journal of Educational Psychology*, 46, 164–173.

Woodrow, D. (2001) 'Learning Preferences of PGCE Students: Implications for Recruitment of Mathematics Teachers', in Proceedings of 'Key Stage 3 Mathematics Teachers: the Current Situation, Initiatives and Vision' Conference, Buckingham: Open University.

9 Modern foreign languages

Kevin Williams

If we were to design school curricula *ab initio*, it is unlikely that modern languages would be assigned the prominent role that they currently enjoy in the curriculum of the United Kingdom or of elsewhere within the English-speaking world. Much concern has been expressed about the difficulty of motivating school learners, as well as the low level of achievement of many of them (see, for example, Association for Language Learning, 1998 and Nuffield Foundation, 2000). Yet only recently, with the likely removal of their compulsory status at Key Stage 4, has the profile of modern foreign languages (MFLs) within the National Curriculum been called into question. This shows that we do not come to the task of curriculum design *ex nihilo*, but rather we are inheritors of a tradition that has assumed the shape it has for a variety of reasons. Like the tourist who asks a countryman how to get a destination and receives the reply, 'If I were going there, I wouldn't start from here', we have to start from here. Although we are not prisoners of our past, there is a sense in which we have to make the best use of what circumstances offer us.

In contrast with the Nuffield Report (2000), the most recent official document entitled *Modern Foreign Languages* (DfEE/QCA, 1999a) does not invoke spurious claims regarding the vocational usefulness of learning MFLs. Elsewhere I have explored in some detail the deficiencies in the utilitarian arguments for teaching them on a compulsory basis over an extended period of schooling to young citizens of the English-speaking world (Williams, 2000) so I shall mention them only briefly here. Obviously I do not deny the usefulness of mastery of the languages of those countries to whom one is hoping to sell goods or services. Yet this knowledge cannot be said to be of utility to the vast majority of English-speakers. There is a conspicuous lack of hard evidence that foreign language skills will increase productivity and employment. In any event, the level of competence acquired by most young people in school would not be of great value in the workplace. After five years' study, only school leavers who are in the top ten or perhaps twenty per cent of the ability range would have a sufficiently reliable grasp of a language even for low-level vocational purposes.

The relative absence of vocational reasons for learning other languages, and the consequence of this for motivating young English speakers present at once a challenge and opportunity to justify their place in the school curriculum. It may in fact be a matter of articulating a rationale for the area because, as Norbert Pachler notes, in English-speaking countries, the identification of such a rationale 'remains elusive' (Pachler, 2001, pp. 70–72; see also Williams, 2001, pp. 43–47). Even in France, the rationale for learning English is not an issue, and debate about language learning is conducted on the assumption that every pupil will learn English (see Baumard, 2002b, p. 25). A positive outcome of the global hegemony of English is that if MFLs are to be included in the curriculum in the Anglophone world, then a case has to be made primarily on educational grounds (that is, related to personal enrichment) rather than on grounds of putative usefulness. Justification of curriculum pursuits is also open to re-negotiation to take account of changed circumstances. This occurred in the case of the classical languages where, on account of the decline in the numbers taking the subjects, the aims of studying Greek and Latin were re-formulated to embrace the study of the civilisations of Greece and Rome rather than simply of their respective languages.

There is one questionable aspect of the traditional justification for teaching Latin imported into the aims of foreign language study. This is the attribution to such study of a role in teaching the 'basic structures of language' and in improving 'listening, reading and memory skills' and in leading to 'more accurate' speaking and writing in the mother tongue (DfEE/QCA, 1999a, p. 14). This is akin to the argument that the study of Latin contributes to the improved use of English. Admittedly, knowledge of Latin may enhance the grammatical sensitivity of some very able students and thereby improve their use of English. Also, study of any language does heighten awareness of language as a system of meaning. But until we have detailed and plausible research evidence, it remains mere assertion to maintain that the writing skills of those who know Latin, Greek, or MFLs are better than those who do not. Moreover, apart from their questionable plausibility, these aims do not relate sufficiently sharply to general aims.

Five principal aims for teaching MFLs can be identified, and I argue that these aims lend themselves to more imaginative, forceful and precise formulation than is to be found in the different official documents dealing with their place in the National Curriculum. These aims have two major aspects, the experiential and the ethical. The experiential has three strands: (1) to provide pleasure; (2) to form a basis for further learning; and (3) to engender cultural decentring. The two aims of the ethical strand are to: (1) to foster individual openness to others; (2) to give symbolic expression to the openness of UK society to other cultures. Four of the aims apply to individual learners and the fifth has a societal character. Although the four individual aims are educationally very positive, it may not be possible to realise them due to lack of interest or ability on the part of learners. For this reason I argue that there is a strong case for making study of MFLs compulsory for a year but that it is unjustifiable to extend obligation beyond this year. Where it is apparent that personal well-being is not being promoted through the MFL curriculum, then young people should not be obliged to continue their studies. In brief, this aspect of the curriculum should form part of the entitlement of every young person but compulsory exposure to it should be limited.

Pleasure as an aim

The first of the experiential aims is to provide pleasure and satisfaction and also to contribute to the cultivation of confidence. This relates to the general Aim 1 of the post 2000 English school curriculum, that is, that the 'school curriculum should develop enjoyment of, and commitment to, learning' (DfEE/QCA, 1999b, p. 11). Aim 1 also speaks of the importance of developing the 'confidence' of young learners 'in their capacity to learn and work independently and collaboratively' (ibid.) but, as will be made clear, 'confidence' in this statement is used in a more limited sense than I use it. The idea of pleasure and enjoyment is not sufficiently emphasised in the main statement and hardly features in the document, *Modern Foreign Languages* (DfEE/QCA, 1999a). This is a pity, and seems to reflect a view of school as arena of serious, indeed, solemn commitment rather than of pleasure and even fun, where the possibility of young people learning French, for example, because they believed it would enhance their attractiveness to the opposite sex would not be entertained. It is worth dwelling on the pleasure and satisfaction that can be a feature of speaking another language. Anyone who has successfully managed to speak even a little of a foreign language on holidays will testify to the sense of accomplishment and achievement that this provides. There is a memorable description of the kind of pleasure I have in mind in the novel, *The Chateau* by William Maxwell (2000). The protagonist, Harold, is a young American recently arrived in France with his wife and in a state of some anxiety he embarks on his first extended discourse in French in company. At the end of the story the listeners laugh and Harold is overjoyed: as the author expresses it: 'he felt flooded with pleasure' (ibid., p. 47). The metaphor 'flooded' suggests something akin to sexual delight and communicates the quality of the pleasure that can be a feature of successfully communicating in another language. It is a pleasure and a satisfaction, which can be experienced by people whose aptitude for languages is very limited.

Even minimal mastery of a foreign language can also make a significant contribution to the development of self-confidence. The sense of achievement to be derived from managing successfully to communicate in a language other than one's mother tongue not only enhances general self-confidence but it also promotes the confidence required to speak the language even better. Indeed, rather than accent or intonation, it is a person's confidence which is the most important attribute in language learning. Eric Hawkins (1987, pp. 56–58) also makes some interesting observations on the potential of foreign language study to offer to some low achievers a completely new linguistic experience at school, without the connotations of failure associated with the native tongue. As well as the other educational benefits which foreign language learning may confer, the general self-confidence and self-image of slow learners who enjoy success are likely to improve.

Of course, achievement in most human activities contributes to the development of self-confidence, and I should not wish to claim that foreign language study is necessary to the development of self-confidence. What, however, is peculiar to the activity is its potential to promote confidence in relating to other people. Use of role play and drama in teaching, for example, can make of the activity a positive and immediate means of personal development. This forges a curricular link between language education and personal, social and health education (PSHE). This is not to claim that MFLs are a necessary part of PSHE, but they can make a significant contribution to it. One reason for the connection between mastery of foreign languages and the development of self-confidence derives from the high status of such knowledge through its traditional association with being well educated.

Learning to learn

The second experiential aim of language learning is to develop the capacity to engage in further learning. It relates to the general aim of preparing 'pupils for the next steps in their education, training and employment' (DfEE/QCA, 1999b, p. 12) and to the statement in the booklet, *Modern Foreign Languages*, which refers to laying 'the foundations for future study of other languages' (DfEE/QCA, 1999a, p. 14). There are good grounds to believe, as Hawkins (1987) argues, that the learning of one foreign language will provide a model that may help in the study of others. Moreover, the benefits of this learning are not specific to any age group. Above all, there is something to be said for making use of the willingness and capacity to learn which many young people exhibit in order to introduce them to a foreign language. Although the complex evidence on the effect of prior study of a foreign language in school on future compe-tence can hardly be said to be encouraging, much of the evidence relates to teaching conducted in the conventional classroom context of five short classes per week extended over a number of years, where what is learned in the classroom is not rein-forced by hearing the language spoken in the community. Obviously in learning foreign languages, the degree of exposure to the language and level of reinforcement received play a decisive role. Accordingly 'given the right learning conditions' we find that 'learners exposed to early second language instruction probably have some advant-age in the very long run over those whose exposure begins later' (Singleton, 1989, p. 267).[1] This suggests, as I shall argue in the conclusion, that we may have to re-consider the arrangements for teaching languages.

Moreover, even if the linguistic advantages may not be great, recent research indi-cates that children's capacity to make sounds and to discriminate between them is enhanced. Enhanced also are their attitudes to otherness and difference (see Blondin, C. *et al.*, 1998; Baumard, 2002a, pp. 22–24; Cédelle, 2002, pp. 26–27)[2] – attitudes that are salient both in the third strand of the experiential aims and in the ethical aims. This suggests that it might not be appropriate to wait until Key Stage 3 before including foreign languages in the curriculum, especially as children from five to ten can experience the frisson of pleasure that is sometimes a feature of communicating in another language. At this point we must consider the third strand of the experiential aims.

Experience and cultural decentring

It is to the credit of the authors of official documents that they conceive languages as forms of cultural expression rather as than de-contextualised skills.[3] These documents are informed by an appropriately holistic epistemology which takes into account the cultural background or *Vorhabe* in which language has its place. This conceptualisation allows the documents to highlight the potential contribution of MFLs to citizenship education. The curricular outreach of MFLs with regard to civic education is not, however, conspicuously reciprocated. For example, reference to the cross-curricular role of MFLs receives less than a full sentence in *Education for Citizenship and the Teach-ing of Democracy in Schools* (DfEE/QCA, 1998, p. 53). Perhaps one reason for this is because, like the very general personal qualities promoted by study of other subjects, the civic qualities (sensitivity towards, and respect for, other cultures) promoted by study of MFLs do not lend themselves to formal assessment. It is not realistic to assess the quality of a learner's relationship with another culture. Perhaps another reason for the failure to appreciate the civic potential of MFLs is the absence of compelling illus-tration of how learning languages can promote civic qualities and this is something I hope to demonstrate later in this section of the chapter.

By offering a unique way of experiencing a culture, use of its language has the potential to prompt what I propose to refer to as cultural decentring. The spirit of this process is reflected in the view of Quintus Ennius that knowledge of three languages gave him three hearts (*Quintus Ennius tria corda habere sese dicebat, quod loqui Graece et Osce et Latine sciret*) (Gellius, 1928, p. 262). The same point is made by Luxembourg writer, Jean Portatet, who speaks of growing up with two languages – Italian, the language of his home and Luxembourgeois, the language of his native place. Negotiating the two languages made him feel, he writes, that '*deux êtres vivaient en moi*' (two beings lived in me) (Séry, 2002, p. 6). The encounter with another speech community offered by knowledge of its language constitutes a crucial element in cultural decentring. This process goes beyond mere respect for diversity or cultural outreach, or as it is put in the general aim statement, 'knowledge, understanding and appreciation of their own and different beliefs and cultures' (DfEE/QCA, 1999b, p. 11); rather it is the engendering of a sense of an insider's experience of the lebenswelt of other cultures. Cultural decentring can be said to be valuable on account of the perspectives that it can offer both on a different culture and also on the learner's own culture. It can allow learners to achieve a critical distance from their own culture and provide what has been described as an 'unsettling' of perspectives assumed in their native culture (see Smith and Carvill, 2000, pp. 119–120). This is not to claim that we can acquire a God's eye view of our own culture, but rather that we can be enabled to stand slightly to the side of it. It may, but this is a contingent rather than a necessary feature of the process, serve to reduce ethnocentric bias and make young people more critical of their own culture and more open-minded and tolerant of other cultures both within and outside the UK. In the context of the distinctions made in Chapter 1 (p. 7), the aim in cultural decentring is therefore twofold. It is both to provide pupils with occurrent experiences of other cultures and also with enduring mental states of sensitivity to them.

Three further points need to be made here. First, cultural decentring can be promoted through the mother tongue but, where teaching is conducted exclusively in the language of the learners, they do not have to undergo the individual decentring which goes with having the insider's experience that is a feature of learning an actual language. Without such learning we are talking of attenuated and second hand experience. It is like suggesting that courses in mutual understanding given to children in church-sponsored schools can have the same potency in promoting social integration as attendance at common schools. Second, other subjects also have the potential to prompt this decentring (civics, PSHE, history, literature, geography) but by providing an experience of a culture from the inside, MFLs offer a special entrée into that culture. Third, decentring can occur in very different degrees – from using a few Spanish phrases on holidays to the kind of experiences described in the following two examples.

In order to go beyond aspirational assertion about the propensity of language learning to engender cultural decentring, it is necessary to illustrate this in some detail.

The civic world of Rome

Earlier I expressed some scepticism about the argument for teaching Latin on grounds of its potential contribution to improving proficiency in the use of the mother tongue. By contrast, one of the most compelling arguments for teaching it relates to its capacity to engender cultural decentring. In a wonderful short story entitled 'Regulus', Rudyard Kipling (2000) illustrates how both in theory and in practice this great Ode of Horace's was taught in this perspective. The particular aim in this case was to enhance civic and moral understanding. The story shows how the Ode actually provides the boys with images of courage and forbearance that they apply in their own lives. In this context, arguably what is in question is more the civic and moral potency of literature rather than of the study of Latin because access to this Ode can be secured via translations. Yet, although I would want to raise some questions about the contribution of a knowledge of Latin to the endeavour, I would also want to say that it is of real significance. What can we identify as the peculiar contribution of knowledge of Latin to this learning? It seems to me that an encounter with the poem in an English translation would be a different experience from encountering it in the original. Reading a poem in English, as Stanley Burnshaw (1964) points out in his discussion of literature in translation, 'offers an experience in *English* poetry' (Burnshaw, 1964, p. xiii; my italics). To be sure the ideas may be carried across into English but 'poems are not made of ideas . . . they are made of words' (ibid.). Can we therefore say that learners have a different experience through the encounter with the words of the original? I think that we can because it is only through reading the Latin text that learners will come to hear the voice of Horace himself and experience some of the excitement of acquiring an insider's knowledge. To enter at once into the thought and into the language requires therefore a twofold imaginative leap. And this is precisely what the young people in Kipling's story show themselves capable of by using Latin to apply to their own lives what they have learned from the poem.

Becoming Congolese

The second example of the role of language in cultural decentring is taken from the widely acclaimed novel, *The Poisonwood Bible*, by American author, Barbara Kingsolver (Kingsolver, 1999). The novel illustrates very vividly how coming to understand a culture and learning its language are related. This it achieves through a representation of contrasting attitudes towards encountering other cultures and through highlighting the difference between individuals in their capacity to engage in cultural decentring.

An American family arrives in the Congo in the early 1960s because the father wishes to pursue his mission of evangelising the natives. Reverend Price, the father, subscribes to a rigid and stern Protestantism that makes no allowance for any deviation from a strict theological and moral code. Unable to make any kind of personal connection with African culture, he fails entirely to exhibit any understanding of, or sympathy towards, native culture and religion and cannot comprehend the antagonism displayed by natives towards Christianity. One significant reason for his failure to evangelise the local people is his inability to speak their language. The Kikongo word, *bängala*, contains many layers of meaning (most precious, most insufferable and poisonwood) and his cry of 'Tata Jesus is *bängala*!' (ibid., p. 571) at the end of his sermons invariably leads to shrieks of laughter.

His attitude is contrasted with that of Leah, his second daughter. Her willingness to decentre from her own culture is conveyed by her learning of the native languages, and she embarks on this project from her earliest days through Pascal, her first childhood friend. Part of their companionship consists in his telling her the Kikongo words for 'everything we saw and some things I hadn't thought to look for' (ibid., p. 128). She is intrigued by the different words for rain and in learning them she learns a further lesson about Western inhibitions concerning sexuality. '*[M]awala* is rain far off in the distance that doesn't ever come. When it booms thunder and beats down the grass, that is *nuni ndolo*, and the gentler kind is *nkazi ndolo*. These he calls "boy rain" and "girl rain" pointing right to his private parts and mine without appearing to think a thing in the world was wrong with that' (ibid., p. 128). This is an obvious illustration of how cultural decentring and moral learning can be part of learning a language.

Married to a local, she reflects as an adult with children on the difficulties she experienced coming to grips with the multiple meanings of Kikongo words. But through understanding these meanings, she has come to penetrate the interconnectedness of different aspects of life within the culture. The word *nzolo* 'means dearly beloved; or a white grub used for fish bait; or a special fetish against dysentry; or little potatoes. *Nzole* is the double sized pagne that wraps around two people at once'. Finally Leah has come to 'see how these things are related' (Ibid.).

> In a marriage ceremony, husband and wife stand tightly bound by their *nzole* and hold one another to be the most precious: *nzolani*. As precious as the first potatoes of the season, small and sweet like Georgia peanuts. Precious as the fattest grubs turned up from the soil, which catch the largest fish. And the fetish most treasured by mothers, against dysentry, contains a particle of all the things invoked by the word *nzolo*: you must dig and dry the grub and potatoes, bind them with a thread from your wedding cloth, and have them blessed in a fire by the *nganga* doctor. Only by life's best things are your children protected – this much I surely believe. Each of my peanut-brown babies I called my *nzolani*, and said it with the taste of fish and fire and new potatoes in my mouth. There is no other possibility now.
>
> (Ibid.)

Leah's assimilation into Africa is communicated by the fact that in speaking Lingala, one of the other Congolese languages, she has come to assume a different personality in it. In English she is described as 'sarcastic', whereas in Lingala she is said to sound 'sweet and maternal' (p. 490). She expresses her appreciation of difference as follows: 'Everything you're sure is right can be wrong in another place. Especially *here*' (p. 572). In this example, knowledge of the language has been one important vehicle of a very strong version of cultural decentring. It has allowed her achieve a critical distance from her own culture and provided an 'unsettling' of the perspectives assumed in her native culture (Smith and Carvill, 2000, pp. 119–120) and, by making her more open-minded and responsive to another culture, it has eliminated ethnocentric bias.

Although we as readers can share in the insights of the fictional Leah, what we acquire is a form of 'knowledge that' rather than 'knowledge of', that is, experiential or insider's knowledge. The experience of speaking the language has been a crucial feature of Leah's capacity to decentre. Likewise in the classroom context, using a foreign language provides pupils with an occurrent experience of another culture and also, it is hoped, enduring mental states of openness to it. This aspect of the aims of MFL education links to the next series of aims: the ethical.

Ethical aims

There are two strands to the ethical aims: the first has a relationship to individual learners and the second a general social character. The first strand links to the previous one and concerns the significance of language as the literal expression of metaphorical openness to others. There is a relationship between responsiveness to other cultures and knowledge of their languages. Willingness to learn the language of the other is the most important signal of a willingness to enter into her *Lebenswelt*. I am reminded of an incident concerning her first visit to Japan recounted by Kusi Okamura, an Irish journalist whose parents are Japanese. Feeling guilty because of her inability to speak Japanese, she is reassured when the immigration officer, after perusing her passport, welcomes her in Irish. By using the language of the country in which she grew up, he makes her feel that she has come to her other home (Okamura, 2000, p. 3). It is also salutary and humbling, especially for English-speakers, to try to communicate in another language as it alerts us to what it is like for strangers in our country and, indeed, for those who because of disability have difficulty in communicating. Again, the status of English as the world's lingua franca actually provides a more compelling moral imperative for including MFLs in the curriculum than applies in non-Anglophone countries. Yet a note of caution must be entered here. By learning a language, we do not automatically have to adopt an uncritical attitude towards the culture where the language is spoken. It does not mean that we have to suspend critical judgement regarding reprehensible practices (use of capital punishment or demeaning of women) wherever these are to be found.

The second strand of the ethical aims has a general social character and might be called the symbolic.[4] Including foreign language in the curriculum gives symbolic expression to a willingness to move beyond national solipsism to affirm the openness of the UK to other cultures. This openness reflects two kinds of inclusiveness: the first refers to the inclusion of languages, indigenous and immigrant, within the UK and the second to the inclusion of a range of languages from other cultures. It is, for example, one of the tragedies of British-Irish history of the twentieth century that the failure until recent times by the Unionist/British establishment in Northern Ireland to affirm the Irish language in public and within the school curriculum contributed to the alienation of the Nationalist minority from the state. By allowing a language a role in the public space, of which the school system is a vital part, speakers of that language, or even those who do not actually speak it but who have roots in the culture in question, feel recognised and respected. The ethical aims are therefore related to the notion of recognition of the other – psychologically and politically.

Pedagogical issues

On account of their educational significance, the four individual aims suggest that there is a case for ensuring that an opportunity be available to all young people to learn, or at least to try to learn, another language. At a minimum, considerations of justice require that all young people should be entitled to do so. But there are important limitations to the scope of application of this claim. Endeavouring to achieve the four individual aims does not require that all young people should have to do a language as part of a compulsory curriculum beyond, at most, one year. Furthermore, no more extensive requirement is necessary in order to give expression to the ethical/symbolic aim.

Entitlement and compulsion

Elsewhere I have defended this position on compulsion in some detail (Williams, 2000) but in view of what I have identified as the positive personal benefits of foreign language education, I shall rehearse the three main points briefly. In the first place, by twelve years of age, after a year's study, a young person is old enough to make a decision based on familiarity about whether she wishes to continue to study a foreign language. Second, the utility argument for compulsion is very weak because the knowledge of MFLs cannot be said to be of utility to the vast majority of English speakers. Finally, I would question the potential fruitfulness of any compulsion extending beyond one year. By all means, we should insist that young people have some experience of learning another language; this should be part of every young person's entitlement. But it is misguided to insist that all young people spend more than one year at a subject in which some have no interest or for which they show no aptitude. The outcome of the efforts of a significant minority of students taking GCSE French is negligible (see Williams, 2000). The educational potential of the four individual aims is so rich and indeed exciting that we should not deny any student the opportunity to study another language, however low her ability. But this is different from trying to force reluctant learners, against their wishes, to do so. In spite of our best efforts, these learners are unlikely to derive much profit or pleasure as a result of such compulsion. By removing their compulsory status, we are not foreclosing all future possibilities for people to learn languages. After all, there are many other contexts in which they can be learned. So where it is apparent that, due to lack of interest or ability, personal well-being is not being promoted through the MFL curriculum, then young people should not be obliged to continue their studies. Entitlement should therefore be as extensive as possible but compulsion limited to one year. Allowing young people to give up MFLs after Key Stage 3 is indeed wise but it would be even wiser to take the more radical step of limiting compulsion to just one year.

Organising the learning of languages

Experience and observation suggest to me, as research has long confirmed (see, for example, Hawkins, 1987, pp. 190–195), that foreign languages are best learned intensively over a short period of time by learners with immediate practical motivation. But English-speaking young people seldom have this motivation and the school curriculum is not usually organised in such a manner as to facilitate the intensive study of a language. We should not be surprised at the lack of positive outcomes from teaching a foreign language four or five times per week to pupils in a classroom where the language receives no reinforcement in the children's family or community. The situation where even very young children are exposed to second or third languages in a bilingual or quasi-bilingual situation is very different. Given the context in which it takes place, it is hardly surprising that the results of a system of teaching foreign languages in five short classes per week extended over a number of years to conscript learners have been discouraging. In spite of the committed and professional work of their teachers, the proficiency of the majority of students is unimpressive (see Williams, 2000, pp. 15–17). For many young people, therefore, conventional curricular arrangements provide a most unsuitable context in which to learn a foreign language.

All of this suggests that the institutional arrangements for teaching languages will have to be reconsidered. Some form of sustained exposure to the language, other than the conventional five forty/forty-five minute lessons per week, will be required in order that students derive maximum benefit from the activity. We might adopt some version of the arrangement used with students taking summer courses who study the language in question for a few hours each morning.

The issue of resources

However we set about it, learning foreign languages requires substantial investment of resources. It is one thing to produce handsome documents and reports encouraging MFL education; it is another to give expression to the aspirations through realistic provision of resources. Yet official documents make me a little uneasy about the seriousness of the Department for Education and Skills towards the provision of time, resources and personnel. As long ago as 1988, we read that: '(d)esirable curriculum change to establish the position of modern foreign languages in the National Curriculum will have to be achieved broadly within the planned level of resources' (Department of Education and Science/Welsh Office, 1988, p. 7). The authors recommend that schools should teach diverse foreign languages but admit that:

> (c)onstraints on resources will, to some extent, affect how quickly it can be brought about. Preparing schools and teachers to offer a different or alternative first foreign language will present the education service with difficult decisions about priorities.
>
> (Ibid., p. 10)

After fifteen years it is still not clear how the position of foreign languages can be enhanced and greater variety of languages provided without increasing resources, unless other subjects are downgraded or removed. The Nuffield Report (Nuffield, 2000), for all of its platitudinous assertions, shows the kind of costly resource provision necessary if the promotion of language learning is to be taken seriously. If politicians and policy makers really believe that entitlement to this learning is important, then it is time to provide these resources or to cease the rhetoric about it.

Notes

1   For a full discussion of the issues involved see Singleton (1989), Hawkins (1987) pp. 11/12, 180–195) and Blondin, C. *et al.* (1998).
2   Baumard (2000a) gives a helpful account of recent research including that of Blondin, C. *et al.* (1998).
3   See Department of Education and Science/Welsh Office (1988), Department for Education and Employment/Qualification and Curriculum Authority (1999a) and other documents between these dates. See Williams (2000, p. 24) for these references.
4   I am grateful to David Smith for alerting me to these aspects of foreign language education and to Deirdre Clancy, Gareth Byrne and John White for comments on the text.

References

Association for Language Learning (1998) Submission to the Nuffield Inquiry (Rugby, The Association for Language Learning).

Baumard, M. (2002a) 'La France se paye de mots', *Le Monde de L'Éducation* 300 (février).

Baumard, M. (2002b) 'L'anglais: le choix obligatoire', *Le Monde de L'Éducation* 300 (février).

Blondin, C. *et al.* (1998) *Foreign Languages in Primary and Pre-School Education: A Review of Recent Research within the European Union*, London: CILT.

Burnshaw, S. (1964) *The Poem Itself: 150 European Poems: Translated and Analysed*, Harmondsworth: Penguin.

Cédelle, L. (2002) 'La souplesse des élèves bilingues n'affecte pas la raideur de l'école', *Le Monde de L'Éducation* 300 (février).

Department of Education and Science/Welsh Office (1988) *Modern Languages in the School Curriculum: A Statement of Policy*, London: HMSO.

Department for Education and Employment/Qualification and Curriculum Authority (1998) *Education for Citizenship and the Teaching of Democracy in Schools*, London: HMSO.

Department for Education and Employment/Qualification and Curriculum Authority (1999a) *Modern Foreign Languages*, London: HMSO.

Department for Education and Employment/Qualification and Curriculum Authority (1999b) *The National Curriculum Handbook for Teachers in England*, London: HMSO.

Gellius, A. (1928) *Noctes Atticae/The Attic Nights of Aulus Gellius*, translated by John Rolfe, London: Heinemann.

Hawkins, E. (1987) *Modern Languages in the Curriculum*, Cambridge: Cambridge University Press.

Kingsolver, B. (1999) *The Poisonwood Bible*, London: Faber & Faber.

Kipling, R. (2000) *The Complete Stalky and Co.*, Oxford: Oxford University Press.

Maxwell, W. (2000) *The Chateau*, London: Harvill.

Nuffield Foundation (2000) *Languages: the Next Generation: the Final Report and Recommendations of the Nuffield Languages Inquiry*, Oxford: Nuffield.

Okamura, K. (2000) 'Home to a foreign place', The *Irish Times, Weekend Supplement*, 1 July.

Pachler, N. (2001) 'In other journals', *Language Learning Journal*, 24 (Winter).

Séry, M. (2002) 'Polyglotte mais "francographe"', *Le Monde de L'Éducation*, 300 (juillet/août).

Singleton, D. (1989) *Language Acquisition: The Age Factor*, Clevedon/Philadelphia: Multilingual Matters.

Smith, D.I. and Carvill, B. (2000) *The Gift of the Stranger: Faith, Hospitality and Foreign Language Learning*, Grand Rapids/Cambridge: Wm. B. Eerdmans.

Williams, K. (2000) *Why Teach Foreign Languages in Schools? A Philosophical Response to Curriculum Policy*, London: Philosophy of Education Society of Great Britain.

Williams, K. (2001) 'Towards a rationale for foreign language education: re-stating my reservation', *Language Learning Journal*, 24 (Winter).

10 Music

Charles Plummeridge and Keith Swanwick

Introduction

When the Subject Working Group for Music published its interim report (Department of Education and Science, 1991) there followed a lively and sometimes acrimonious debate about the position of music in education and the aims and values embodied in the content of the proposed programme. Whilst there was widespread support for the inclusion of music in the new curriculum from the musical establishment, parents and the general public, it soon became apparent that there were many different opinions about the nature and purpose of music in schools. There was also much confusion and misunderstanding over current practices, trends and issues. None of this was altogether surprising. Music is a value-laden enterprise and much more complex than can be captured in a single curriculum subject. Over the past 150 years music in schools has become a collection, or family, of activities forming three major clusters: general class music, which is timetabled along with other school subjects and is effectively mandatory for all pupils until the end of Year Nine; instrumental teaching, for a minority of usually self-selected pupils who are either withdrawn from other subjects during the school day or have instrumental instruction out of normal school time; choral groups and various instrumental ensembles, which again are usually organised out of normal school time.

In this chapter we argue that the various pursuits constituting what is thought of as 'music' are generated and realised in a variety of specific social settings and contexts. This diversity, both of activity and context, is a major problem for curriculum designers and for teachers, and raises doubts as to the possibility of 'authenticity' in much classroom music. A related issue is the disjunction between the affective elements of musical response and school classroom settings. Music is distinctive amongst most curriculum subjects in that it has a particularly strong out-of-school presence in the lives of students, especially those in secondary schools. For many young people music is a source of great personal fulfilment. However, the extent to which teachers are able to draw on this commitment is problematic and it is questionable how far students' interests can be further enhanced within the present curriculum structure.

Music in schools: aims and practices

The origins of music in schools extend back to antiquity and are strongly linked to choral singing. Contemporary conceptions of class teaching have been particularly influenced by nineteenth century principles and practices. Bernarr Rainbow maintains that one of the reasons for introducing class singing lessons into the elementary schools was the expectation, on the part of some prominent churchmen, that such a move would eventually lead to more refined congregational participation in Sunday worship (Rainbow, 1989). Thus the methods of famous teachers like John Curwen and Sarah Glover fitted in well with the general educational aim of furthering Christian ideals. Many of the Victorian reformers, often as a result of their own classical education, also believed in the power of music to foster civilised behaviour, and musical activity came to be regarded as a suitable and sober leisure pursuit. These musical and social aims continue to permeate educational thinking, although in modified form, and can be aligned with recent formulations of curriculum aims and values, especially those concerned with 'valuing oneself, other people and society'. For example, in the current documentation it is stated:

> [Music] encourages active involvement in different forms of amateur music making . . . developing a sense of group identity and togetherness. It also increases self-discipline.
>
> (DfEE/QCA, 1999)

Numerous innovations during the first half of the twentieth century contributed to a considerable expansion of general class music teaching with an increasing emphasis on the importance of developing young people's musicianship and their deeper awareness of the cultural heritage. Accordingly, students were to be taught to 'read' and 'write' the 'language' of classical tonality, and to appreciate those musical works that represented 'the best' of the European tradition. The aims of music education as a curriculum subject, as set out by the Incorporated Society of Musicians (1947), were twofold. First, through a carefully structured course in singing, aural training, creative work and appreciation covering the years of compulsory schooling, children would (or should) acquire a range of musical competences. Second, it was intended that students would come to value and enjoy music as a social activity. But most importantly all should be educated 'as musicians'. Such a view was unquestioned; it was expressed some thirty years later by Ian Lawrence and would probably still be endorsed by many present-day music educators. 'The difficulties in defining objectives in music education are increased by arguments which overlook its central aim which must be to educate musicians, regardless of whether they [the students] wish to devote their lives exclusively to music' (Lawrence, 1978).

However, throughout the 1960s and 1970s a number of progressive educators challenged these prevailing aims and practices. Amongst others, Robert Witkin and Malcolm Ross advocated a style of music teaching in which children were to express their thoughts and feelings through the medium of sound as part of an education concerned with the nurturing of both cognitive and affective capacities (Witkin, 1975; Ross, 1975). On this view, the aim of music and arts education became not the acquisition of traditional skills and techniques, but rather the development of the life of 'inner feeling' and qualities of mind: creativity, imaginativeness and sensitivity. Over the past twenty years progressive aims have been largely rejected although associated practices have been modified and incorporated into a curriculum scheme, the aim of which is to enable children to experience many musical styles and genres through performing, composing and listening. The purpose is for students to gain what has been described by John Paynter as musical understanding and by Keith Swanwick as a grasp of what it is to participate in musical discourse (Paynter, 1992; Swanwick, 1999). This perspective on class teaching is informed by the notion of music as one of several distinct ways of knowing or realms of meaning, a view which finds support from a variety of philosophical, psychological and sociological sources. From this position, the study of music, as a curriculum subject, is justified as part of a broad education in and for a pluralist society.

Alongside these approaches to general class music teaching, individual and group instrumental tuition has developed as an important although always optional dimension of musical education at school level. Initially encouraged in nineteenth century independent schools, this type of instruction was soon adopted in the maintained sector and greatly expanded by most Local Education Authorities after the second world war. There has been relatively little discussion over the aims of instrumental tuition and styles of teaching have often reflected the conservatoire tradition of training students to achieve the highest possible standard of individual performance. However, more recently there has been a growing tendency to regard instrumental tuition as a way of introducing children to the 'world of music' rather than a form of specialist instruction. This approach was commended some years ago by The Music Advisors' National Association, who recommended that instrumental teachers relate their work to the structure and pedagogical style of the National Curriculum (MANA, 1995). At the same time, it is interesting to note that certain eminent figures, including Sir Simon Rattle and Sir Peter Maxwell Davies, in offering support for music in schools, have emphasised the need for educational institutions to cultivate young performers and thereby maintain and strengthen the country's musical heritage. It would seem that long established ideas regarding the aims of instrumental tuition, within an educational context, still seem to persist amongst musicians and it is quite possible that some music teachers hold similar views. As a result of financial policies associated with the local management of schools, instrumental tuition was somewhat curtailed during the 1990s. However, following widely reported concern and criticism from musicians and the music profession, the government has now provided new funding for this elective aspect of music education.

The third aspect of music in schools is often described as 'extracurricular'. As with the introduction of instrumental teaching, the formation of choirs, orchestras and bands was originally an independent sector initiative, but today these musical groupings are organised in almost every school. Concerts, plays, operas and other artistic presentations are regular events and regarded as embodying the values that underpin the cultural and social life of the school community. Extra-curricular activities are also seen as valuable in that they provide opportunities for students to work together in the pursuit of common goals and so engender a sense of co-operation and corporate identity. In spite of the argument that these activities cater for only a small number of children and are therefore of an elitist nature, it is widely accepted that a school's musical 'reputation' will arise from students' achievements in pursuits beyond class work programmes. However, most teachers would regard class teaching, instrumental tuition and extra-curricular activities as inter-related forms of music education.

The National Curriculum

The variety of musical activity in schools, as outlined above, has been given only limited attention in the design and development of the statutory National Curriculum.

The Subject Working Group recognised the value of extra-curricular work, but music was to be regarded essentially as a class subject for all pupils between the ages of 5 and 14. According to the most recent version of the curriculum document, music is a powerful form of communication and one that brings together intellectual and feeling capacities; it helps pupils to understand themselves and others, develops in individuals a sense of group identity, and increases self-discipline, aesthetic sensitivity and creativity (DfEE/QCA, 1999). There is nothing in such statements that is particularly controversial and all are in keeping with the overall aims and values as set out in the primary and secondary handbooks. Music is said to contribute to spiritual, moral, social and cultural development, and again this is an ideal that has its origins in the nineteenth and early twentieth centuries. The critical question is how far, and in what ways, can these stated aims and values be realised through the statutory music curriculum in its present form.

Central to the National Curriculum is the intention that students will acquire skills and knowledge through performing, composing and listening activities and experience a wide range of musical styles and genres. The aim is the development of a range of competences and a broad musical understanding. These principles are presented in slightly different ways in the three versions of the Order but underlying them is the traditional idea of promoting a type of general musicianship. Consequently, the design of the music curriculum has always been based on the view that musical progress is linear and dependent on students' systematic development of appropriate skills, the acquisition of which enables learners to participate in the different activities at increasingly higher levels. This is a well-known approach to musical studies and one that underpins the structure of the instrumental grade syllabuses and examinations. However, a fundamental flaw in the music curriculum scheme is the failure to recognise the complexity of the different types of musical skills and that the learning of such skills requires certain necessary conditions. Most obviously, cumulative skills can only be acquired when there are frequent and regular periods of practice. One of the best-known sequential skill-based schemes of musical education is the Kodaly system, which has proved to be very successful in Hungarian schools; it involves the learning of aural, vocal and literacy skills through daily and highly rigorous instruction. The wide range of vocal, manipulative, literacy and aural skills implied in the Order cannot possibly be developed in a systematic way when students have but one lesson each week. Furthermore, staffing resources in schools are not always sufficient for the implementation of the specification in a way that will ensure children's consistent and progressive musical development as stated in the documentation. This was a main finding of research carried out by Lawson, Plummeridge and Swanwick who investigated the workings of the music curriculum in some 40 primary schools (Lawson *et al.*, 1994). Many teachers in primary schools also complain that with ever-increasing emphasis on the teaching of numeracy and literacy skills there is less time for music and other foundation subjects. That this is a genuine concern is supported by the findings of an extensive survey recently reported by Maurice Galton and John MacBeath (Galton and Macbeath, 2002).

The introduction of the National Curriculum could have been an opportunity for a major review of music in schools. In fact, it has simply preserved a rather unsatisfactory status quo: class music for all, with instrumental tuition and extracurricular activities as options. The content of class music lessons is very similar to many previous schemes set out by individual teachers and numerous LEA guidelines during the 1980s. Questions arise not only about the feasibility of the programme but also how far the present curriculum is actually in the best interests of all students. There is a long history in Britain of negative attitudes to music as a curriculum subject on the part of pupils, especially in secondary schools, first highlighted over thirty years ago in a famous Schools Council (1968) report and more recently by writers such as Francis (1987) and Ross (1995). In a report of a study of the arts in five secondary schools, Ross and Kamba (1997) assert that for music 'the enjoyment factor remains unchanged and disappointingly low'. However, Lucien Jenkins has referred to research carried out on behalf of the newly established National Music Education Forum which suggest that over 70 per cent of students enjoy their class music lessons (Jenkins, 2002). Unfortunately, these research findings are not publicly available and there is no substantial evidence at the present time to show that large numbers of students in secondary schools have more positive attitudes towards music as a curriculum subject. In fact, recent research reported by John Harland (2000) and his colleagues indicates that at secondary level class music lessons are lacking in appeal for a substantial number of students.

From the perspective of the inspectorate there is little sign of the National Curriculum being implemented effectively across the country in the intended manner. According to Janet Mills, music in secondary schools following the introduction of the new programme was particularly uneven, with wide variation in curriculum content, and with teachers often having low expectations of students (Mills, 1994). Inspectors have also raised questions about the quality of students' work, the conditions under which music is taught and the morale of secondary music teachers. Among several negative observations were teachers' underestimation of students' abilities, too much time spent on non-musical activities and poor performance of badly chosen material (Ofsted, 1992–1993). In 1995, inspectors (Ofsted, 1995) reported that the curriculum in Year 7 was often less challenging than that in primary schools, and its demand increased insufficiently in Year 8. A year later achievement was still thought to be too low, and pupils' understanding of musical concepts, shown through composition, talk and performance, did not develop beyond that expected in Year 5 and Year 6 (Ofsted, 1996). The following year inspectors stated that standards 'remain poor in too many schools at Key Stage 3' (Ofsted, 1997). Of course, there are some well-known examples of good practice identified by Ofsted which are in keeping with the design and content of the curriculum scheme (Ofsted, 1998). However, after ten years of central control there is no compelling evidence to suggest that students' achievements (an obviously central aim) in class music lessons have risen in any significant way.

Music in school and community

Yet music can be, and frequently is, a powerful force in society and in the lives of many people. In a study of music in the new town of Milton Keynes, Ruth Finnegan found that there were several brass bands, choirs, small bands – including pop, rock, folk, jazz groups – four classical orchestras and several chamber ensembles (Finnegan, 1989). There was music making in many of the churches. These activities were not located geographically or in clearly defined local communities. Rather, they were musical 'pathways', chosen by individuals according to their interests. These people, representing all age groups, formed virtual communities through a shared musical focus. There are, of course, many ways of making and engaging with music and people develop preferences for some rather than others. And so it is in schools. Playing the violin, or flute or guitar in an orchestra or band may be fine for some but certainly not for everybody. Similarly, there are those who are committed to jazz or rock but do not have much interest in the singing of Anglican chant or Elizabethan madrigals. One of the overall aims of the new curriculum is the development of students' strengths and interests. In music these are extremely diverse and the principle that one prescribed curriculum scheme can be suitable for all students seems unrealistic. No doubt, there will be some individuals who delight in almost any form, style or genre of music making but teachers know that such students are likely to constitute a very small minority.

Music is not a single entity, or subject, easily reduced to work in conventional classrooms, but a multiplicity of diverse activities. These activities take place in different contexts and each requires some specialist know-how, a suitable group size and a particular type of equipment. Unfortunately, music in the classroom often becomes a closed system, lacking in authenticity and concerned with the production of what Malcolm Ross calls 'pseudo music' (Ross, 1995). Indeed, many of the innovations of the post-war years, initially greeted with great enthusiasm and optimism, have led to forms of music making that bear little resemblance to the world of music 'out there'. For example, the introduction during the 1960s of 'new' classroom instruments provided for a sound world almost unique to schools but it was one far removed from styles of music with which students were familiar. And it may well be that this is one of the reasons why students become disenchanted with music as a subject within the curriculum. Over many years, one attempt to make musical experience more relevant and authentic for students has been to introduce elements of popular music into formal programmes. But in order to become 'institutionalised', popular music has to be modified, abstracted, analysed and taught in ways that will fit into classrooms, timetables and prescribed objectives. Consequently, its impact is reduced, and an inappropriate style of learning is imposed as the socio-cultural context is shorn away. Of course, the same kind of problem applies to any type of music and music making. Playing and singing various forms of African music, or the verse anthems of Purcell, or the 12-bar blues in the classroom cannot capture the original learning environments and musical and social contexts that contribute so powerfully to the meaningfulness of these very different musics.

It may well be that the popularity of outreach programmes, increasingly offered by orchestras, opera houses, community groups and other agencies, is due to the fact that they provide more genuinely authentic experiences for students. No doubt the growth of these initiatives is mandated by conditions of funding and there is, as yet, only limited information about their effects. However, where there has been systematic evaluation of such programmes the findings have been encouraging. For example, in a series of five linked projects commissioned and run by the South Bank Centre in London in collaboration with six secondary schools, Year 7 students worked with a number of professional musicians over three years. A study throughout the duration of this project by Swanwick and Lawson included interviews with the participants, observation at the Centre and in schools, and repeated monitoring using a simple attitude inventory for students (Swanwick and Lawson, 1997). The findings indicate that the attitudes of students towards music in school became more positive and teachers gained in musical confidence throughout the project. More recently, Stephen Moss in the *Education Guardian* reports optimistically on a number of links between orchestras and schools and on the advent of 'Creative Partnerships', a scheme to bridge schools and cultural organisations (Moss, 2002).

There is clearly considerable potential for future collaboration between educational and musical agencies but to draw more on resources of this kind requires a fundamental and critical review of the structure and function of schools. At present there is a possible conflict between the style of the National Curriculum and outreach projects as approaches to curriculum development. According to Kushner:

> Here are two distinct approaches to curriculum innovation which appear to be in tension – the one a nationally engineered, standardised approach to a curriculum devised in non-school settings and imposed with the force of law; the other a locally diverse basket of activities devised in collaborations between professional musicians in school and joined on a voluntaristic basis.
>
> (Kushner, 1994)

Kushner sees these collaborative activities as educationally rich, permitting children to engage with music in their own way and at their own speed. There may be little if any curriculum sequencing towards pre-specified learning outcomes. These projects tend to be broadly process-based rather than geared to narrowly defined and standardised 'products'. They also operate at various levels. For example, involvement over time with an opera production can offer different kinds of participation and have different meanings for individuals. Complex music may be 'deconstructed' by working with features and processes prior to, during and after experience of a performance. Such musical activities are not only more open-ended but they may also be perceived as 'authentic', involving 'real' instruments, 'real' music, 'real' musicians and 'real' music-making settings.

In many of this country's state secondary schools a teacher has five to seven classes of up to 30 children each day, perhaps upward of 600 different pupils every week. He or she is expected to be a versatile musician, able to work in the music of a number of cultures and at the same time function as a systematic educator, making sure that each individual is engaged in an integrated music curriculum at a challenging level. In addition to this 'normal' teaching commitment there is the management of instrumental teaching schemes running on a parallel timetable, the direction of several extra-curricular groups and the production of musical events throughout the year. These activities are usually planned and prepared in out-of-timetable time and are rarely offset against the normal teaching load. As has often been pointed out the school music teacher is expected to be both director of music and class instructor. This dual role is becoming ever more demanding, both in terms of organisational duties and subject expertise. Teachers cannot be authorities in every musical genre and may find themselves veering uncomfortably between their own music specialisms and an insecure generalism. It is impossible for single schools and individual teachers to provide access to music-making involving, for example, the use of gamelan, steel pans, and standard Western orchestral instruments, and to diverse activities based on many different styles and genres which might include rock, pop, jazz, Indian music and the musics of Africa and the Pacific. Students can often miss out on musically authentic experiences, and it is perhaps for this reason that 'school music' may appear to many young people as a subculture separated from music 'out there' in the world, abstracted by the constraints of classrooms, curriculum and formal assessment.

The future

One effect of the imposition of a centralised curriculum is that education is increasingly equated with formal schooling. Under these conditions, class music teaching has become a curious mixture of activities taken out of different contexts. A central aim continues to be the development of a kind of general musicianship that has its roots in conservatoires and some university music departments. It leads to a type of musical study that may be relevant in higher education where people are being educated as musicians. But it would seem to be inappropriate for many students in school and in the light of the new overall aims there is a need to consider alternative forms of practice and organisation. In most schools there is already an extensive programme beyond the classroom and for many students this is where they have their most meaningful musical experiences. There is also a rich variety of musical activity outside the school which could be drawn on more effectively for educational purposes. This would, of course, necessitate greater co-ordination of resources in and out of school and new attitudes regarding the organisation of activities. It has to be recognised that schools and colleges cannot be musical islands. They need to be part of a music network and might best be seen as facilitating agencies rather than sole 'providers'. There are many musicians in communities who could contribute to school programmes and it should be possible to avoid further perpetuating a separate musical sub-culture in schools, detached from music in the wider world. This is especially important with reference to the aim of promoting students' interests, since these are many and increasingly varied and cannot be catered for in every school.

There will be resistance to change, not least because our institutions are historically locked into rigid systems. Most teaching takes place in school classrooms. Yet, as we have indicated, there is musical richness beyond school gates if only we could more systematically find and utilise it. To achieve this would require changes in organisation, timetabling and the employment of teaching staff. Options are essential to match the range of authentic engagement and the music curriculum may need to be thought of in terms of a modular rather than sequential structure. The advantage of this is flexibility. Musical projects can be started at a level relevant to a particular group of pupils and using available expertise and resources. There can be culminating points, which may be a series of small group performances, a whole class composition assembled from group contributions or a recorded performance of related items composed by children and 'professional' composers. Necessary techniques would be developed for the particular task in hand, rather than working to a generalised concept of 'musicianship'. A range of instrumental teachers and community musicians could be involved in this kind of process which, in turn, would require alternative kinds of educational transactions. For example, Lucy Green has identified some of the pedagogical implications arising from the way rock musicians learn their craft (Green, 2001). These include playing and listening to music of one's own choice, playing by ear and working with friends who share the same values, thus shifting the emphasis from the organisation of teaching to the facilitating of learning.

Schools might coordinate access to a range of authentic and viable instrumental and vocal groupings led by general class teachers, instrumental teachers and community musicians. Students above primary level could then elect into at least one of these projects. Within the context of such specific activities they would be able to perform, compose and listen to and discuss music from many sources. In this way a broad music education could be achieved, though anchored to an identifiable chosen activity. There are opportunities here for the newly emerging cohort of instrumental and vocal teachers being trained in higher education and by such bodies as the Associated Board of the Royal Schools of Music. Some of these activities could be on school premises, though by no means all. This sharing of available resources in the community would be of great value, both to primary school teachers who often feel uncertain about their general musical competence and to secondary teachers, who by themselves are not able to encompass the range of 'musics' that could be opened to the students.

Conclusion

The National Curriculum documentation does not include a justification for music as a curriculum subject but its importance is stated in both intrinsic and extrinsic terms. It is maintained that through the present type of curriculum programme students will develop their music understanding. We have argued that not only is the linear structure impracticable but it is questionable whether a course of study based on a fairly traditional view of general musicianship is in the best interests of all students between the ages of 5 and 14. Furthermore, music cannot be generalised into a single 'subject' but, is a collection of different activities and associated skills which are realised in a variety of social contexts. This has implications for the authenticity of student encounters and highlights the need to provide experience of music that feels 'real'.

Quite clearly, participation in musical activity can lead to the realisation of overall curriculum aims in both general and distinctive ways. But in order to meet these different types of aims there is a strong argument in favour of more flexible programmes of music education, especially in secondary schools. Reference has been made to the possibilities for students arising from closer links between the school and the local musical community. This is not to suggest that there should be no class music but the policy of insisting that all students follow the same type of core programme does not take into account individual strengths and interests. Some will want to be active participants, others may find more fulfilment through combined arts projects or programmes of cultural studies. The present curriculum is dominated by the notion of common, sequential musical development but there may be much to be said for modular courses designed to meet the needs of particular groups. We have emphasised the importance of recognising student's interests which is one of the stated aims of the new curriculum. At the same time it is necessary also to acknowledge that education is concerned with introducing young people to new interests and experiences. It would therefore be important to see that there is a range of musical experience across any series of modules and that activities within projects are as comprehensive as possible.

It is not our purpose here to propose in detail an entirely new form of organisation for music in schools. We have simply highlighted some strategies that could prove to be a more effective means of realising the overall aims that now inform the National Curriculum. According to Maxwell Price, the Qualifications and Curriculum Authority is currently investigating how to effectively relate statutory and elective programmes in ways that will further enhance musical experience (Price, 2002). The organisation *Youth Music* has funding for three years from 2002 to promote a range of projects in and out of schools. At the same time the *Paul Hamlyn Foundation* is developing a major initiative to examine the current music experience of young people aged 11 to 19, within and outside formal education. All such developments are to be welcomed and might eventually lead to a situation that allows for greater flexibility in the design and operation of school music programmes. In this way, participation in musical activities could become more genuinely meaningful. Such a scenario would also be in keeping with the newly stated curriculum aims, which focus on valuing ourselves, others, the environment and the society in which we live.

References

Department of Education and Science (1991) *National Curriculum Music Working Group Interim Report*, London: HMSO.

DfEE/QCA (1999) *Music. The national curriculum for England*, London: HMSO.

Finnegan, R. (1989) *The hidden musicians: music-making in an English town*, Cambridge: Cambridge University Press.

Francis, L.J. (1987) 'The decline in attitudes towards religious education among 8–15 year olds', *Educational Studies*, 13.

Galton, M. and Macbeath, J. (2002) *A life in teaching: the impact of change on primary teachers' working lives*, London: National Union of Teachers.

Green, L. (2001) *How popular musicians learn: a way ahead for music education*, London and New York: Ashgate Press.

Harland, J. *et al.* (2000) *Arts education in secondary schools: effects and effectiveness*, Slough: NFER.

Jenkins, L. (2002) 'Editorial', *Music Teacher*, 81, 5.

Kushner, S. (1994) 'Against better judgement: how a centrally prescribed music curriculum works against teacher development', *International Journal of Music Education*, 23, 34–45.

Lawrence, I. (1978) *Composers and the nature of music education*, London: Scolar Press.

Lawson, D., Plummeridge, C. and Swanwick, K. (1994) 'Music and the National Curriculum in Primary schools', *British Journal of Music Education*, 11, 3–14.

MANA (1995) *Instrumental teaching and learning in context*, London: Music Advisers' National Association.

Mills, J. (1994) 'Music in the National Curriculum: the first year', *British Journal of Music Education*, 11, 191–196.

Moss, S. (2002) 'Bring it all Bach', The *Guardian*, 8 October, pp. 4–5.

Ofsted (1992–1993) *Music – Key Stages 1, 2 and 3*, London: HMSO.

Ofsted (1995) *The Annual Report of Her Majesty's Chief Inspector of Schools, 1993/4*, London: HMSO.

Ofsted (1996) *The Annual Report of Her Majesty's Chief Inspector of Schools, 1994/5*, London: HMSO.

Ofsted (1997) *The Annual Report of Her Majesty's Chief Inspector of Schools, 1995/6*, London: HMSO.

Ofsted (1998) *The arts inspected*, London: Heinemann.

Paynter, J. (1992) *Sound and structure*, Cambridge: Cambridge University Press.

Price, M. (2002) 'QCA – Qualifications and Curriculum Authority', *Schools Music Association Bulletin*, 149.

Rainbow, B. (1989) *Music in educational thought and practice*, Aberystwyth: Boethius Press.

Ross, M. (1975) *Arts and the adolescent. Schools Council Working Paper No 54*, London: Evans.

Ross, M. (1995) 'What's wrong with school music?', *British Journal of Music Education*, 12, 185–201.

Ross, M. and Kamba, M. (1997) *State of the arts in five English secondary schools*, Exeter: University of Exeter.

Schools Council (1968) *Enquiry one: the young schoolleavers*, London: HMSO.

Swanwick, K. (1999) *Teaching music musically*, London and New York: Routledge.

Swanwick, K. and Lawson, D. (1997) *An evaluation of the South Bank Centre music education project – 1994 to 1997*, Institute of Education, University of London.

Witkin, R. (1975) *The intelligence of feeling*, London: Heinemann.

11 Physical education

Dawn Penney

Physical education (PE) is in something of a paradoxical position in the National Curriculum. It is a subject that many people still regard as marginal to 'core' and 'more academic' subjects and that pupils themselves may well see as quite different – and often a welcome break – from other subjects. Yet it has enjoyed the status of being a statutory element of the National Curriculum throughout all four key stages. Why was it accorded this relatively privileged position? What are the alleged publicly valued purposes of physical education that underpin this? How do they bear on the perceived marginality of the subject? And what are the linkages between the dominant purposes and the content of the physical education curriculum as outlined in official texts of the National Curriculum for physical education (NCPE), and the subject as taught in schools? These are among the questions that this chapter will pursue in critically reflecting on the current physical education curriculum for England and possible directions for future development. Following the format of previous chapters, it will consider the extent to which physical education, as developed in policy and practice via the NCPE, can be seen as engaging with the new aims for the National Curriculum and as representing a socially and culturally relevant vehicle for realising them.

What is it that we understand PE to be?

> Physical education in its present form has been a part of the school curriculum for so long that it is difficult to conceive of it in any other way.
>
> (Boorman, 1998, p. 91)

A particular conception of physical education – as a curriculum subject comprising and understood to be a collection of activities, and invariably equated with 'sport' – was already well established as the norm in schools in England prior to the National Curriculum (Kirk, 1992). This was particularly true of PE in secondary schools, with the transition from primary to secondary PE marking an end to play or game experiences associated with general movement skills rather than adult sports. The move to secondary PE is to a highly specialised domain, but also to what pupils and parents alike would regard as 'real PE' – participation in a series of sporting experiences, with teaching directed towards improving competence in them. This secondary model became the reference point for defining the subject, and articulating a statutory entitlement, within the National Curriculum. To date there has been neither the political scope for, nor any apparent professional interest in, conceptualising physical education differently (Evans and Penney, 1995; Penney and Evans, 1999). The familiar, recognisable curriculum form comprising a collection of activities – perhaps regarded as the only possible form – has been retained and repeatedly legitimated in the development of the NCPE. In Goodson's (1997) words, the 'givenness' of the curriculum has been firmly enshrined in legislation. Echoing comments made in this collection about other curriculum subjects, I will argue that *content* – in the shape of activities – that has come to gain the status of 'core and unquestionable' has also had (and continues to have) an overwhelming influence in terms of curriculum *purposes* and therefore teaching and learning priorities. Those purposes are, I contend, notably narrow and relate to still widely held 'common sense' views not only of what the subject is, but also of what it is about: improving one's performance in particular activities and finding out in an invariably very public manner if those activities are ones in which one will feel confident and competent enough to remain an active participant.

The activities referred to here arise from the traditions of the élite public schools in England, have been deemed central to English 'national identity', and frequently continue to be gender-stereotyped (Kirk, 1992; Evans and Penney, 1995; Penney and Evans, 1999; Williams and Bedward, 2002). The simplistic image and understanding of the subject is not only restrictive in its focus on activities, but also extends to which activities are deemed to have a legitimate, and in some cases privileged, position.

This applies particularly to the different provision within physical education for boys and for girls. The NCPE has always featured some flexibility in its requirements, not least of which has been the scope for stereotypical views about physical education, activity and sport to be either challenged or reinforced (Talbot, 1993; Penney, 2002a). This flexibility allows choices about the range of areas of activity (such as games activities, gymnastic activities or outdoor and adventurous activities) and the specific activities within these (such as football, rugby, netball within games) that are offered as the statutory entitlement for either boys or girls; about the time that will be accorded to particular activities/areas of activity; about staffing; and about grouping arrangements. Flexibility has thus enabled schools and teachers to provide boys with a noticeably different entitlement from girls. This has led to the retention of firmly established traditions in provision and learning priorities.

In this chapter I will suggest that debates about the contribution of physical education to the fulfilment of the new aims for the National Curriculum, and furthermore, to the learning and lives of all children, must consider issues of curriculum content and structure that to date have been beyond the legitimate boundaries of debate. If physical education is to be a subject that plays a key role in embodying the new aims in children's curriculum experiences and that has lifelong meaning and relevance to more than just a minority of pupils, physical educationalists may need to consider a radical reorientation and re-structuring of their subject and in that process embark on a possibly uncomfortable review of their own professional identities. As Young (1998) has stressed, for subjects to develop as 'connective specialisms', whereby we move beyond a view of them as ends in themselves and instead direct attention towards the complex contexts in which the knowledge to which they give access might be applied, we need to reconsider our role as specialists.

What are the aims and purposes of physical education?

Statements about physical education – internationally, nationally and within individual schools – characteristically embody *a number of* aims for the subject, relating to pupils' learning and lives within and beyond schools. They emphasise that it is about much more than the physical – that it can play a key role in helping young people 'to develop spiritually, morally, culturally, mentally *and* physically' (Blunkett, 1999, my emphasis). The Physical Education Association of the United Kingdom (PEAUK) maintains the view that physical education:

- provides opportunities for young people to develop their knowledge, skills and understanding of the body and its movement;
- develops physical awareness, skills and competence and contributes to healthy growth and physical development;
- develops artistic and aesthetic understanding in and through movement;
- influences the development of healthy lifestyles and lifelong habits;
- provides opportunities to promote spiritual, moral, social and cultural development and develops personal qualities such as self-esteem, independence, citizenship, tolerance and empathy;
- provides opportunities to promote key skills such as communication (verbal and non-verbal), application of number, IT, working with others, improving own learning and performance and problem-solving;
- makes a strong contribution to the development of pupils' language through the extensive use of speaking and listening skills.

(PEAUK, 2001)

In the official statement of the 'importance of physical education' that was incorporated in the revised National Curriculum, the subject is portrayed – as in the PEAUK document – as a vehicle that will encourage and enable involvement in physically active and healthy lives in a variety of social contexts. The impression created is of a foundation of skills, knowledge and understanding that will have relevance across learning contexts and beyond schools:

> Physical education develops pupils' physical competence and confidence, and their ability to use these to perform in a range of activities. It promotes physical skilfulness, physical development and a knowledge of the body in action. Physical education provides opportunities for pupils to be creative, competitive and to face up to different challenges as individuals and in groups and teams. It promotes positive attitudes towards active and healthy lifestyles. Pupils learn how to think in different ways to suit a wide variety of creative, competitive and challenging activities. They learn how to plan, perform and evaluate actions, ideas and performances to improve their quality and effectiveness. Through this process pupils discover their aptitudes, abilities and preferences, and make choices about how to get involved in lifelong physical activity.

(DfEE/QCA, 1999, p. 15)

If we now relate these points to the new aims of the National Curriculum (see Chapters 1 and 2), physical education could certainly claim to have particular value (and somewhat unique potential because of the practical contexts of teaching and learning) in relation to 'promoting pupils' commitment to learning and confidence in their capacities to learn'. It could no doubt also be argued that via various activities and activity contexts it addresses 'the capacity to solve problems, think rationally, critically and creatively'; helps pupils 'to become creative, innovative, enterprising and capable of leadership'; contributes to the 'development of pupils' sense of identity and their understanding of cultural heritage'; 'passes on enduring social values'; 'promotes pupils' integrity and autonomy'; addresses issues of 'discrimination and knowledge of different beliefs and cultures'; and develops abilities 'to work for the common good', 'respond positively to challenges and also to change and adversity', and make 'informed choices' about current and future lifestyles (and, in particular, participation in activities).

But does it? Where, when and how are these various aims and interests reflected in the curriculum, teaching and learning of physical education? Do pupils leave physical education with this extensive range of skills, knowledge and understanding, positive self-identities and attitudes?

'Core' skills, knowledge and understanding

A notable new characteristic of the revised National Curriculum was the common structure that it established for the programmes of study in the various curriculum subjects, comprising aspects of knowledge, skills and understanding to be taught through a defined range of 'contexts, activities, areas of study and range of experiences' ('breadth of study') (DfEE/QCA, 1999, p. 12). It is worth relating the new content identified for physical education to the above claims about the contribution of the subject to children's lives. We also need to see what potential this revision of the National Curriculum has for redirecting teaching and learning beyond a dominant (and by no means unique to the UK) concern with psychomotor development and skilled performance in particular areas (Kirk, 1992; Locke, 1992; Crum, 1983). Here we return to the commonsensical understanding of what physical education is 'surely' all about, captured vividly in the then Secretary of State Kenneth Clarke's response to aspects of the Interim Report for the NCPE in 1991. The Secretary of State explained categorically that he was 'not at all convinced' by the structure provided by the *three* attainment targets proposed by the working group, of (i) planning and composing; (ii) participating and performing and (iii) appreciating and evaluating (DES/WO, 1991a). Clarke requested that the group reconsider their proposals 'with a view to coming up with a single attainment target for physical education which reflects the *practical nature of the subject*' (Clarke in DES/WO, 1991a, my emphasis). He added 'I should be grateful if you could ensure that the active element is predominant' and reminded the working group that the programmes of study 'should focus on the active side of PE' (ibid., 1991a). Ultimately the NCPE featured a single attainment target in which both pragmatic and political compromises were openly apparent. The attainment target remained un-named, with the explanation that it 'should encompass the planning and evaluation of activities, but the main emphasis should be on participation, reflecting the active nature of the subject' (DES/WO, 1991b, p. 1; see Evans and Penney, 1995; Penney and Evans, 1999).

Reflecting on the implementation of the 1992 and 1995 versions of the NCPE, Laker (2000) has observed that 'teachers are required to concentrate on the physical aspects [in comparison to cognitive, affective or social] and the evidence suggests that this is in fact what happens' (p. 21). Other research has further reinforced a picture of the NCPE having a limited impact on teachers' priorities in curriculum planning and teaching, of 'performing' being privileged over 'planning' and 'evaluating'; and of the subject remaining both structured around and directed towards performance in activities/sports (Curtner-Smith, 1999). So, did the new aspects of skills, knowledge and understanding and their development in the programmes of study within the new NCPE provide a new (and broader) direction for curriculum planning, teaching and learning? Elsewhere I have questioned whether the four aspects below, and their expansion in the text of the programmes of study for the various key stages and in the level descriptions of attainment in the subject that were also introduced with the new NCPE, adequately embrace the whole range of the aims put forward for physical education. I have suggested that the new requirements continue to reflect a far more specific vision, informed by an understanding of physical education as about, first and foremost, the development of performers in specific activities (Penney and Chandler, 2000; Penney, 2002b).

The four aspects of knowledge, skills and understanding that the new NCPE established as the focus for teaching and learning in the subject are:

- Acquiring and developing skills;
- Selecting and applying skills, tactics and compositional ideas;
- Evaluating and improving performance;
- Knowledge and understanding of fitness and health.

(DfEE/QCA, 1999, p. 6)

At first glance, this may appear unproblematic as a basis from which physical education could seek to contribute to the new aims of the National Curriculum. Opportunities could be created and encouragement provided for teaching and learning to be 'outward looking', with a focus on the relevance, application and continued development of skills, knowledge and understanding in *multiple* 'communities of practice' (Lave and Wenger, 1991). Attention could be on the opportunities for 'legitimate peripheral participation' in at least three such communities of practice – of sport, exercise and leisure/recreation (Kirk, 1999; Kirk and Macdonald, 1998) – and on connections between many varied forms of physical activity and lifestyles. However, when we trace the four aspects through the texts of the programmes of study and of the newly established level descriptions, I contend that a less positive picture emerges. A dominant purpose of the subject comes to the fore and other aims (particularly those concerned with social development) become clearly positioned as the marginal or absent 'other'.

The following statement in a publication that accompanied the revision of the NCPE, entitled 'Terminology in Physical Education' sought to clarify the specific purpose of the physical education curriculum:

> The purpose of a PE curriculum is to provide the range of tasks, contexts and environments so that an individual's skills can be tuned, adjusted, adapted, modified and refined. The challenge of teaching is to provide information, ideas and encouragement for each pupil to become competent and confident in each new task, context and environment and then to extend them again.
>
> (QCA, 1999, p. 1)

Concern with increasing physical competence in specific activity contexts also comes out in the level descriptions for attainment in the subject. Take, for instance, the text for level 8, which may be deemed a 'target' or at least key reference point for teachers and learners:

Pupils consistently distinguish and apply advanced skills, techniques and ideas, consistently showing high standards of precision, control, fluency, and originality. Drawing on what they know of the principles of advanced tactics or composition, they apply these principles with proficiency and flair in their own and others' work. They adapt it appropriately in response to changing circumstances and other performers. They evaluate their own and others' work, showing that they understand the impact of skills, strategy and tactics or composition, and fitness on the quality and effectiveness of performance. They plan ways in which their own and others' performance could be improved. They create action plans and ways of monitoring improvement. They use their knowledge of health and fitness to plan and evaluate their own and others' exercise and activity programmes.

(DfEE/QCA, 1999, p. 42)

Marginalised here is the broad range of learning (spiritual, moral, cultural, mental as well as physical) that may be – and is invariably claimed to be – developed through participation in physical activities and challenges. The limited vision is of pupils' developing as performers, of their gaining skills, knowledge and understanding that will enable them to improve as such and assist others in doing likewise. Attention is directed towards mastery of particular, predefined skills, knowledge and understanding relevant to the pursuit (by oneself or others) of élite performance in sport. The curriculum, from this perspective, can be linked to notions of apprenticeship. However, the apprenticeship is highly specific and, furthermore, openly positions pupils in a sporting and social hierarchy. It will always be a minority of pupils who are in the sporting élite and to whom this orientation of the curriculum is arguably appropriate or likely to be of interest. In the new NCPE, linked with the introduction of new statutory requirements for citizenship there is recognition of 'other roles' in physical activity and sport (particularly leadership roles) and there is encouragement for this 'other learning' to be addressed. Yet it is hard to escape the notion that this is indeed 'other' and marginal to performance, and that a hierarchy of learning will be mirrored in a hierarchy of learners. It is interesting to note that the requirement for teaching to address the development of leadership skills at Key Stage 4 does not fall under the banner of 'acquiring and developing skills'. Instead it is associated with 'evaluating and improving performance'. The role of leadership, and the social and communication skills central to it, is clear: it supports but is also inherently subordinate to performance.

Also embedded in the level descriptions (and indeed, the order as a whole) is a tension that is found throughout policy and curriculum development in physical education between discourses of education, sport and health. The above level 8 description reflects the differential status of these discourses. That of sport, and more specifically, élite performance in sport, is repeatedly privileged, and provides the reference point for the development and expression of other discourses (see Penney and Evans, 1997, 1999). It is only certain discourses of health, for instance, that have an approved place in the NCPE. Attention is upon the fitness required for, or developed by, participation in sport. Mental, social and emotional dimensions of health are largely overlooked, while a simplistic and uncritical association runs through the text: sport = activity = health.

Activities (particularly 'traditional' team games) that have a politically valued and established place in the curriculum are portrayed as somehow automatically furthering interests relating to health and to social behaviour and values, irrespective of how the activities are taught or of the particular focus of teaching and learning. Readers will have their own reflections about the degree to which their games lessons in childhood made a positive contribution to their physical activity levels or to their attitudes towards physical activity and towards fellow pupils. Should we need it, research reaffirms that if we are seriously interested in pupils' physical activity levels and their interests in lifelong engagement with physical activity, the activities which feature in physical education, how they are taught and with what aims, are all worthy of review (Fairclough, 2002; Corbin, 2002; Yelling *et al.*, 2000; Yelling and Penney, 2002). Meanwhile, headlines such as 'Couch potatoes grow as games lose out' (Thornton, 1999) continue to feature in the media and discourses of health that relate to broader conceptualisations of well-being and prompt us to pursue activity/health/healthy lifestyle/healthy bodies dynamics from a critical perspective remain absent from the NCPE texts (Penney and Harris, 2002).

The centrality of activities

Throughout the development of the NCPE it has been assumed that a particular mix of activities (bringing with them increased 'breadth' and improved 'balance' in the physical education curriculum) is an assured way of addressing multiple aims. The failure to acknowledge the importance of pedagogy in relation to what will be learnt through any particular activity seems quite astounding. But perhaps it is not so surprising. Maintaining a myth of total compatibility between a particular collection of activities and the realisation of multiple aims, is crucial to maintaining physical education 'as we know it' and to the continued privileging of performance in politically valued, culturally specific sports as the reference point for thinking about the subject. We need to understand why there is a continual emphasis on a *collection* of activities, all of which are portrayed as notably *different* from one another. Here we confront what (and who) underpins the 'boundary maintenance' that is at the heart of and that actively reinforces the 'strongly classified' physical education curriculum (Bernstein, 1990, 1996).

In distinguishing activities from one another, we shift to a view of them as vehicles of learning. But the contexts are highly specific: particular learning demands particular vehicles. Thus, the multiple-activity curriculum model, and with it the dominance of discourses of sport, is again endorsed. Crucially, so is the need for sufficient curriculum time to incorporate these multiple activities and for 'specific specialists' – experts in particular activities – to teach the subject. Advertisements for physical education teachers in England confirm that expertise is still firmly tied to specific activities and that issues of gender are intertwined with activity-based professional identities and curriculum provision (Flintoff, 1993; Brown and Rich, 2002).

The document 'Terminology in Physical Education' (QCA, 1999), produced to coincide with the publication of the new NCPE, presented teachers with an authoritative clarification of learning associated with particular activities:

- *dance activities* were identified as contexts 'where pupils use their imaginations and ideas to create, perform, appreciate and develop dances with awareness of historical and cultural context. The artistic intention makes use of rhythm, space and relationships, expressing and communicating ideas, moods and feelings' (p. 1);

- *games activities*, a context in which 'pupils will select, apply and adapt skills, strategies and tactics, on their own and in teams, with the intention of outwitting the opposition in a range of different game types' (p. 2);
- *gymnastic activities*, a context 'where pupils will devise aesthetically pleasing sequences using combinations of skills and agilities which they repeat and perform with increasing control, precision and fluency' (p. 2);
- *athletic activities*, one in which 'pupils will perform and refine a range of dynamic skills, with the intention of improving personal and collective bests in relation to speed, height, distance and accuracy' (p. 2);
- *outdoor and adventurous activities*, a context in which 'pupils will develop individually and in teams, the ability to analyse, plan and then respond effectively and safely to physical challenges and problems they encounter in familiar, changing and unfamiliar environments' (p. 2); and
- *swimming activities and water safety*, a context 'where pupils will develop their confidence and ability to stay afloat and to swim unaided for sustained periods of time, selecting, adapting and refining their skills so that they can swim safely and engage in a variety of activities in and around water' (p. 2).

Learning is thus identified as *specific to* the area of activity, with the potential commonality in learning across activities effectively denied. It is with this background in mind that I now return to the new NCPE, before moving on to issues about possible future developments.

As indicated, the four aspects of skills, knowledge and understanding provide a new, and potentially powerful, framework for the subject. What is interesting, but given some of the preceding discussion may now seem entirely understandable, is that the aspects were subsumed within the familiar curriculum framework of activities (or areas of activity). The detail of the programmes of study loses explicit focus on the four aspects. Instead, extensive commentary is provided about the areas of activity that comprise the *breadth of study* for the subject (i.e. dance activities, games activities, gymnastic activities, swimming activities and water-safety, athletic activities, and outdoor and adventurous activities). In this respect the order for physical education looks very different from that for other subjects, like music for instance, where the commentary relating to breadth of study is minimal.

The programmes of study for physical education were clearly written when the curriculum was still conceptualised in an 'activity-based' form. The retention of this curriculum form and the development of the four aspects *through it*, produces a legitimisation of a focus on activity-specific purposes. In the text of the programmes of study the four aspects operate only within each of the *different* areas of activity taken separately. The defining knowledge boundaries within and around the subject are actively reaffirmed and simultaneously a view of knowledge as bounded, fixed and to be transmitted/acquired comes to the fore. The requirements relating to gymnastic activities in Table 2 show a specificity in teaching and learning, and an orientation towards performance in the activity, which is mirrored in each of the other areas. The specificity retains knowledge boundaries, legitimates the dominant curriculum form and the specialisms within the subject. The idea that teaching and learning in physical education extend beyond and cut across specific activities or areas of activity remains little developed. In this context, the notion of 'entitlement' itself takes on a particular

Table 2 Activities: the defining form and defining focus. Gymnastic activities

Key Stage 1 Pupils should be taught to . . .	Key Stage 2 Pupils should be taught to...	Key Stage 3 Pupils should be taught to . . .	Key Stage 4 Pupils should be taught to . . .
Perform basic skills in travelling, being still, finding space and using it safely, both on the floor and using apparatus; Develop the range of their skills and actions [*for example, balancing, taking off and landing, turning and rolling*]; Choose and link skills and actions in short movement phrases; Create and perform short, linked sequences that show a clear beginning, middle and end and have contrasts in direction, level and speed.	Create and perform fluent sequences on the floor and using apparatus; Include variations in level, speed and direction in sequences.	Create and perform complex sequences on the floor and using apparatus; Use techniques and movement combinations in different gymnastic styles; Use compositional principles when designing their sequences [*for example, changes in level, speed, direction, and relationships with apparatus and partners*].	Compose and perform sequences, both on the floor and using apparatus, in specific gymnastic styles, applying set criteria; Use advanced techniques and skills with precision and accuracy; Use advanced compositional concepts and principles when composing their sequences.

meaning. We shift from potential visions of an entitlement to

> a form of curriculum which will cater appropriately to the growth and develop-
> ment of every capacity, which will promote the acquisition of those understandings
> which will facilitate intelligent participation in democratic processes, which will
> offer genuine social and political empowerment, and which will in general enrich
> and enhance the life potential of every individual.
>
> (Edwards and Kelly, 1998, p. 16)

to the far more economic and pragmatic view, of access to a minimum common core of activities (Boorman, 1998). It is doubtful whether this is an entitlement – and thus a curriculum framework – that can enable PE effectively to contribute to the fulfilment of the new aims for the National Curriculum and provide for the learning needs and interests of all pupils. In any case, the idea is flawed from the outset, as policy makers and teachers have recognised that there are not the time or resources to include all six areas of activity throughout all key stages. With a so-called 'full PE entitlement' out of the question, the compromise reached – of variations in the range of areas of activity that must be incorporated within the various key stages – denies access to specific types of learning at particular points in children's education. This is especially true of the primary years, where some children may progress through Key Stages 1 and 2 without having experienced athletic activities or outdoor and adventurous activities at all (DfEE/QCA, 1999).

The future of physical education in the curriculum

> No-one thinks education should look the same in twenty years' time as it does
> now. There is widespread agreement on the need for a strategy capable of trans-

forming what young people learn and how they learn. There is no consensus on what such a strategy might look like, less because people disagree on the need for one than because there are few competing strategic visions to act as the focus for debate.

(Bayliss, 1999, p. 3)

Curriculum – the specification of what is to be taught in schools – is a powerful, perhaps the most powerful, driver of education.

(Ibid., p. 2)

In this final section, I will raise a number of points that have remained beyond the boundaries of current debate about the prospective form, content and focus of a NCPE, but that all help to show how physical education can most effectively contribute to the realisation of the new aims of the National Curriculum and, furthermore, seek to transform itself into what we might term a 'connective specialism' (Young, 1998) that is inherently more inclusive. The questions I wish to raise are:

1   why the current areas of activity?
2   why the identified 'four aspects'?
3   what role for aesthetic goals and personal qualities?

1   The short history of the NCPE has featured many heated discussions about the pragmatic difficulties of including the six areas of activity in both school curricula and initial teacher training. They have led to politically-based compromises involving the statutory inclusion of *some* areas, veiled in a rhetoric of flexibility and choice. Yet the debate has not extended to either the rationalisation, re-orientation and re-categorisation of activities, or to the total dissolution of boundaries between activities. Do we need categories at all? There is certainly a question mark over the appropriateness of the current six areas to patterns of physical activity in both young people and adults (Roberts, 1996). The six areas and activities dominant within them, like football and netball, do not map well on to such popular adult recreational activities as walking, jogging, cycling, swimming, yoga, other exercise classes or martial arts. Neither are they closely linked to activities found in contemporary youth culture such as roller-blading or skateboarding. Equally, the dominant activities ill fit the physical activities and skills belonging to adult working and domestic life. We need strength, knowledge and understanding to lift objects safely in housework, DIY or gardening. This could justifiably be deemed an essential life skill. Why should this not be part of physical education? This and other activities are effectively excluded by the six-area framework, or at least struggle to have a legitimate place in it. Activities like the martial arts *do* feature in PE curricula elsewhere. This highlights the cultural specificity of the NCPE. It is something to challenge if we are serious about providing an education that engages with ethnic and cultural diversity.

Just as we might consider different, fewer or additional activity-based divisions, we can also envisage a physical education curriculum in which the choice of activities is entirely a matter for schools, teachers and pupils to negotiate. Is experience of any particular activity something *essential* to stipulate in a National Curriculum? Is it beneficial from a lifelong perspective to be forcing all children to participate in specific activities? Could not core skills, knowledge and understanding be acquired via a number of routes? But it is an open question whether more opportunities for choice would cater better for individual learning needs.

2   As I have already suggested, we can question whether, as currently identified, the four aspects adequately encompass the range of learning that physical education claims to address and whether they provide a firm foundation from which the subject can positively engage with the new aims of the National Curriculum. Do they promote an inherently inclusive curriculum, or is their orientation such that provision is for a particular few learners? Elsewhere I have pointed to the contrasting features of physical education (or 'health and physical education') curricula internationally, that give explicit status to what in England remains an absent, 'other' learning (Penney, 2001). If we are serious in seeing physical education as a subject via which pupils will, as the PEAUK claims, develop artistic and aesthetic understanding in and through movement, or personal qualities such as self-esteem, independence, citizenship, tolerance and empathy, should these not feature as 'core aspects' of learning, with statutory requirements for teaching and descriptions of attainment to match? What is needed is a series of reconceptualisations: of the subject and its fundamental purposes, of physical education teachers and learners, of the curriculum and the inherent entitlement it provides.

3   I have suggested that matters such as 'artistic and aesthetic understanding in and through movement' or 'personal qualities' could and should be core aspects of learning in physical education. Both could provide a focus for programmes of study and, therefore, units of work. These labels are important. Units need to be firmly identified with these kinds of objective, not with specific activities. I have an open mind about the range of activities that could or should feature in 'thematically focussed' units. Here conventional associations undoubtedly spring to mind. Surely 'artistic and aesthetic understanding in and through movement' means gymnastics and/or dance? But does it? Are only these things relevant? Pick any physical activity and you can find artistic and aesthetic qualities. If children engage in a range of activities, these qualities can be developed more fully. With such an approach we may provide more points of connection with more children's current and future lives. As things are now, for most of us gymnastics and/or dance may well be only a childhood memory – as something dropped at the earliest opportunity.

Similar things could be said about PE's role in promoting personal qualities, such as 'independence, citizenship, tolerance and empathy' or 'social skills'. It would be good to see teaching and learning relating to these issues planned for and privileged. Physical activity settings do provide rich potential for addressing progressively more complex and challenging work of this kind, yet currently that potential remains inadequately explored and only partially realised: a matter of accident not design. All too often we hear of participation in team games being linked with the development of certain personal qualities in a simplistic and highly problematic fashion. Learning experiences in games must be planned explicitly so as to cultivate personal qualities without such stereotypes getting in the way.

The review I have in mind is radical, demanding a reconsideration of what should constitute the central features of the physical education curriculum and their interrelationships. There needs to be a fundamental re-orientation, such that 'the *contribution to learning* that we see the subject as providing, rather than the activities through which we may ultimately achieve that contribution, should become the explicit defining feature of the subject, and should provide the framework for curriculum development' (Penney and Chandler, 2000, p. 77). I would argue that such a shift would significantly enhance the chances of physical education providing 'a coherent set of experiences, not a heterogeneous conglomerate whose cohesiveness is left to chance' (Edwards and Kelly, 1998, p. xv).

Conclusion

It has been argued that the post–2000 National Curriculum for England is revolutionary – or at least potentially more radical – in that for the first time there is a common framework of curricular aims. In this chapter we have seen that the revised statutory order for physical education has similar new characteristics that could be a basis for re-orientating thinking, curriculum planning, teaching and learning – away from activities (or sports) as ends in themselves and towards a view of them as merely vehicles capable of facilitating and providing the contexts for a rich array of learning. But we have also seen mirrored within the subject the type of tensions that arise in relation to the curriculum as a whole – between aims and the basic, subject-based, structure and organisation of the curriculum. The general theme of this book is how far the current subject-based curriculum can fit with the new aims. We may ask similarly searching questions of the long-established activity-based curriculum of physical education. It is a subject in which boundaries between self-separated knowledge communities remain embodied in the organisational form of the curriculum and in teachers' own professional identities. Any change from this may well be considered not merely strange but also threatening. If all we are interested in is performance in sport and sport performers, then maintaining the status quo in curriculum terms is justified. But if we have hopes that teaching and learning will extend beyond out-dated boundaries and connect with the needs, interests and lives of all children and their roles in the transformation of communities and societies (Bentley, 1998; Quicke, 1999; Young, 1998), the status quo is not an option. Quite simply, we will retain a situation in which

> although many people have school experiences of physical education which provide the entrance to a lifetime passion for physical activities of all types, these same experiences for others generate an ongoing aversion to anything remotely physical. In between these two extremes are a multitude of people whose experiences have given rise to a loathing of one activity and delight in another.
>
> (Boorman, 1998, p. 88)

Whether the future development of the National Curriculum will have space for a concerted shift from this familiar pattern remains to be seen. As Locke (1992) observed a decade ago 'there must be people who are sufficiently dissatisfied with what *is* to take the risks of exploring what might be' (p. 369).

References

Bayliss, V. (1999) *Opening Minds. Education for the 21st Century*, London: The Royal Society for the Encouragement of Arts, Manufactures and Commerce.

Bentley, T. (1998) *Learning Beyond the Classroom. Education for a Changing World*, London: Routledge.

Bernstein, B. (1990) *The Structuring of Pedagogic Discourse. Volume IV Class, Codes and Control*, London: Routledge.

Bernstein, B. (1996) *Pedagogy, Symbolic Control and Identity. Theory, Research, Critique*, London: Taylor & Francis.

Blunkett, D. (1999) Letter of introduction, in QCA (1999) *The Review of the National Curriculum in England. The Secretary of State's Proposals*, London: QCA.

Boorman, D. (1998) 'The physical: a new millennium, a new beginning?', in Edwards, G. and Kelly, A.V. (eds) *Experience and Education. Towards an Alternative National Curriculum*, London: Paul Chapman Publishing.

Brown, D. and Rich, E. (2002) 'Gender positioning as pedagogical practice in teaching Physical Education', in Penney, D. (ed.) *Gender and Physical Education. Contemporary Issues and Future Directions*, London: Routledge.

Corbin, C.B. (2002) 'Physical activity for everyone: what every physical educator should know about promoting lifelong physical activity', *Journal of Teaching Physical Education*, 21, 128–144.

Crum, B.J. (1983) 'Conventional thought and practice in physical education: problems of teaching and implications for change', *QUEST*, 45, 336–356.

Curtner-Smith, M.D. (1999) 'The more things change the more they stay the same: factors influencing teachers' interpretations and delivery of National Curriculum physical education', *Sport, Education and Society*, 4, 1, 75–97.

Department for Education and Employment (DfEE)/Qualifications and Curriculum Authority (QCA) (1999) *Physical Education. The National Curriculum for England*, London: QCA.

Department of Education and Science/Welsh Office (1991a) *National Curriculum Physical Education Working Group Interim Report*, London: DES.

DES/Welsh Office (1991b) *Physical Education for ages 5–16. Proposals of the Secretary of State for Education and the Secretary of State for Wales*, London: DES.

Edwards, G. and Kelly, A.V. (1998) 'Education as development through experience', in Edwards, G. and Kelly, A.V. (eds) *Experience and Education. Towards an Alternative National Curriculum*, London: Paul Chapman Publishing.

Evans, J. and Penney, D. (1995) 'Physical education, restoration and the politics of sport', *Curriculum Studies*, 3, 2, 183–196.

Fairclough, S. (2002) 'Promoting lifetime physical activity through physical education. Are we providing the right opportunities?', *British Journal of Teaching Physical Education*, 33, 2, 38–42.

Flintoff, A. (1993) 'Gender, physical education and initial teacher education', in Evans, J. (ed.) *Equality, Education and Physical Education*, London: The Falmer Press.

Goodson, I. (1997) *The Changing Curriculum. Studies in Social Construction*, New York: Lang Publishing Inc.

Kirk, D. (1992) *Defining Physical Education: The Social Construction of a School Subject in Postwar Britain*, London: The Falmer Press.

Kirk, D. (1999) 'Physical culture, physical education and relational analysis', *Sport, Education and Society*, 4,1, 63–73.

Kirk, D. and Macdonald, D. (1998) 'Situated learning in physical education', *Journal of Teaching Physical Education*, 17, 376–387.

Laker, A. (2000) *Beyond the Boundaries of Physical Education. Educating Young People for Citizenship and Social Responsibility*, London: RoutledgeFalmer Press.

Lave, J. and Wenger, E. (1991) *Situated Learning: Legitimate Peripheral Participation in Communities of Practice*, New York: Cambridge University Press.

Locke, F.L. (1992) 'Changing secondary school physical education', *QUEST*, 44, 361–372.

Penney, D. (2001) 'The revision and initial implementation of the National Curriculum for Physical Education in England', *The Bulletin of Physical Education*, 37, 2, 93–134.

Penney, D. (2002a) (ed.) *Gender and Physical Education. Contemporary Issues and Future Directions*, London: Routledge.

Penney, D. (2002b) 'Physical education: who is learning what for life?'. Paper presented at the *Busan Asian Games Sport Scientific Congress*, Busan, Korea, 24–27 September, 2002.

Penney, D. and Chandler, T. (2000) 'Physical education: what future(s)?', *Sport, Education and Society*, 5, 1, 71–87.

Penney, D. and Evans, J. (1997) 'Naming the game. Discourse and domination in physical education and sport in England and Wales', *European Physical Education Review*, 3, 1, 21–32.

Penney, D. and Evans, J. (1999) *Politics, Policy and Practice in Physical Education*, London: E&FN Spon.

Penney, D. and Harris, J. (2002) 'Policy, pedagogy and the politics of the body and health'. Paper presented at the *Australian Association for Research in Education Conference*, December 2002, Brisbane.

Physical Education Association of the United Kingdom (2001) *PEAUK Policy Statements*, http://www.pea.uk.com/menu.html; accessed 21 January 2001.

Qualifications and Curriculum Authority (1999) *Terminology in Physical Education*, London: QCA Publications.

Quicke, J. (1999) *A Curriculum for Life. Schools for a Democratic Learning Society*, Open University Press: Buckingham.

Roberts, K. (1996) 'Young people, schools, sport and government policy', *Sport, Education and Society*, 1, 1, 47–57.

Talbot, M. (1993) 'A gendered physical education: equality and sexism', in Evans, J. (ed.) *Equality, Education and Physical Education*, London: The Falmer Press.

Thornton, K. (1999) 'Couch potatoes grow as games lose out', *Times Educational Supplement*, 5 March, p. 8.

Williams, A. and Bedward, J. (2002) 'Understanding girls' experience of physical education: relational analysis and situated learning', in Penney, D. (ed.) *Gender and Physical Education. Contemporary Issues and Future Directions*, London: Routledge.

Yelling, M., Penney, D. and Swaine, I.L. (2000) 'Physical activity in physical education: a case study investigation', *European Journal of Physical Education*, 5, 3, 45–66.

Yelling, M. and Penney, D. (2002) 'Physical activity in physical education: pupil activity rating, reason and reality'. Paper presented at the *British Educational Research Association Annual Conference*, 12–14 September, University of Exeter.

Young, M.F.D. (1998) *The Curriculum of The Future. From The 'New Sociology of Education' to a Critical Theory of Learning*, London: Falmer Press.

12 Religious education

Michael Hand

Religious education (RE) currently enjoys the status of a compulsory curriculum subject in state schools in England and Wales. Though it is not part of the National Curriculum, and therefore not subject to a nationally prescribed syllabus, it is part of the basic curriculum to which all children are entitled. The question I should like to raise in this chapter is whether RE merits this status. Is the study of religion sufficiently central to the task of preparing children for adult life to justify the existence of a separate and compulsory curriculum subject?

There is, at present, a broad consensus among policy-makers on two distinct justifications for the study of religion in schools. The first is that an understanding of religious individuals and communities better equips pupils for life in a multicultural society. Whether or not pupils hold religious beliefs themselves, they will live and work among people who do, and they will be better able to communicate and negotiate with such people if they understand their beliefs and values. Religion is an inescapable fact of social life, and knowing something about it can only be advantageous to people in their efforts to live together in harmony.

The second justification is that the study of religion is morally educative. Religions are here construed as repositories of moral wisdom upon which pupils may be encouraged to draw. By reflecting on the moral teachings propagated by religious communities, or the exemplary lives of characters in religious narratives, pupils can acquire the inclination and ability to make sound moral judgements. It is important to note that the study of religion is thought to be capable of serving this morally educative function regardless of whether or not pupils hold religious beliefs.

These two justifications are clearly reflected in the two Attainment Targets for RE recommended in the SCAA model syllabuses (1994) and the QCA non-statutory guidance (2000). *AT1: Learning about religions* articulates the objective of equipping pupils with an understanding of religious individuals and communities. It requires that pupils should come to have knowledge and understanding of religious beliefs, teachings, practices and lifestyles. *AT2: Learning from religion* expresses the aim of promoting moral development. It requires that pupils, through their engagement with religious traditions, should ask and respond to questions of identity, purpose, values and commitments.

My discussion will proceed in three stages. I shall begin by sketching the history of RE in Britain, with a view to explaining how the current consensus on these two justifications came about. I shall then examine the validity of the approved justifications and argue that neither constitutes an adequate reason for compulsory RE. I shall conclude by suggesting an alternative rationale for a compulsory curriculum subject dedicated to the study of religion.

Religious education since 1944

Religious instruction, subject to a parental right of withdrawal, was made compulsory by the Education Act of 1944. With state control of the curriculum having been withdrawn from elementary schools in 1926, and soon to be withdrawn from secondary schools in 1945, it thus became the *only* compulsory subject in British schools.[1]

What was the justification for this legislative decision? The answer is to be found in the 1938 Spens Report and the 1943 White Paper *Educational Reconstruction*. Both documents argued for a more pronounced role for RE on the basis of its power to instil moral virtue. The former characterised RE as 'the education which inculcates duty and reverence' and asserted that it therefore belongs 'in the forefront' of the curriculum (Board of Education, 1938, p. 170). The latter identified and endorsed 'a very general wish, not confined to representatives of the Churches, that religious education should be given a more defined place in the life and work of the schools, springing from the desire to revive the spiritual and personal values in our society and our national tradition' (Board of Education, 1943, para. 36).

From the beginning, then, compulsory RE was explicitly justified in terms of its contribution to pupils' moral development. As the subject was understood in 1944, however, this contribution was not to be made by inviting pupils to find inspiration in the moral teachings of a range of religious traditions, but by initiating them into the Christian faith. The intention was that schools should induct pupils into Christian belief and practice, and thus furnish them with good reasons for abiding by Christian moral principles.

The need for effective moral education was keenly felt in wartime Britain. The second world war was seen, in part, as a moral crusade against totalitarianism, demanding from British subjects an unwavering commitment to the principles of democracy. Christianity was widely held to be the sturdiest foundation upon which to build such commitment. In a statement issued in 1941, the Archbishops of Canterbury and York urged that 'in this present struggle we are fighting to preserve those elements in human civilisation and in our own national tradition which owe their origin to Christian faith' (cited in Loukes, 1965, p. 23). Rosalind Strachan writes:

> The war was seen as a clash of ideologies. To some it was a war between Nazi and Christian, but to most it was a war between totalitarianism and democracy. Therefore, people were forced to ask themselves what was the basis of this democratic tradition for which so many men had fought and died. And to the majority Christian ethics seemed to be the basis of British democracy . . . it was vital that the children of the nation should learn about the Christian faith in order that they, as citizens of the future, might have the necessary moral fibre to uphold the democratic way of life.
>
> (Cited in Niblett, 1966, p. 20)

It is now widely recognised that the 1944 Act was 'legislating for a society that had ceased to exist' (Cox and Cairns, 1989, p. 4). Even in the 1940s, Britain was a Christian country only in a residual sense. People paid lip-service to Christian belief and retained a respect for Christian moral teaching, but church attendance was in steady decline and 'Christianity had already ceased to have a prior, determining hold upon the affections of the majority of the British population' (Parsons, 1994, p. 169). It was simply unrealistic to suppose that schools could succeed in bringing the nation's youth back into the Christian fold. Nevertheless, the conception of RE as moral education by means of Christian nurture remained the dominant influence on policy and practice until the end of the 1960s.

The first wave of reforms in RE, associated with the work of Loukes (1961, 1965), Goldman (1964, 1965) and Acland (1963, 1966), represented an important departure in the methods by which the subject was taught, but not in its underlying aim. Developments in both educational theory and Christian theology led to a new pedagogical emphasis on the experiences, feelings and ideas of pupils. The focus shifted from formal instruction to the exploration of personal experience, from imparting biblical knowledge to showing the relevance of religion to pupils' lives. But if the life-world of the child was the new starting-point for RE, its end-point was still commitment to the Christian religion. The Agreed Syllabuses which prescribed the new approach may have introduced 'greater relevance and reality into religious education', but they remained 'Christian documents written by Christians and aiming at Christian education' (Schools Council Working Paper 36, 1971, p. 32).

As late as 1967, the Plowden Report endorsed the view that the aim of RE was to pass on Christian faith and morality. RE, it said, 'should recognise that young children need a simple and positive introduction to religion. They should be taught to know and love God and to practise in the school community the virtues appropriate to their age and environment' (DES, 1967, para. 572). It is interesting to note that a significant minority of the Central Advisory Council for Education dissociated themselves from these recommendations, arguing in a Note of Reservation to the main report that Christian beliefs are too controversial for their transmission to be justified, and that it is neither necessary nor desirable to tie moral education to Christian nurture.

It was not until the second wave of reforms, associated with the work of Cox (1966), Smart (1968) and Smith (1969), that the aim of nurturing Christian faith was finally abandoned. By the end of the 1960s it was clear that, even in its child-centred guise, RE was an ineffective tool of Christian renewal. More importantly, it had become increasingly difficult to ignore the large immigrant communities in Britain which practised religions other than Christianity. It was no longer possible to keep up the pretence that Britain was a Christian country, that Christian nurture in schools was a natural extension of the Christian upbringing children received in the home. Urban schools now admitted significant numbers of pupils from non-Christian religious backgrounds. Edwin Cox writes:

> The immigrant children posed particular problems in schools. Were they to be taught Christianity like the others as part of their enculturising process, or were they to be educated in the faiths which were being practised in their homes? What is more, was there not needed some inter-faith education, so that the more or less Christian native population could understand and sympathise with the religious beliefs and practices of their new schoolfellows, and so that the followers of the newly arrived religions could understand each other and the indigenous population?
>
> (Cox and Cairns, 1989, p. 18)

The response to these developments was a complete reconstruction of RE in British schools. The aim of nurturing Christian faith was replaced with the aim of advancing understanding of world religions; the method of making connections between pupils' experience and Christian teaching was replaced with the systematic study of religious phenomena. The new approach, sometimes referred to as the 'phenomenological' or 'explicit religion' approach, was modelled on the academic discipline of religious studies, which began to appear in institutions of higher education from the late 1960s (King, 1990). The RE of the 1970s and 1980s thus:

> eschewed confessionalism, advocated the value of studying a variety of world religions, possessed an increasing sense of its own identity as a distinct and genuinely academic subject, and was self-consciously responsive and relevant to the increasingly religiously plural nature of late-twentieth-century Britain.
>
> (Parsons, 1994, p. 179)

With the new aim of imparting knowledge of world religions came a new justification for compulsory RE. Britain was now a multicultural society, and it was important that citizens of different colours and creeds learned to understand and respect each other. By equipping pupils with knowledge and understanding of a range of religious beliefs and practices, RE could enhance their capacity to live peacefully and productively among people of different faiths. This justification, as we have seen, is still advanced by policy-makers today.

But what of the original, moral justification for compulsory RE? Did not the abandonment of Christian nurture necessitate the uncoupling of RE from moral education? For a time, at least, it was held that it did. In 1971 the Schools Council Project on Religious Education in Secondary Schools produced an influential Working Paper which explicitly rejected the construal of RE as a vehicle of moral education:

- Moral knowledge is autonomous: it is perfectly possible to have moral education without reference to religious sanctions or presuppositions.
- Schools should beware of linking morals too closely with one religious viewpoint, since some pupils who abandon that viewpoint may be left with no considered basis for morality.
- You cannot successfully take the moral code from a religion and leave the rest: the moral code of a religion is part of an organic whole; it is not the same thing when lifted out of its religious context.
- There is no reason why moral education in school should be regarded as the responsibility of the RE department

(Schools Council Working Paper 36, 1971, p. 70)

Despite this admirably clear-headed rejection of the moral agenda, RE did not manage to shake off its association with moral education entirely during this period. Indeed, even the authors of Working Paper 36 conclude their discussion with the odd concession that 'the RE teacher has a special contribution to make to moral education, showing the links between moral problems, and moral concepts, and religious beliefs' (ibid., p. 70). Nevertheless, the task of promoting moral development remained marginal to the main business of RE in the 1970s and 1980s, and the connection would perhaps have withered away altogether had it not been unexpectedly revived by two developments associated with the 1988 Education Reform Act.

The first of these developments was the 're-Christianising' of the RE curriculum. When the Education Reform Bill went before the House of Lords, it did little more than reassert the minimal requirements of the religious clauses of the 1944 Act; by the time it left the Lords, amendments had been added requiring that the daily act of collective worship in schools 'shall be wholly or mainly of a broadly Christian character', and that any Agreed Syllabus for RE coming into effect after the Act 'shall reflect the fact that the religious traditions in Great Britain are in the main Christian'. There is no doubt that the conservative Christian lobby responsible for these amendments were trying to recast RE in a confessional mould, or that the amendments found support because of the still widely-held assumption that religion is the proper foundation of morality. One peer speaking in support of the Act remarked:

> What is important is that the religious foundation of morality should be maintained. It was the 17th century which coined an aphorism, 'No Bishop, no King'. Our own could coin another. 'No religion, no morality', and certainly history affords no example of a society which has permanently maintained morality without a religious base.
>
> (Parliamentary Debates (*Hansard*) Vol. 496, No. 20, p. 417)

Although, by this time, the reintroduction of an overt policy of Christian nurture in schools was out of the question, in the years following the Act a more insidious idea began to gain ground. If pupils could not be inducted into the Christian faith itself, they could perhaps be inducted into a national culture historically rooted in the Christian faith. The vestiges and trappings of Christian belief, though hardly a substitute for the real thing, may yet afford some kind of foundation for moral virtue. This, at any rate, was the justification for compulsory RE offered by Nick Tate, Chief Executive of the SCAA, in 1996:

> Although many can accept that truth in moral matters can be independent of God, the loss of the religious base for morality has weakened its credibility. As the Archbishop of Canterbury has recently said, people ever since the Enlightenment 'have been living off the legacy of a deep, residual belief in God. But as people move further away from that, they find it more and more difficult to give a substantial basis for why they should be good'. This is one reason why religious education must continue to be a vital part of every child's curriculum.
>
> (Tate, 1996, para. 23)

The suggestion, then, was that by delivering an RE curriculum which 'reflects the fact that the religious traditions in Great Britain are in the main Christian', teachers could transmit a culture characterised by 'the legacy of a deep, residual belief in God', which would in turn furnish pupils with the motivation to be morally good.

The second of the developments which revived the connection between RE and moral education was a surge of interest in the notion of 'spiritual development'. The 1988 Act charged schools with promoting 'the spiritual, moral, cultural, mental and physical development of pupils'. Although an almost identical clause had been included in the 1944 Act, it was only after 1988 that policy-makers and educationists began to take a serious interest in what might be entailed by the obligation to promote pupils' spiritual development.

Two influential Discussion Papers on the topic were published in the early 1990s by the National Curriculum Council (1993) and the Office for Standards in Education

(1994). As attempts to clarify the meaning of spiritual development, both are woefully inadequate. John Beck observes that 'the discourse of the documents is vague, platitudinous, and tends to mix unjustified assertion with equivocation' (Beck, 1998, p. 62). The NCC paper identifies eight aspects of spiritual development: beliefs; a sense of awe, wonder and mystery; experiencing feelings of transcendence; search for meaning and purpose; self-knowledge; relationships; creativity; and feelings and emotions (NCC, 1993, pp. 3–4). It is not at all clear how these various aspects are supposed to be related to each other, or what reason there is for viewing them as aspects of a single developmental process.

Notwithstanding their conceptual shortcomings, two points emerge clearly from the documents. The first is that there is a large area of overlap between spiritual development and moral development. Spiritual development has to do with 'encounters with good and evil' and 'the search for values by which to live' (NCC, 1993, p. 3). It is concerned with 'how an individual acquires personal beliefs and values' and 'the basis for personal and social behaviour' (Ofsted, 1994, p. 8). In the NCC paper, the phrase 'spiritual and moral development' is frequently used 'in a manner calculated to suggest that the two constitute an indissolubly linked double entity – like Siamese twins' (Beck, 1998, p. 61).

The second point is that spiritual development involves engagement with religious traditions. As evidence that pupils have 'benefited from provision intended to promote spiritual development', the Ofsted paper advises inspectors to look for 'knowledge of the central beliefs, ideas and practices of major world religions and philosophies' and 'an understanding of how people have sought to explain the universe through various myths and stories, including religious, historical and scientific interpretations' (Ofsted, 1994, p. 9). The NCC paper states that pupils should respond to:

> the ultimate questions of life and death ... in the light of knowledge and understanding of the wisdom of others. Pupils should be challenged by hearing the claims to truth offered by people with a different religious or philosophical perspective on life.
>
> (NCC, 1993, p. 7)

Spiritual development, then, is tied to moral development on the one hand and the study of religion on the other. The idea seems to be that religious traditions are the most illuminating guides in the 'search for values by which to live'. Unsurprisingly, the documents agree that RE should therefore be expected 'to play a major part in promoting pupils' spiritual development' (Ofsted, 1994, p. 8).

The re-Christianising of the RE curriculum and the surge of interest in spiritual development combined to put the moral justification for compulsory RE firmly back on the agenda. If RE could not instil moral virtue by means of Christian nurture, it could perhaps do so either by inducting pupils into a Christian national culture, or by inviting them to draw upon the ancient moral wisdom stored up in the religions of the world. It is this latter notion of turning to religious traditions for moral guidance which underpins *AT2: Learning from religion* in the current SCAA model syllabuses and QCA non-statutory guidance.

So it is that policy documents today endorse two distinct justifications for compulsory RE: a social justification dating back to the late 1960s and based on the need to prepare pupils for life in a multicultural society; and a revised version of the moral justification which has been associated with compulsory RE since its introduction in 1944.

The moral justification

Having shed some light on the origins of the two contemporary justifications for compulsory RE, I turn now to consider their validity. I begin with the more controversial of the two, the contention that the study of religion is morally educative.

It is sometimes argued that it was a mistake to construe RE as a vehicle of moral education even when its aim was to induct pupils into the Christian faith, on the grounds that the supposed connection between religious beliefs and moral principles is illusory. There is, on this view, a logical gap between moral principles and religious beliefs such that the former cannot properly be derived from the latter. Statements of the form 'X is the will of God' neither entail nor justify statements of the form 'One ought to do X'. The fact that God wants something done does not make it the right thing to do. There may be a contingent correspondence between what God wants and what is right, but to establish such a correspondence one would need an independent method of validating moral principles.

The problem with this argument is that it depends on the more general claim that moral conclusions cannot be derived from factual premises of *any* kind. This claim was first advanced by Hume, who famously held that propositions 'connected with an *ought*, or an *ought not*' cannot be derived from those joined by 'the usual copulations of propositions, *is*, and *is not*' (Hume, 1740, p. 302). It was then taken up by Kant, who maintained that morality 'is of itself entirely *a priori* and independent of empirical principles' (Kant, 1788, p. 48). Kant admitted that *some* prescriptions are justified by empirical facts about desired outcomes and the means of securing them, but insisted that the difference between moral and non-moral prescriptions lies precisely in the fact that the former cannot be so justified.

Unfortunately, the consequence of divorcing morals from facts, which Hume embraced and Kant struggled to avoid, is that morality floats free of reason altogether. It becomes impossible to give rational grounds for moral judgements because there is nothing left to constitute such grounds.

The only plausible accounts of rational moral discourse are those which recognise that moral judgements depend for their truth or falsity on empirical facts about human beings and the consequences of their actions. Roughly, moral judgements are true when the actions they enjoin advance the cause of human flourishing, happiness or well-being. But as soon as it is acknowledged that morality rests on factual claims about the conditions under which human beings flourish, it becomes obvious that there can be no sharp division between the spheres of religion and morality. For claims about the conditions of human flourishing are the stock-in-trade of religion.

In fact, there are at least two ways in which religious beliefs might underpin moral judgements. First, it might be held that human flourishing consists, wholly or partly, in some form of relationship with God. The requirements of such a relationship will therefore be the determining ground of one's moral principles. Second, it might be held that God is a legitimate moral authority. Whatever one takes to be the conditions of human flourishing, one might judge that an omniscient God is in a better position than fallible men and women to determine the principles of action that are most effective in satisfying them. In either case, the believer will derive her moral principles directly, and properly, from her religious beliefs.

Religions, then, can and do equip believers with moral principles and reasons for abiding by them. When, from 1944 to the late 1960s, RE openly sought to induct pupils into the Christian faith, it made good sense to justify the subject in terms of its contribution to moral development. It may have been unrealistic to think that RE could succeed in its Christian mission, and there may be objections of educational principle to the enterprise of religious nurture, but there was nothing incoherent in the supposition that to pass on Christian faith is also to pass on a set of rationally justified moral principles.

At present, however, the aim of nurturing faith is explicitly eschewed in policy documents and Agreed Syllabuses for RE. The means by which RE is supposed to promote pupils' moral development is not Christian nurture, but the academic study of world religions. Pupils are not expected to adopt religious beliefs, but they are expected to draw guidance from moral teachings based on those beliefs. It is this expectation which seems to me to be quite incoherent. Not only is it a rather short-sighted educational policy to ask pupils to accept moral principles cut loose of their rational justification, but it is not clear what possible grounds we could offer them for doing so.

The point is that one only has reason to submit to the moral teachings of a religion if one holds that religion to be true. *If* one believes that there is a divine being whose moral judgements are significantly more reliable than ours, and who issues injunctions through the texts and institutions of a religious tradition, *then* it is reasonable to abide by those injunctions. But in the absence of such a belief, there is no reason at all to regard religious texts or institutions as morally authoritative. On the contrary, one has good reason to regard their moral teachings with suspicion, since they are predicated on beliefs one does not share.

I conclude that the moral justification for compulsory RE ought to be rejected outright. Although there are various ways in which religion may underpin morality, there is no logical connection between the academic study of religion and the adoption of moral principles.

But perhaps there are defenders of the morally educative function of RE who will be prepared to concede the logical ground and base their defence on purely practical considerations. Such people will agree that promoting moral development has no logical connection with advancing understanding of world religions, but point out that there is no reason why RE teachers cannot perform logically unconnected tasks. They will argue that moral education must be explicitly addressed somewhere on the curriculum, and that RE lessons are as good a place as any.

It is true that, until recently, none of the other subjects on the timetabled curriculum offered a natural home to moral education. In 2000, however, two new subjects were introduced into the National Curriculum: personal, social and health education (PSHE) and citizenship.[2] Both subjects are heavily weighted towards moral learning, the former in the personal domain, the latter in the civic. In PSHE pupils 'gain greater knowledge and understanding of spiritual, moral, social and cultural issues through increased moral reasoning, clarifying their opinions and attitudes in discussions with their peers and informed adults and considering the consequences of their decisions'. In citizenship they 'develop knowledge, skills and understanding through, for example, learning more about fairness, social justice, respect for democracy and diversity at school, local, national and global level, and through taking part in community activities'. It is therefore no longer the case that RE affords the only curriculum opportunity for explicit moral education.

Moreover, there are good reasons for *not* providing moral education under the curriculum heading of RE and alongside the study of religion. For this can hardly fail to create an association in pupils' minds between morality and religion. Since we know that religion will not play a significant part in the adult lives of the majority of pupils, such an association is patently undesirable. Most pupils will ultimately reject religion, in practice if not in principle, and the more closely they associate religion with morality, the more likely they are to throw out the moral baby with the religious bathwater. This is just the anxiety expressed 30 years ago by the authors of Schools Council Working Paper 36: 'Schools should beware of linking morals too closely with one religious viewpoint, since some pupils who abandon that viewpoint may be left with no considered basis for morality' (Schools Council Working Paper 36, 1971, p. 70).

This is not to cast aspersions on the many innovative and effective programmes of moral education currently devised and delivered in schools under the banner of RE. It is merely to point out that RE is not the ideal place for such programmes, particularly now that there are other curriculum subjects which have moral education as part of their remit.

The social justification

What of the other official justification for compulsory RE, the claim that citizens of multicultural Britain are significantly advantaged in their dealings with one another by an understanding of religious beliefs and practices? This claim is certainly not beset by the sort of philosophical difficulties attending the moral justification, and it is hard to deny that *some* familiarity with the major world religions is socially beneficial to members of multicultural societies. Nevertheless, I should like to advance two considerations which count against the adequacy of the social justification for compulsory RE.

First, religion in contemporary Britain is a far less significant social phenomenon than it once was. Membership of religious organisations and attendance at religious services continue to decline steadily. In 1980, only 19 per cent of the adult population belonged to a church, mosque, synagogue or temple; by 1990 the figure had fallen to 17.5 per cent. In 1999 only 7 per cent of British people were attending a weekly religious service.[3]

It is true that a rather higher percentage of the population reports some sort of belief in God; but the God they believe in appears to be quite irrelevant to their lives. Just as large numbers of people retain a nominal affiliation to the Church of England without ever setting foot inside a church, so they assent to the existence of God without ever being moved to worship or pray. The ineffectual character of this residual religious attachment is encapsulated in an interview extract from a research study carried out in the late 1960s:

> Do you believe in God?
> Yes.
> Do you believe in a God who acts upon the world?
> No, just the ordinary one.
>
> (Abercrombie *et al.*, 1970; cited in Davie, 1994, p. 1)

Whether belief in this 'ordinary God' qualifies as religious belief at all is open to question. It is tempting to suggest that it is not so much a conviction that there exists an all-powerful deity, 'the maker and preserver of all things', as a loose subscription to

Christian moral principles and a vague affirmation of British cultural heritage. Be that as it may, the import of the statistical evidence is clear: Britain is now a country in which the great majority of people neither belong to religious institutions nor engage in religious activities. It is therefore difficult to see why a detailed knowledge of religious traditions should confer a significant social benefit on pupils.

The second consideration is that there are many more kinds of difference between people than differences of religion. People differ from one another in gender and sexuality, class and culture, race and ethnicity, personality and intelligence. Is it not just as important to equip pupils with an understanding of these differences? If there is a social case for compulsory RE, there would seem to be an equally strong social case for compulsory gender studies, cultural studies, ethnology and psychology. And perhaps these subjects *should* be added to the school curriculum. Or perhaps the introduction of compulsory curriculum subjects simply to familiarise pupils with types of social difference would be taking a sledge hammer to crack a nut.

I contend that eleven years of compulsory RE is far in excess of what preparation for social diversity requires. There is indeed a social case for equipping pupils with a basic knowledge of the major world religions, just as there is for equipping them with a basic knowledge of the various other ways in which people differ from one another; but these tasks could readily be incorporated into a general programme of civic education. And since the introduction of citizenship into the National Curriculum, they have been so incorporated. The statutory programme of study for citizenship in secondary schools requires that 'pupils should be taught about the diversity of national, regional, religious and ethnic identities in the United Kingdom and the need for mutual respect and understanding'. At the primary level, where citizenship and PSHE are combined, 'pupils should be taught that differences and similarities between people arise from a number of factors, including cultural, ethnic, racial and religious diversity, gender and disability'. The level of religious understanding pupils need for effective participation in multicultural society is therefore both insufficient to justify a dedicated curriculum subject and satisfactorily catered for elsewhere in the curriculum.

An alternative rationale

I conclude that neither of the approved justifications for compulsory RE is adequate. I should like finally to propose an alternative rationale for the study of religion in schools which does, I think, justify its status as a compulsory curriculum subject.

The rationale is this: pupils should be given opportunities to consider religious propositions, and be equipped to make informed, rational judgements on their truth or falsity, on the grounds that some of those propositions *may in fact be true*. Religions make claims about the world with far-reaching implications for the way life should be lived; if there is a genuine possibility that some of those claims are true, it is arguable that pupils have a right to be made aware of them and provided with the wherewithal to evaluate them. I call this the possibility-of-truth case for compulsory RE.

That there is a possibility of some religious propositions being true is in one sense uncontentious, since it is clearly not the case that all religious propositions have been decisively falsified. Even the most resolute of unbelievers is normally content to say that religion is massively implausible rather than demonstrably false. But the case for compulsory RE plainly requires a stronger kind of possibility than this. It requires not merely that religion has yet to be conclusively disproved, but that it is, in some of its manifestations, rationally credible. The case turns on the claim that some religious propositions are sufficiently well supported by evidence and argument as to merit serious consideration by reasonable people.

This is, admittedly, a controversial verdict on the state of religious apologetics. But it is, I think, *less* controversial than any other verdict. Although there are those who find the arguments in support of religious propositions rationally compelling, and others to whom they seem entirely without force, neither of these verdicts is easy to justify. One suspects that they reflect a prior commitment to the truth or falsity of the propositions in question. The most even-handed view of the arguments is that they have some, but not decisive, rational force. They do not place one under a rational obligation to accept their conclusions, but they carry enough weight to make those conclusions rationally credible.

In addition to this claim about the plausibility of some religious propositions, the possibility-of-truth case for compulsory RE depends on two further claims. The first is that religious judgements *matter*, in the sense of making some practical difference to people's lives. The second is that making religious judgements rationally requires a facility with distinctive kinds of evidence and argument.

That religious judgements matter can hardly be disputed. A person's religion, or their decision to reject religion, is a fundamental determinant of their personal identity, of their picture of the world and the shape of their inner life. It has major implications, as we noted earlier, for their conception of human flourishing and for the moral authorities they are prepared to recognise. Religious believers typically characterise their religious judgements as the most important judgements they will ever make. Non-believers are more inclined to play down their importance, but only because they find religious truth-claims so implausible; they readily admit that, if there *were* an omnipotent deity with ultimate control over human destiny, his existence would demand a massive reorientation of thought and conduct.

That making religious judgements rationally requires a facility with distinctive kinds of evidence and argument is also difficult to deny. It is true that the kinds of evidence and argument adduced by the defenders and opponents of religion are not completely unlike those adduced in other fields: they would hardly be recognisable as evidence and argument if they were. But the domain of natural theology would appear to be at least as different in its evidential and argumentative forms from the domains of science, history and literary criticism as the latter are from each other. Consider, for example, the use made by religious apologists of such distinctive kinds of evidence as testimonies to miraculous events, private experiences of 'transcendence' or 'oneness', and 'marks of design' in the natural world. For distinctively theological forms of argument, think of the ontological argument that God is a being whose existence is included in his essence, or the axiological argument that God is a necessary postulate of moral reasoning, or the theodical argument that evil has its origin in the exercise of free will. These kinds of evidence and argument are markedly different from those involved in other types of theoretical inquiry.

These three claims, then, form the basis of the possibility-of-truth case for compulsory RE. Because some religious propositions are rationally credible, and it matters whether one judges them to be true or false, we have an obligation to ensure that children encounter them and learn how to evaluate them in school. Because the ability to evaluate religious propositions involves a facility with distinctive kinds of evidence and argument, imparting this ability requires a programme of study of the same order of magnitude as those we devote to other types of theoretical competence. This seems to me to constitute an adequate justification for separate and compulsory RE, at something like the currently recommended level of provision.[4]

It does not follow that the curriculum reformer has no work to do in this area. On the contrary, it is clear that, if compulsory RE were to be justified in these terms, syllabuses would need to look rather different from the way they do now. The focus would be on coming to understand the meaning of religious propositions and learning how to make informed, rational judgements on their truth or falsity. The emphasis would shift from *empathising* to *evaluating*, from trying to imagine what it is like to hold certain beliefs to asking what grounds there are for doing so. There would be much less attention to the differences between particular religions and much more to the differences between religion and irreligion. Pupils would be actively encouraged to question the religious beliefs they bring with them into the classroom, not so that they are better able to defend or rationalise them, but so that they are genuinely free to adopt whatever position on religious matters they judge to be best supported by the evidence.

Acknowledgements

My thanks to John White, whose trenchant criticisms of compulsory RE provoked much of the thinking contained in this chapter.

Notes

1 For an illuminating account of 'the end of the compulsory curriculum' in 1926 and 1945, see White, 1975.
2 PSHE and citizenship at Key Stages 1 and 2, and PSHE at Key Stages 3 and 4, are included in the revised National Curriculum as non-statutory guidelines; citizenship at Key Stages 3 and 4 became statutory in August 2002.
3 These figures are calculated from data reported in *Social Trends 30, 31 and 32* (HMSO, 2000–2002).
4 The SCAA model syllabuses (1994) recommend 36–45 hours of RE per year throughout the period of compulsory schooling.

References

Abercrombie, N., Baker, J., Brett, S. and Foster, J. (1970) 'Superstition and religion: the God of the Gaps', in Martin, D. and Hill, M. (eds) *A Sociological Yearbook of Religion in Britain*, 3, London: SCM.
Acland, R. (1963) *We Teach them Wrong*, London: Gollancz.
Acland, R. (1966) *Curriculum or Life*, London: Gollancz.
Beck, J. (1998) *Morality and Citizenship in Education*, London: Cassell.
Board of Education (1938) *Report of the Consultative Committee on Secondary Education (Spens Report)*, London: HMSO.
Board of Education (1943) *Educational Reconstruction*, London: HMSO.
Cox, E. (1966) *Changing Aims in Religious Education*, London: Routledge & Kegan Paul.
Cox, E. and Cairns, J. (1989) *Reforming Religious Education: the religious clauses of the 1988 Education Reform Act*, London: Kogan Page.
Davie, G. (1994) *Religion in Britain Since 1945*, Oxford: Blackwell.
DES (1967) *Children and their Primary Schools: a Report of the Central Advisory Council for Education (Plowden Report)*, London: HMSO.

Goldman, R.J. (1964) *Religious Thinking from Childhood to Adolescence*, London: Routledge & Kegan Paul.

Goldman, R.J. (1965) *Readiness for Religion*, London: Routledge & Kegan Paul.

HMSO (2000) *Social Trends 30*, London: HMSO.

HMSO (2001) *Social Trends 31*, London: HMSO.

HMSO (2002) *Social Trends 32*, London: HMSO.

Hume, D. (1740) *A Treatise of Human Nature*. Edition: Oxford: Oxford University Press, 2000.

Kant, I. (1788) *Critique of Practical Reason*. Edition: trans. Beck, L.W., New York: Macmillan, 1993.

King, U. (ed.) (1990) *Turning Points in Religious Studies: Essays in Honour of Geoffrey Parrinder*, Edinburgh: T&T Clark.

Loukes, H. (1961) *Teenage Religion*, London: SCM.

Loukes, H. (1965) *New Ground in Christian Education*, London: SCM.

NCC (1993) *Spiritual and Moral Development: a Discussion Paper*, London: National Curriculum Council.

Ofsted (1994) *Spiritual, Moral, Social and Cultural Development: a Discussion Paper*, London: Ofsted.

Niblett, W.R. (1966) 'The Religious Education clauses of the 1944 Act: aims, hopes and fulfilment', in Wedderspoon, A.G. (ed.) *Religious Education 1944–1964*, London: George Allen & Unwin.

Parsons, G. (1994) 'There and back again? Religion and the 1944 and 1988 Education Acts', in Parsons, G. (ed.) *The Growth of Religious Diversity: Britain from 1945*, London: Routledge.

QCA (2000) *Religious Education: Non-statutory Guidance on RE*, London: Qualifications and Curriculum Authority.

SCAA (1994) *Model Syllabuses for Religious Education*, London: School Curriculum and Assessment Authority.

Schools Council Working Paper 36 (1971) *Religious Education in Secondary Schools*, London: Evans/Methuen Educational.

Smart, N. (1968) *Secular Education and the Logic of Religion*, London: Faber.

Smith, J.W.D. (1969) *Religious Education in a Secular Setting*, London: SCM.

Tate, N. (1996) 'Education for adult life: spiritual and moral aspects of the curriculum'. Paper delivered to the SCAA Conference on Education for Adult Life, London: SCAA.

White, J. (1975) 'The end of the compulsory curriculum', in *The Curriculum: The Doris Lee Lectures 1975*, London: Institute of Education.

13 Science

Edgar Jenkins

Science teaching must take place in a laboratory; about that at least there is no controversy.

(Solomon, 1980: 13)

Science cannot produce ideas by which we could live. Even the greatest ideas of science are . . . inapplicable to the conduct of our lives.

(Schumacher, 1973: 71)

The level of global investment in school science education in the second half of the twentieth century was very high. Its consequences include a doubling of the number of scientists and engineers every 10–15 years since 1950 and the study of more science by a larger number of students than at any time in the past. In many education systems, including those of England and Wales, some form of science has become a compulsory component of the curriculum up to the statutory school leaving age, with the case for 'science for all' being justified by reference to personal 'scientific literacy' and to national economic prosperity. In brief, it is claimed that some knowledge of science is a *sine qua non* of effective citizenship in the modern world and that school laboratories and classrooms now constitute the front line in the battle for economic survival in an increasingly global market. To monitor the return on their investment, governments have also invested heavily in large-scale and expensive international comparisons of student achievement in science.[1] The results of these studies are seen as having significant policy implications, despite the limitations and, some would argue, fatally flawed nature of, the studies themselves (for a range of comments, see Shorrocks-Taylor and Jenkins, 2000).

In the case of England, the results of these international studies indicate that students' levels of achievement in science (although not in mathematics) compare quite favourably with those of students in the other countries participating in the projects. From this perspective therefore, school science education in England under the National Curriculum might be judged to lack any serious weaknesses. I want to argue, however, that such a judgement is less than complete.

If, for example, student choices are used as an indication of student enthusiasm for, and interest in, science, the signs are less than encouraging. In England, as in most industrialised countries, the physical sciences are not popular choices for more advanced study, whether at school or beyond, and there are difficulties in recruiting undergraduates to courses in physics and chemistry. Physics in particular continues to be an unattractive option for girls. Moreover, this lack of interest or enthusiasm seems not to relate to science in general but to school science in particular. It can be contrasted, for example, with the record levels of attendance at 'hands-on' science centres, museums and exploratories, with the flourishing market for popular science books and the increased attention given to science by the broadcast and print media.[2]

More fundamentally, I believe that such a judgement overlooks shortcomings in the way school science is currently conceived. Some of these shortcomings have their origin in the terms upon which science was first schooled in the second half of the nineteenth century. Others derive from a number of unsustainable claims made in the National Curriculum about the contribution that science can reasonably hope to make to the education of young people in the early years of the new millennium. In this chapter, I argue that if National Curriculum science is to appeal to the majority of students, i.e. to become less exclusive, these shortcomings must be acknowledged and addressed.

The construction of school science

By the time the Taunton Commission reported in 1868, the curriculum of the English grammar school had been the subject of controversy for well over half a century. By the early 1860s, however, the nature of the debate about the inclusion of scientific subjects in that curriculum had changed. The conflict of studies had begun to abate and the ardent protagonism of advocates like Herbert Spencer and the vigorous response of his opponents were gradually giving way to a greater perception of the complexity of the problems of curriculum reform and to a broader and more rational analysis of the issues involved. By 1867, when a committee of the British Association for the Advancement of Science gave attention to the 'best means for promoting scientific education in schools', it was possible to claim that there was 'already a *general* recognition of science as an element in liberal education' (BAAS, 1868, p. xxxix). What was needed was a clear rationale for school science that would command widespread support, point the way forward and command the necessary resources. The report of the BAAS committee in 1867 provided just such a rationale, identifying five grounds on which the case for teaching science in schools could rest. Science offered an excellent means of mental training and its inclusion in the school curriculum would lead to a more balanced education. Moreover, the 'methods and results of science' had 'so profoundly affected all the philosophical thought of the age', that an educated man (*sic*) was 'under a very great disadvantage' if he remained unacquainted with them. In addition, the study of science could give pleasure, and scientific knowledge affected materially 'the present position and future progress of civilisation', i.e. such knowledge was useful. This five-point rationale was accompanied by an important distinction drawn between scientific *information* and scientific *training*. While both of these aspects were recognised as important, the principal benefit of a scientific education was identified as the development of 'the scientific habit of mind'.

Despite the unqualified reference to schools in its title, the BAAS report was principally, and often explicitly, concerned with the position of science in the curriculum of the public schools. In the broader range of post-elementary institutions, the BAAS opined that the study of natural science was essential 'whether as a means of disciplining the mind or for providing knowledge useful for the purpose of life' (BAAS, 1870, p. xliii). However, such claims were not immediately transferable to other types of school, notably trade or elementary schools, designed to serve different social functions and in which science might be taught with different ends in view. As far as elementary schools were concerned, the passage of the 1870 Education Act led the Association to supplement the disciplinary and utilitarian arguments by reference to the importance of science in the 'technical education of the working classes' and 'the industrial progress of the country' (*Nature* quoted in Layton, 1981: 199). This supplementary argument reflected the desire of the BAAS to draw as widely as possible upon the reservoirs of talent upon which the future well-being of science itself depended. As an article in *Nature* noted, other countries had found it necessary to 'give a taste for science in elementary schools, so that the youth of the country may be induced to take advantage of the more advanced schools' (*Nature*, 1870: 149).

The introduction of a new subject into the school curriculum requires that attention be given to such matters as curriculum content, pedagogy, examinations and resources, including the supply of teachers. All these aspects of science teaching were addressed with some vigour during the last quarter of the nineteenth century, although with varying degrees of success. Textbooks were written, new teacher training courses developed, syllabuses constructed upon which students could be examined, and laboratories designed and built. By 1902, there were over a thousand school science teaching laboratories, most of which had been built since 1877 (Abney, 1904: 875) and grant-supported students destined for the teaching profession were rapidly becoming a major source of income for the expanding sector of higher education.

By 1904, the *Regulations* of the Board of Education required the new local authority secondary schools in receipt of grant aid to devote at least seven and a half hours each week to the teaching of science and mathematics, with the proviso that the teaching in science be both 'theoretical and practical'. Although this time requirement was abandoned three years later in favour of a ruling that the instruction provide for 'due continuity', the position of some form of science in the curriculum of publicly-maintained secondary schools was secure. The practice and rationale of science teaching in these schools followed that which had been pioneered in a few of the public schools and it was firmly cast in a pre-professional mode. The science taught was essentially a preparation for the further study of science in higher education. The methods used quickly came to be standardised and based upon organised courses of laboratory work, supported by practical demonstration. Generations of students learnt scientific laws and definitions by heart and were taught to present their laboratory work in paragraphs headed 'Test, Observation and Inference', or 'Title, Apparatus, Method, Observation, Results and Conclusion'.

In contrast, in the public elementary schools, which provided the formal education of the overwhelming majority of students, the position was much less satisfactory. Specialist facilities were virtually unknown and, for most of the students attending such schools, science took the form of 'Observation Lessons and Nature Study'. Much of the work done here was little more than thinly disguised religious or moral instruction which made no attempt to introduce students to the scientific study of the natural world (Jenkins and Swinnerton, 1998).

The legacy

Since science was first schooled in the second half of the nineteenth century, so much has changed, not least in the social and political context of education, that emphasising continuity with, rather than the differences from, the past might seem perverse. Yet, in the case of school science teaching such an emphasis is not difficult to justify. For example, the neglect of science in the education of young children, referred to above, was not remedied until the introduction of the National Curriculum in 1989, despite important curriculum initiatives by the Nuffield Foundation and the Schools Council in the 1960s and 1970s. More broadly, the terms upon which science was first accommodated within the curricula of both elementary and secondary schools have strongly influenced the practice and rationale of school science education throughout most of the twentieth century and key elements of that influence remain evident in the science that must now be taught to all students in maintained primary and secondary schools in England and Wales.

For most of the twentieth century, for example, school science curricula were strongly differentiated by social class. As with other subjects in the curricula of public and grammar schools, science was taught to those who had 'some profession in view'. Syllabuses and examinations were under the control of Examination Boards in which an academic, university influence was paramount, and the form and content of secondary school science courses reflected their role in preparing students for more advanced study in a related discipline. They presented science in its heroic Enlightenment mode, driven by intellectual curiosity without thought of possible applications. Its heroes were the likes of Newton, Faraday, Maxwell and Darwin, its philosophy was essentially positivist and its history triumphalist in tone.[3] The distinction between this kind of science education and that provided for the majority of students (where it was provided at all) reflects two different strands within the history of school science education. It was the elementary and modern schools, and not the grammar schools, that sought to meet the needs of their students by setting aside disciplinary structures and developing and teaching courses with such titles as gardening, nutrition, food science, hygiene, health education and human or social biology. It was these same schools that pioneered, with varying degrees of success, the teaching of science by topic or project and the development of schemes of work around such themes as the home or the environment. Where courses such as social or human biology were accommodated in grammar and public schools, they were usually taught either as options or restricted to so-called less able students. This social differentiation in the rationale of school science education reflected the different social functions ascribed to different types of school.[4]

With the advent of comprehensive schooling and the introduction of the National Curriculum, it was the discipline-based, academic tradition that prevailed, leaving a significant proportion of science teachers to complain that they were no longer able to meet the needs of many of their students (Donnelly and Jenkins, 1999a).

School science curricula have also been differentiated by gender and, like the distinctions derived from social class, such differentiation endured for most of the last century, with particular kinds of science courses being judged 'appropriate' for girls (e.g. botany, human biology, general science). The result was an impoverished science education for most girls for much of the twentieth century (Jenkins, 1979). Today, when the National Curriculum does not distinguish between boys and girls, attention has shifted, although not exclusively, to strategies for encouraging more girls to study the physical sciences beyond the compulsory school leaving age.

A partial and out-dated view of science

In the second half of the nineteenth century, secondary school science was defined in terms of chemistry and physics, or more precisely, aspects of these disciplines such as inorganic and organic chemistry, mechanics, properties of matter, heat, light and sound. Biology as an integrated discipline was a much later arrival, finding a place in the curricula of many secondary schools only in the 1950s and 1960s. There were several reasons for this. They include the later maturity of biology as a scientific discipline, the relationship between school biology and the requirements for entry into medical schools, and, significantly, the belief that biology did not lend itself to quantitative work in the school laboratory (Jenkins, 1979). Had science been schooled a generation earlier, geology would have had a particularly strong claim for inclusion in the curriculum. It, together with a number of other scientific disciplines, continues to receive little or no attention in school science courses which, for the most part, continue to be dominated by concepts and techniques drawn from physics, chemistry and biology.[5] Numerous attempts at integration, known by a variety of umbrella titles such as general science or integrated science, have done little to challenge this domination, despite some acknowledgement of the educational claims of earth, space or environmental science. In addition, few of these attempts at integration have met with long-term success and the adoption of other significant initiatives, notably in the earth sciences, has also been modest. Given this, the specification of *science*, rather than physics, chemistry and biology, as the component of the National Curriculum is of particular significance. It reflects more than a response to an overcrowded timetable. It is an attempt to construct by legislative means a subject from disciplines that have different curriculum histories and pedagogical traditions, and one that, at secondary level, will be taught for the foreseeable future by graduates whose scientific expertise lies, not in science, but in one of its more specialised fields.[6]

In limiting attention to the traditional basic sciences of physics, chemistry and biology,[7] the National Curriculum fails to introduce students to the roles that science has come to play in the modern world.[8] Today, basic or fundamental science is a relatively small part of the research endeavour and the notion that science stands pure and separate from all involvement with society has largely disappeared. Much scientific research is strategic, with priority attached to establishing a body of knowledge out of which specific products and processes may emerge in due course. Science has become 'worldly' in every sense of the word, with some commentators describing the commercialisation and industrialisation of science as a new system of knowledge production (Gibbons *et al.*, 1994). That system is characterised by the emergence of *ad hoc* and more fluid institutional structures, the generation of knowledge in the context of use and the validation of such knowledge by criteria other than peer review. Another important aspect of scientific research in the modern world relates to the work of regulatory and legislative agencies, standard setting organisations and expert commissions, a field sometimes referred to as mandated science (Levy, 1989). Mandated science is thus often intimately related to the notion of risk assessment, an undertaking that brings together the uncertainty and complexity of the real world in a way that National Curriculum science has largely ignored. As far as students are concerned, it is in this context of uncertainty and complexity that they most frequently encounter science-related issues outside school. What is the risk of contracting lung cancer from passive smoking and how is such risk assessed? How safe is it to live under high voltage power lines, to use the contraceptive pill or to use a drug like cannabis? What is a safe level of alcohol intake? At what point can a food additive be declared unsafe? What are the risks and benefits associated with genetically modified organisms? What does it mean to say that British beef is safe to eat? Some of these examples are of particular interest since there are differences in medical, scientific and legal opinion within or between different countries or communities.

Addressing questions of this kind might be thought central to the notion of citizenship in the modern world, a notion to which the National Curriculum attaches sufficient importance to make it a compulsory subject. Attempts to link the science curriculum with citizenship have a long history. They include the general science movement, the radical socialist ideas of Hogben, Bernal and Haldane, the science, technology and society (STS) movement and a range of courses concerned with the 'public understanding of science'. Such initiatives have, at best, achieved only short-term or marginal changes in mainstream secondary school science education, and some recent developments (e.g. NEAB, 1998) have been directed at older students to whom the constraints of the National Curriculum do not apply. No doubt this lack of success owes much to the allegiance of many secondary school science teachers to their disciplines but there has also been a failure of the professional, and especially the academic, scientific community to acknowledge the diverse roles that science plays in the modern world and to address the implications of this diversity for science for all.

Practical work in the laboratory

Perhaps the most enduring contemporary legacy of the manner in which science was schooled in the nineteenth century is the emphasis in the National Curriculum upon practical work in the school laboratory. As noted above, the 1867 BAAS report was careful to distinguish scientific information from scientific training. The latter was universally assumed to require some sort of investigative work undertaken by students in a specialised teaching laboratory. In the early years of the twentieth century, that requirement was given substance in the teaching of scientific method, promoted with great vigour, but only limited success, by Henry Edward Armstrong (Armstrong, 1903; Brock, 1973). By the mid-twentieth century, the emphasis in a variety of initiatives designed to reform science teaching was on helping students to 'see the nature of science by engaging in scientific activity' (Pimentel, 1960: 1) and on getting students 'to think in the way practising scientists do' (Halliwell, 1996: 242). The 1980s saw the advent of science curriculum projects with titles like *Process Science* (Screen, 1986) and *Science in Process* (ILEA, 1987), the distinction implied in the title between 'process' and 'content' mirroring that drawn, with the aid of different terminology, in the 1867 BAAS report. In 1985, the publication of a statement of official policy for school science advised that 'Each of us needs to be able to bring a scientific approach to bear on the practical, social, economic and political issues of modern life' (DES, 1985: para. 7), although it was careful to avoid referring explicitly to scientific method. Most recently, 'Scientific enquiry'/Sc1 has been codified as the first of the four Attainment Targets that comprise the science component of the National Curriculum in England, the remaining three being essentially concerned with content.

Teachers in both primary and secondary schools are now required to teach their students a range of 'investigative skills' and to use these to obtain, present, consider and evaluate evidence in contexts taken from the remaining three Attainment Targets of the science National Curriculum. They are also required to assess their students' competence at 'Scientific enquiry', i.e. to judge which of the eight levels of description best fits each student's performance.[9] In this way, Sc1 reduces the practical, technical, affective, social, imaginative and creative activity of 'doing science' to terms that allow students' work to be mapped against descriptions of levels of attainment that have no empirical basis, however logical they may seem as a basis for determining progression. In the case of primary schools, it has also led to equating scientific experimentation with the somewhat strange notion of the 'fair test'. It is worth emphasising that, unlike the remaining three Attainment Targets that are well-grounded in secondary school science teachers' professional practice, Sc1 is essentially a creature of the National Curriculum.

The emphasis upon laboratory activity within secondary school science teaching under the National Curriculum raises a number of problems and questions. Most of these have been explored in a voluminous and, for the most part, highly critical literature that addresses categories on the boundaries of pedagogy, assessment and the philosophy of science (e.g. Woolnough, 1991; Hodson, 1993; Wellington, 1998). Among the questions relevant to the present chapter are the following: to what extent does the 'Scientific enquiry' mandated by the National Curriculum reflect the kind of enquiry undertaken by research scientists and to what extent should it attempt to do so? To what extent are students led to believe that the experiments they undertake, the results they obtain and the 'conclusions' that they draw, engage them in something that might be called scientific practice, and what are the implications of such a belief? Much scholarly work in the sociology, history and philosophy of science published in the last quarter of a century suggests that the neat classical picture of deductions being made from theories and then tested by observation and experiment rarely corresponds to the way in which scientific research is conducted. Moreover, 'only a minority of scientists have received instruction in scientific methodology, and those that have seem no better off' (Medawar, 1982: 80).

How then might the emphasis on scientific enquiry in the National Curriculum be justified? The answer perhaps lies in the claim, made in the National Strategy for teaching science in years 7, 8 and 9, that 'Scientific enquiry has a central place in [school] science ... because the skills and processes of scientific enquiry are useful in many everyday applications' (DfES, 2002: 11). The evidence, however, seems to be that such 'skills and processes' are likely to be useful only when addressing scientific problems. 'Grand strategies of discovery do not seem to be transferable across disciplines' (Ausubel, 1964: 298) and

> when we investigate learning transfer directly across situations, the results are constantly negative, whether analysing performance levels, procedures or errors.[10]
>
> (Lave, 1988: 68)

Perhaps, therefore, justification should be sought elsewhere, e.g. in the view that engaging students in scientific enquiry helps them to learn important scientific concepts and theories. Again the evidence is hardly supportive. Such concepts and theories do not acquire meaning through experience and, as abstractions, they bear a complex relationship to any observations and conclusions that students might make when their teachers engage them in scientific enquiry. There is also evidence that some students are confused by the outcomes of the practical investigations they are required to undertake and sometimes come to scientifically erroneous conclusions that they see as supported firmly by the 'evidence' they have gathered (Donnelly *et al.*, 1996: 177).

Enough has perhaps been written above to indicate that the rationale invoked to support practical work undertaken by students in the school laboratory encompasses a confused mixture of objectives that embrace the cognitive, affective and motor domains and that questions can be asked about the extent to which any of these objectives can be realised. Woolnough's overall judgement is that,

> Much practical work is ineffective, unscientific and a positive deterrent for many students to continue with their science. It is ineffective in helping students to understand the concepts and theories of science. It is unscientific in that it is quite unlike real scientific activity. And it is boring and time-wasting for many students who find it unnecessary and unstimulating.
>
> (Woolnough, 1995: 3)

Much, however, is not all, and there is nothing in Woolnough's judgement to suggest that all practical work conducted by students in their science lessons must be open to the criticisms that he identifies. Other types of practical activity are readily identifiable (e.g. role play, drama, simulation, using the Internet and multimedia) but they have made little headway against a belief, underpinned by the National Curriculum, that conducting 'experiments' at the laboratory bench (or 'fair tests' in the primary classroom) is really what matters in school science education. The following comment from a teacher would command widespread support from others in the science teaching profession and beyond.

> It's what science is all about really . . . getting on with some experiments. Science is a practical subject . . . you know, end of story, I think.
>
> (quoted in Donnelly, 1995: 97)

As a result, what is perceived as unlikely to lend itself to experimental work of this kind is rarely welcomed by science teachers, and a wide range of non-laboratory-based pedagogies do not receive the attention they deserve,[11] a neglect that, paradoxically, may be sustained, if not encouraged, by the status of science as a compulsory subject within the National Curriculum up to the age of 16.

Science and technology

School science has traditionally been concerned with pure, rather than applied, science, despite numerous attempts to accommodate the latter within the curriculum. During the twentieth century, these attempts include the 'alternative road' of the secondary technical schools, programmes such as the Schools Council Project in Technology, the Technical and Vocational Education Initiative (TVEI) and the establishment of technology as a component of the National Curriculum (McCulloch *et al.*, 1985; McCulloch, 1989).[12] As far as science teaching is concerned, technological artefacts have been used to confirm the power and usefulness of scientific ideas or called in aid of the principal task of introducing and teaching scientific principles.

While such an approach may serve to increase the motivation of some students, attempts to teach science through its technological applications have, in general, met with little success. Students are unlikely to be interested in a scientific idea if they are not also interested in the application presented to illustrate it. Those who are bored by an everyday application of a potentiometer, lens or thermostat are not likely to be attracted by the underlying physics, although there are always some students who will find the latter more appealing than the former. There is also the risk that students' understanding may remain anchored in the particulars of a technological artefact or system to the neglect of a grasp of the underlying theoretical principles.

Today, technology occupies a place in its own right in the National Curriculum, although defining the subject for pedagogical purposes has been fraught with difficulty (Layton, 1995). However, according to that curriculum, it is through science that pupils are to be led to 'understand how major scientific ideas contribute to techno-logical change – impacting on industry, business and medicine and improving quality of life' (DfEE/QCA, 1999: 15). This is an ambitious goal, the realisation of which requires an understanding of the highly complex relationships between science, technology and commerce. Those relationships have been much studied by scholars in the last quarter of a century or so (e.g. Staudenmaier, 1985), but few, if any, science teachers are likely to possess the insights necessary to do more than pay lip service to this aspect of the National Curriculum.

School science is essentially concerned with knowledge of the material world, whereas technology and commerce are concerned with practical action in what might be called the 'made world'. The relationship between these two worlds cannot be understood in terms of technology as the straightforward application of science. The relationship is symbiotic, interactive and marked by equality rather than by the sub-servience of technology to science that the National Curriculum is at some risk of implying. In addition, scientific concepts that describe an idealised world cannot simply be applied to the world of real materials within which atoms are not point masses and gases and other materials do not behave in an ideal way. Whereas in science, data are related to general and abstract theories, technological data are determined by, and related to, the specifics of technological practice. As Staudenmaier has shown, 'before scientific concepts can contribute to technological knowledge, they must be appropri-ated and restructured according to the specific demands of the design problem at hand' (Staudenmaier, 1985: 104). Aitken has summed up the central issue in the following way.

> Information that is generated within one system exists in a particular coded form, recognisable by and useful to participants in that system. If it is to be transferred from one system to another – say from science to technology... – it has to be translated into a different code, converted into a form that makes sense in a world of different values.
>
> (Aitken, 1985: 18–19)

To offer two crude illustrations, knowledge of electromagnetic theory is not sufficient to build a motor or construct a power generating system, and the building of a jet engine requires more than an understanding of thermodynamics and Newton's laws. This 'more' is not simply something that has to be added on. It is a distinctive and creative activity, accommodating not only scientific principles but also problematic data, engin-eering theory, commercial, economic and perhaps political considerations, and a range of technical skills. It is also likely to involve the generation of unique, context-bound technological concepts.[13] The task facing science teachers wishing to help students understand how major scientific ideas contribute to technological change is, therefore, particularly demanding.

The notion that scientific knowledge can rarely be 'applied' in any straightforward manner to the solution of technological problems has implications beyond technology itself, not least for GCSE courses in applied science. However, it has a direct bearing on the requirement of the National Curriculum that school *science* help students 'learn to discuss science-based issues that may affect their own lives, the direction of society and the future of the world' (DfEE/QCA, 1999: 15). Such a requirement can be seriously misleading. Science in the everyday world usually turns out to be much less certain and much more contingent than school science, and many other factors usually come into play when science-based issues are being discussed. As with technology (and problem-solving more generally), these factors are not additional but intrinsic to the issue under discussion and there is no unique solution to the problems involved. Establishing a basis for wise action or decision-making in relation to science-based issues in the real world thus requires a wider knowledge base than that provided by the science component of the National Curriculum. Such action or decision-making does not recognise the boundaries between the natural sciences or between these and the social sciences and other forms of knowledge and understanding. It does not sit comfortably with a subject-based curriculum. It may embrace the authority, or lack of it, to be attached to the source of any data, together with a range of uncontrolled, contingent or uncertain elements that characterise everyday life in the real world but which are rigorously excluded in the laboratory. It also requires something more comprehensive and more complex than the 'scientific thinking' prescribed by the National Curriculum.

Towards an inclusive science education

The preceding paragraphs have presented a number of criticisms of the current version of the National Curriculum. I have suggested that it is too much a prisoner of its past, in its failure to reflect the range and diversity of science in the modern world, its uncritical attachment to practical procedures in the laboratory, its over-valorising of scientific thinking, and the naïvety of its assumptions about the role that scientific knowledge can realistically play in problem-solving in the world outside the classroom or laboratory.

Nonetheless, compulsory science for all is an enormous opportunity and it is one that should be seized and turned to greater educational advantage than is presently the case. What might be a way forward? For some, it lies in making school science courses more relevant by developing programmes of science, technology and society education. Important though such programmes might be, they amount to a redefinition and reclassification of school science that does damage to what Donnelly has referred to its ontic characteristics.[14] He identifies these as the elimination of the personal, a demarcation from ethics and the absence of reflexivity (Donnelly, 2002: 135–141). From this perspective, the natural sciences offer no place for such characteristics as judgement, purpose or personality *in their account of the material world*. The goal of the natural sciences is an understanding of that world that is mind-invariant, or to use an unfashionable word, objective. Such understanding does not accommodate ethical or moral considerations, although it is self-evidently the case that science engages with ethical issues and that ethical concerns enter into scientific research.

Science, technology and society (STS) programmes typically invite students to engage with political, moral and ethical judgements. These judgements are irreducibly human in character and a significant degree of engagement with them in the context of school science education requires the transformation of the latter into an education *about* science and, more particularly, into an introduction to its history, sociology and politics. For some commentators, this would represent a long overdue development and one that is likely to represent a more successful strategy for relating science to citizenship, especially when the latter is understood in terms of social responsibility (Cross and Price, 1992) or socio-political action (Roth and Désautels, 2002).[15] For these commentators, scientific literacy is essentially a social rather than a scientific issue and it is too complex to be left in the hands of scientists or science educators. However, school science has been, and remains, resistant to a change of this kind which 'identifies life in society itself', rather than science, 'as the starting point for determining the scientific knowledge that should be given priority in the school science curriculum' (Fensham, 2002).

The central task of a compulsory school science education for all is surely to introduce students to the key features of how scientists understand the material world. It is not to train students to think like scientists, save when they are addressing scientific problems, nor is it primarily to engage them in socio-political issues that have a scientific dimension. Such engagement is better undertaken by (or in conjunction with) others whose training and expertise fits them to handle ethical, moral and political controversy, and might be better accommodated within lessons or activities devoted to citizenship or personal and social education. More fundamentally, such engagement again exposes and challenges the limitations of a subject-based curriculum.

Given this central task, the next step is to identify the key features and develop appropriate ways of helping students to understand them. As a minimum, the former requires a broader understanding of what constitutes science in the early years of the twenty-first century. The latter demands greater attention to, and illustration of, the fundamental principles, the 'big ideas', of science and less to its minutiae. It also requires a willingness to accommodate a range of teaching strategies and techniques that do not depend on the laboratory and are not directed towards the acquisition of practical techniques that few students will ever use. Practical investigation has an important role in science teaching but the many claims made for laboratory work need to be confronted with greater honesty than hitherto. A laboratory is not necessary to help students explore such issues as correlation, cause and risk that are fundamental to much of twenty-first century science. As for helping students to understand how scientific ideas contribute to technological development, that is a task best left to the technology component of the National Curriculum where the designing and making of technological artefacts will inevitably highlight the complex relationships between scientific knowledge and practical action to which reference was made above.

Much of what is written above runs contrary to contemporary attempts to broaden school science curricula by including attention to 'STS' issues, highlighting the role of science in technological development or by developing a 'core plus options' model as in the 'Science for the 21st Century' project currently under development.[16] The argument presented in this chapter is a reassertion of the role of the modern sciences in education as an exciting intellectual challenge and adventure and for the development of innovative pedagogies to present them as such.

Notes

1 Notable examples are the Third International Mathematics and Science Study (TIMSS) and the OECD Programme for International Student Assessment (PISA).

2 From a different perspective, it is interesting to note that Britain won 11 Nobel prizes in science and medicine in the 1960s, 13 in the 1970s, four in the 1980s and two in the 1990s. There is unlikely to be a single explanation for this apparent decline, the origins of which must pre-date the introduction of the National Curriculum (*The Economist*, 16 November, 2002, p. 30).

3 Much might be said to defend this picture. Scientific imagination is all too easily undervalued, especially by those who appear to take some pride in neither understanding nor exercising it, and science has much to be triumphant about. In addition, rejecting positivist ideas in the absence of any alternative and well-confirmed picture of how science 'works' does not come without danger.

4 As late as the 1960s, separate science curriculum projects were developed for different groups of students, e.g. Nuffield O- and A-level sciences and the topic based 'Secondary Science' programme. The curriculum differentiation was reinforced by the introduction of examinations leading to the Certificate of Secondary Education (CSE) for which a bewildering variety of non-academic science-based syllabuses was developed.

5 Early versions of the National Curriculum included some topics drawn from earth science. Such inclusion met with strong opposition from the science teaching profession, especially from chemistry teachers. The opposition was based on the reduced time available for teaching chemistry, lack of knowledge of the content to be taught and, significantly, a claim that the topics did not lend themselves to experimental work in the laboratory.

6 Science departments within schools have deployed their specialist staff in a variety of ways in response to this legislative imposition. Most strive to retain specialist teaching at Key Stage 4 and a minority continue to 'deliver' the science component of the National Curriculum by providing separate courses in physics, chemistry and biology (Donnelly and Jenkins, 1999b).

7 In the language of the National Curriculum, these are represented respectively by Physical processes, Materials and their properties, and Life processes and living things.

8 A rather different criticism of the scope of school science, although a somewhat more contentious one, is that it ignores the so-called system sciences. A report of the Earth System Sciences Committee (ESSC) of the National Aeronautics and Space Administration (NASA) in the USA in the late 1980s described 'earth system science' as characterised by treating 'the Earth as an integrated system of interacting components whose study must transcend disciplinary boundaries' (Meyer, 2002: preface). A similar but rather broader criticism has been made by the distinguished American science educator, Paul deHart Hurd. He writes of the 'hundreds of new sciences [that] have been created that are unrepresented in school science curricula', adding that many of these 'focus on human welfare and on social and economic progress' (Hurd, 1998: epilogue).

9 The origins of the specification for assessing students' performance in the first Attainment Target, Sc1, and its predecessors in earlier versions of the National Curriculum are complex. However, it seems clear that the work of the Assessment of Performance Unit (APU) was of seminal importance. It helped to sustain and operationalise the notion of process in the science curriculum, although not necessarily under this name. It was also critically influential in the treatment of laboratory work within the National Curriculum for science (see Donnelly and Jenkins, 2001, especially Ch. 5).

10 The views of Ausubel and Lave are essentially the same as those expressed by the British Association for the Advancement of Science as long ago as 1917 when it judged the educational merits of teaching science method as an objective: 'The scientific method is an abstraction which does not exist apart from its concrete embodiments' (BAAS, 1917: 134).

11 A graduate student teacher of science, gaining experience in a school in which all lessons lasted for 75 minutes, once asked me what teachers of history or English did in lessons of this duration since, unlike him, 'they didn't have laboratories to teach in'.

12 Note also the current introduction of GCSE courses in 'Applied Science'.

13 Layton offers a range of examples, such as 'disability glare' and 'discomfort glare' which do not feature in school textbooks on light (Layton, 1993: 145).

14 In the National Curriculum, the emphasis is almost entirely upon techniques, methods and

validity, i.e. upon the epistemological characteristics of science. The enduring commitment to work in the laboratory serves to distinguish school science from the hermeneutic disciplines, and the contrast with a subject such as history, where discussion of what constitutes historical knowledge is of central concern, is marked.

15 There is also evidence that many students would welcome a shift of the school science curriculum in this direction. See, for example, Campbell, 2002.

16 Following an initiative by the University of York Science Education Group, QCA and the Examination Board, OCR, are developing a Double Award GCSE course, 'Science for the 21st Century', to be piloted in schools from September 2003.

References

Abney, W. de W. (1904) Presidential Address to Section L, *Report of the British Association for the Advancement of Science 1903*, London: Murray.

Aitken, H.G.J. (1985) *Syntony and Spark. The Origins of Radio*, Princeton, NJ: Princeton University Press.

Armstrong, H.E. (1903) *The Teaching of Scientific Method and Other Papers on Education*, London: Macmillan.

Ausubel, D.P. (1964) 'Some psychological and educational limitations of learning by discovery', *The Arithmetic Teacher*, II (5).

BAAS (1868) *Report of the Thirty-Seventh Annual Meeting, Dundee 1867*, London: Murray.

BAAS (1870) *Report of the (Exeter) Meeting, 1869*, London: Murray.

BAAS (1917) *Report*, London: Murray.

Brock, W.H. (ed.) (1973) *H.E. Armstrong and the Teaching of Science 1880–1930*, Cambridge: Cambridge University Press.

Campbell, P. (2002) 'The Citizenship Agenda', *Education in Science*, 200: 17.

Cross, R.T. and Price, R.F. (1992) *Teaching Science for Social Responsibility*, Sydney: St. Louis Press.

DES (1985) *Science 5–16: A Statement of Policy*, London: HMSO.

DfEE/QCA (1999) *Science: The National Curriculum for England*, London: DfEE/QCA.

DfES (2002) *Key Stage 3 National Strategy, Framework for teaching science: Years, 7, 8 and 9*, London: DfES.

Donnelly, J.F. (1995) 'Curriculum development in science: the lessons of Sc1', *School Science Review*, 76(277): 95–103

Donnelly, J.F. (2002) Instrumentality. Hermeneutics and the Place of Science in the School Curriculum, *Science and Education*, 11(3): 135–153.

Donnelly, J.F., Buchan, A., Jenkins, E.W., Laws, P. and Welford, A.G. (1996) *Investigations by Order. Policy, Curriculum and Science Teachers' Work under the Education Reform Act*, Nafferton: Studies in Education.

Donnelly, J.F. and Jenkins, E.W. (1999a) *Science Teaching in Secondary Schools under the National Curriculum*, Leeds: Centre for Studies in Science in Mathematics Education, University of Leeds.

Donnelly, J.F. and Jenkins, E.W. (1999b) *The Expertise and Deployment of Science Teachers at Key Stage 4*, Leeds: Centre for Studies in Science and Mathematics Education, University of Leeds.

Donnelly, J.F. and Jenkins, E.W. (2001) *Science Education: Policy, Professionalism and Change*, London: Paul Chapman.

Fensham, P.J. (2002) 'De nouveaux guides pour l'alphabétisation scientifique', *Canadian Journal of Science, Mathematics and Technology Education*, 2(2): 33–49.

Gibbons, M., Limoges, C., Nowotny, H., Schwartzman, S., Scott, P. and Trow, M. (1994) *The New Production of Knowledge. The Dynamics of Science and Research in Contemporary Societies*, London: Sage.

Halliwell, H.F. (1966) 'Aims and action in the classroom', *Education in Chemistry*, 3: 5.

Hodson, D. (1993) 'Rethinking old ways: towards a more critical approach to practical work in school science', *Studies in Science Education*, 22: 85–142.

Hurd, P. de H. (1998) *Inventing Science Education for the New Millennium*, New York: Teachers College Press.

ILEA (1987) *Science in Process*, London: Heinemann.

Jenkins, E.W. (1979) *From Armstrong to Nuffield: Studies in Twentieth Century School Science Education*, London: Murray.

Jenkins, E.W. and Swinnerton, B.J. (1998) *Junior School Science Education in England and Wales since 1900: From Steps to Stages*, London: Woburn Press.

Lave, J. (1988) *Cognition in Practice*, New York: Cambridge University Press.

Layton, D. (1981) 'The schooling of science in England 1845–1939', in Macleod, R. and Collins, P. (eds) *The Parliament of Science: The British Association for the Advancement of Science 1831–1981*, London: Northwood Science Reviews.

Layton, D. (1993) 'Science education and praxis: the relationship of school science to practical action', in Jenkins, E.W. (ed.) *School Science and Technology: Some Issues and Perspectives*, Leeds: Centre for Studies in Science and Mathematics Education, University of Leeds.

Layton, D. (1995) 'Constructing and reconstructing school technology in England and Wales', in Jenkins, E.W. (ed.) *Studies in the History of Education: Essays Presented to Peter Gosden*, Leeds: Leeds University Press.

Levy, E. (1989) 'Judgement and policy: the two-step in mandated science and technology', in Durbin, P.T. (ed.) *Philosophy of Technology: Practical, Historical and Other Dimensions*, Dordrecht: Kluwer.

McCulloch, G., Jenkins, E.W. and Layton, D. (1985) *Technological Revolution? The Politics of School Science and Technology in England and Wales since 1945*, London: Falmer Press.

McCulloch, G. (1989) *The Secondary Technical School: A Usable Past?*, London: Falmer Press.

Medawar, P. (1982) 'Induction and intuition in scientific thought', in Medawar, P. (ed.) *Pluto's Republic*, Oxford: Oxford University Press.

Meyer, V.J. (ed.) (2002) *Global Science Literacy*, Dordrecht: Kluwer.

Nature (1870) 1: 149.

NEAB (1998) *Science for Public Understanding*, Manchester: Northern Examinations and Assessment Board.

Pimentel, G.C. (ed.) (1960) *Chemistry: An Experimental Science*, San Francisco: Freeman.

Roth, W.-M. and Desautels, J. (eds) (2002) *Science Education as/for Sociopolitical Action*, New York: Peter Lang.

Schumacher, E.F. (1973) *Small is Beautiful: The Study of Economics as if People Mattered*, London: Abacus.

Screen, P. (1986) *Warwick Process Science*, Southampton: Ashford Press.

Shorrocks-Taylor, D. and Jenkins, E.W. (eds) (2000) *Learning from Others. International Comparisons in Education*, Dordrecht: Kluwer.

Solomon, J. (1980) *Teaching Children in the Laboratory*, London: Croom Helm.

Staudenmaier, J.M. (1985) *Technology's Storytellers. Reweaving the Human Fabric*, Cambridge, MA: Society for the History of Technology, MIT Press.

Wellington, J.J. (ed.) (1998) *Practical Work in School Science: Which Way Now?*, London: Routledge.

Woolnough, B.E. (ed.) (1991) *Practical Science. The Role and Reality of Practical Work in School Science*, Milton Keynes: Open University Press.

Woolnough, B.E. (1995) 'Switching students onto science', *British Council Science Education Newsletter*, British Council: London.

14 Conclusion

John White

Chapters 3 to 13 support the suggestion in Chapter 1 of a gap between the new overall aims and the curriculum specifics of many school subjects. If the aims are to be taken seriously, filling the gap must be central to educational policy.

One way of looking at things is this. The new aims put the child and the child's needs as person and as citizen at the heart of schooling. Since 1988 there has been a lot of talk about the school curriculum as an 'entitlement curriculum'. I go along with this: pupils now have rights to a certain kind of schooling. But what is the entitlement *to*? Fundamentally, it is to a curriculum which delivers the overall aims (see also the quotation from Edwards and Kelly on p. 85). As pointed out in Chapter 2, there is more work to be done in shaping these up. Even so, they are a good enough touchstone of whether children are getting the curriculum they deserve.

The grip of custom

Earlier chapters have thrown light on how the actual curriculum has come about. We have seen the tenacity of custom. Contribution after contribution has borne out Raymond Williams' (1965) claim (see p. 45 above) that 'the fact about our present curriculum is that it was essentially created by the nineteenth century'. New patterns have been overlaid on old, but the old show through. We have seen this in the resilience of the 'Victorian' view of history as moral training based on the lives of national heroes (p. 89); in the statement that 'we are still delivering art curricula in our schools predicated largely upon procedures and practices that reach back to the nineteenth century' (p. 31); in the line traceable back from the current dominance of class teaching in music to the nineteenth century desire to improve the quality of choral singing in church (p. 129); and in the fact that methods of teaching science 'based on organised courses of laboratory work, supported by practical demonstration' had crystallised by as early as 1900 into standardised forms familiar today (p. 167).

Following custom is not necessarily a bad thing, of course, as is shown by Bethan Marshall's attachment to the liberal arts and critical dissent traditions which have influenced contemporary English teaching. But life beyond the school gates in the twenty first century is a universe away from what it was in the nineteenth. Curricular patterns which may well have made some kind of sense a century and more ago have now hardened into intra-school activities which have lost touch with the subject as practised in the world outside. Physics, chemistry and biology defined the science curriculum in the late 1800s, but 'today, basic or fundamental science is a relatively small part of the research endeavour' (p. 169). 'School art', based on collections of objects set up in the art room, and with its 'long-running all-time favourite, the sliced pepper' (p. 31), is a long way from the excitements and extravagances of the world of the visual arts. 'Mathematical tasks outside school are always very extended, taking hours, weeks or even years to complete and cannot be represented by the short questions which are the diet of school mathematics lessons' (p. 107). 'Music . . . has a particularly strong out-of-school presence in the lives of students' (p. 128); yet 'music in the classroom often becomes a closed system, lacking in authenticity and concerned with the production of what Malcolm Ross (1995) calls 'pseudo-music' (p. 133).

Recent influences

The coming of the National Curriculum in 1988 did little to disturb these customary patterns. On the contrary, in making what was very close to the 1904 Secondary (grammar) curriculum framework the model, it reinforced them. Things could have been different. As David Lambert points out, geography might well have been absent from the National Curriculum had it not been for 'highly successful lobbying activities by the Geographical Association' (p. 77). After 1988 politicians and the media did their bit towards steering the specifics of the curriculum along traditional paths. The House of Lords ensured in 1988 that RE lessons 'shall reflect the fact that the religious traditions in Great Britain are in the main Christian' (p. 156). The Secretary of State, Kenneth Clarke, prided himself in 1991 that 'the content had been put back into geography' (p. 76), thus meeting the kind of anxiety expressed by the *Sunday Times*'s parent appalled that her child 'could not point to Egypt or even Africa on a map' (p. 80). It was Clarke, too, who narrowed the PE curriculum to its traditional focus on physical activities and away from planning and appreciating (p. 141); and who decreed that the history syllabus had to stop twenty years before the present day (p. 93). In 1994 one of Clarke's successors, John Patten, stated of the history curriculum that 'all children must understand such key concepts as empire, monarch, crown, nobility, peasantry' (p. 89).

Politicians have influenced the curriculum at micro-level not only by specific interventions like these, but also more pervasively by the assessment régime also introduced after 1988. SATs in core subjects have given English, mathematics and science a priority reminiscent in many ways of the nineteenth century's preoccupation with the 'three Rs'. Not only in the core subjects, but across the board, assessment mechanisms have led, as Terry Haydn has indicated for history, to pressures to 'teach to the test' and to 'testing what is easy or possible to test, rather than what is important or useful' (p. 95).

There is too much evidence in preceding chapters that 'the curriculum experience becomes 'stuck' and increasingly disengaged from both the wider discipline and the lived experience of the teacher and students' (p. 79). This is true not only of geography, as here, but more generally. The 'prevailing orthodoxy of approach' that John Steers finds in art and design (p. 31) is echoed throughout the book.

In recent years numerous agencies have been at work influencing the curriculum. First, politicians. Right-wing ones have tried to reinstate traditional content. When in power, those of all stripes have been addicted to the assessment regime, both because of the perceived popularity of league tables among parents, and also to show the electorate quantifiable improvements in results. Politically appointed public servants like Nick Tate of SCAA/QCA have bolstered the call for more traditional content in English and in History (p. 90), as has the right-wing press (p. 65). Some school subject associations

– leaving aside those which have been marginalised – have fought for 'a place in the sun' (p. 75) for their subject, trying to make sure of its inclusion in the National Curriculum, and thereafter engaging in still-continuing 'turf wars' (p. 84) with their rivals for curricular space. University and college teachers of school subjects, often powerful voices within subject associations as in Peter Gill's example of the Mathematical Association (p. 110), have an interest in ensuring that schools give their students an adequate apprenticeship in science, history, music or whatever. Employers in the mathematical field have pressed for teamworking and communication skills (p. 110). Publishers and textbook writers must be delighted when, as with *Key Geography* (p. 78), they can exceed 60 per cent of market share with a book filled with double page spreads that painlessly help teachers to meet their statutory obligations. Finally, faith communities have managed, through their influence in the RE world, to preserve religious teaching in an increasingly secularised society.

Forgotten voices

Since 1988 these and other interest groups have all gone for a piece of the curricular action, sometimes – notably among employers – wanting to bring its nineteenth centuriness up to date, but just as often wishing to preserve it. In all the jockeying and squabbling, the voice of one interest group has been hard to hear: that of the children.

Why do we have a national school curriculum? We have it not as a to-be-preserved part of our national heritage like the Tower of London, or as a vehicle of political ideology or part of a strategy for winning elections; a means of maintaining territory for existing school subjects; making money for publishers; bolstering religious organisations; or improving the specialised attainments of university recruits. Its purpose is to help children – *all* children – to become people of a certain sort. It is there to equip them with personal qualities, kinds of understanding and practical abilities they need as citizens and to lead interesting, fulfilled lives.

A voice that has spoken for children in recent years can be heard, behind the clamour of pressure groups, in the statement of values, aims and purposes at the front of the post-2000 *Handbook* on the National Curriculum. This is why I see this statement as key to children's entitlement, to their curricular rights. It is the yardstick against which we can measure whether the curriculum is cleaving to its proper purposes.

Several contributors to this book have picked up the overall aim statement that 'the school curriculum should develop enjoyment of, and commitment to, learning' (DfEE/QCA, 1999, p. 11). They have also mentioned the lack of interest, the feelings of irrelevance, the disaffection which many pupils currently experience, their 'truanting in mind', as Terry Haydn puts it (p. 92), whether or not they are truanting in body. It is here, above all, that we see the contradictions in present arrangements. The test of whether a national school system is delivering the goods is not whether 80 per cent of pupils rather than 75 are successful in certain SATs, but whether pupils are so switched on to learning that they want to carry on doing it long after they leave school.

Ways ahead

How can things become better?

The new aims

First, the new aims must be taken seriously. This will be difficult. The tug of custom will be as strong as ever. Interest groups will continue to have their own agendas and no incentive to subject their assumptions to critique. Teachers themselves, if their present frantic busyness continues, will be pressured to keep their eye on specific obligations, with too little time for wider thought about purposes. Indeed, to judge by my own and colleagues' experience, some of them have not yet realised that the curriculum now *has* general aims – and this is three years after they came into force.

The good thing is that we have aims at all. For this the present Labour government must take most of the credit. Intentionally or not, it has brought into being a means of holding the curriculum to account. Of all the vehicles of evaluation and assessment that it has taken over from its predecessors or itself introduced, the statement of overall aims is potentially the most powerful. Always assuming, that is, it is taken seriously and not treated as a collection of good-sounding platitudes that everyone can ignore.

The curriculum

Second, present curriculum arrangements must be honestly scrutinised to see how far they can be brought better in line with the aims. This book is a contribution to this task. As well as discussing what can be done in different subjects, it has more general lessons for the curriculum as a whole.

Reversing introversion

The suggestion in Chapter 1 that many of the subjects have an 'intra-subject orientation' (p. 14) has been borne out in subsequent chapters. These have gone beyond analysis of official documentation into current practices in their area, so their verdicts are especially significant. Sometimes this inward-lookingness can be attributed to custom, as with 'school art'. There is no suggestion in John Steers' paper that it is the outside world of architects, graphic artists, film makers and painters who have rooted for the retention of the sliced pepper. Elsewhere, there is more evidence of what we have called 'the apprenticeship model' at work – of the early stages of a specialised initiation designed to bear fruit in higher education or in some other field of élite activity. This comes out very clearly in Dawn Penney's chapter on PE and her contention that its overwhelming emphasis on the mastery of specific physical activities is explained by the demands of élite performance in sport (p. 143). Edgar Jenkins points out that in the post-1904 grammar school tradition which continues to dominate science teaching today, 'the science taught was essentially a preparation for the further study of science in higher education' (p. 167). As for school mathematics, 'a main traditional influence has been the university mathematicians, who actually only represent the interests of a tiny proportion of the population' (p. 109). And in music, as Charles Plummeridge and Keith Swanwick tell us, 'a central aim continues to be the development of a kind of general musicianship that has its roots in conservatoires and some university music departments. It leads to a type of musical study that may be relevant in higher education where people are being educated as musicians. But it would seem to be inappropriate for many students in school' (p. 135).

This last sentence puts the finger on the problem. It is quite understandable that enthusiasts for an academic discipline or activity like sport should want this enthusiasm to be transmitted to a new generation so that mastery in the field can be perpetuated. But this is not a good reason for shaping *general education* on apprenticeship lines. Part of this education – as is reflected in the overall aims – is about opening up different activities as a basis for choice. It requires a different orientation from that of the specialist. This is not to say that children who develop talents and enthusiasms in this field or the other should not be encouraged to take things further. There is a strong case, to which I will return, for building this work into an optional part of the curriculum. But we are talking in this section about the compulsory part of the curriculum, the part that all children have to follow. Here we have absolutely no reason to expect that *every* child must have an apprenticeship as a scientist, musician, geographer, mathematician and sportsperson.

Towards interconnectedness

Another, related, feature of current provision is a tendency towards atomisation. I mean by this a focus on specific skills or pieces of factual knowledge with insufficient emphasis on wider perspectives within the field or between fields. The assessment system, with its bias towards easily testable achievements rather than depth or interconnectedness of understanding, is partly responsible for this, reinforcing as it has done the atomisation embedded in our post-nineteenth century tradition. Bethan Marshall shows how current policies in English teaching attempt 'to atomise and itemise knowledge as if what is learnt in English were akin to historical dates or the periodic table' (p. 68). Examples from elsewhere in the book are the 'investigative skills' tested by the science curriculum (pp. 170–1); the 'piecemeal' nature of the mathematics curriculum noted on p. 111 as being at odds with the connectedness so central to mathematical thinking; the 'fragmented' feel of KS3 geography (p. 78); the HMI warning against mechanical tasks in history 'rehearsing formulaic responses to snippets from sources' (p. 95); and the 'heterogeneous conglomerate' of specific activities in PE, 'whose cohesiveness is left to chance' (p. 149).

The post-2000 curriculum highlights learning across the curriculum. It stresses the contribution each subject should make towards, for instance, moral development and PSHE, and also insists on key skills and thinking skills like those of problem-solving, reasoning and enquiry. In this way it acknowledges the importance of connected learning. But unless the impulse towards connectedness is sparked off within the subjects themselves, external solutions like this will not work. There is another reason why the 'thinking skills' solution in particular will not work: the whole notion that general thinking skills exist is open to serious philosophical and empirical doubt (Johnson, 2001).

To summarise these first two points: all children are entitled to a curriculum which provides them with a general education and does not treat them as proto-specialists. They are all equally entitled to a curriculum which makes sense as a whole and does not fragment into a mass of isolated items. If one looks at the curriculum instrumentally, as some parents do, as a vehicle for improving their child's chances of a 'good' university place, the specialisation and lack of connectedness may not matter so much. These may even be a plus: their child may be at an advantage in being able to cope better than most with this kind of curriculum for the sake of benefits to come. But the school curriculum is for *all* children, not an academic élite, and should be planned accordingly. Not that the curriculum as we know it *really* suits these high-fliers, whose chances of fulfilment in life – as distinct from success in the mini-rat-race towards university – would be better served, as with other pupils, by a schooling more in line with the post-2000 overall aims.

The primacy of the practical

Let me pick up this point about fulfilment in life. I have looked at some aspects of this in Chapter 2, where I argued that for all their gaps and inadequacies the overall aims are on the right lines in placing the pupil's well-being as individual and citizen centre-stage. What comes first here is the sort of person we want a child to become – his or her personal qualities. Rightly, the overall aims put most weight on these.

When we think in this way about the sort of person we want education to promote, we think of a person in the round, a person with a life to lead, a path to follow through all its conflicts, opportunities, contingencies. We do not think, in a more confined way, of someone with a lot of factual knowledge or specialised mental or physical skills. These come into the picture at some point, but further along the road. The first thing we think of is a person as a whole, the person who lives the life.

This means that practical rather than theoretical considerations should be uppermost in our thinking. The realm of the practical – in this sense of the word – is the realm of means and ends. To live life well is to be a certain sort of *agent*. As with any human agent, this means having certain ends in mind and adopting certain means in order to attain them. A good life brings with it constraints on both goals and means, only ethically acceptable ones passing muster. Given the ubiquity of ethical and other kinds of conflict in everyday human existence, it also brings with it reflection on which means to adopt and which goals are to be weighted more heavily than others. As Aristotle among philosophers has seen most clearly, practical rationality is at the heart of the good life for a human being.

These philosophical points may seem in danger of getting abstruse and of deflecting us from curriculum practicalities. But they are very important. They urge us to begin our thinking about the curriculum with the human being as agent, not the human being as knower. For reasons which go deep into Western culture, taking us via Descartes back to Socrates and Plato and having to do with what has been held to be the unique and distinguishing feature of a human being, traditional thought about education has been premised on the acquisition of knowledge. This is reflected in the current school curriculum in the relative weight given to accumulating items of knowledge over thinking about ends and means, planning and evaluating one's actions.

Many of the chapters on specific subjects favour a more practically-orientated curriculum in this sense. This is true whether their main focus is knowledge or something else. Bethan Marshall quotes with approval Medway's view about the English he did at school that 'what counted was its being about life. We got our lessons about life from the books we read in English and from our English teachers who, more than others, shared with us their own takes on the world' (pp. 71–2). Or take music: above primary level Charles Plummeridge and Keith Swanwick set great store by elective musical projects and activities. They write, for instance, about 'small group performances, a whole class composition assembled from group contributions or a recorded performance of related items composed by children and "professional" composers' (p. 135). All these activities are built around planning, the dovetailing of appropriate means and ends.

Likewise, on p. 141 Dawn Penney rues Kenneth Clarke's objection to the 1991 proposal for three attainment targets in PE: (i) planning and composing (ii) participating and performing and (iii) appreciating and evaluating, and his pressure for a single target prioritising performing. John Steers' revitalisation of the art and design curriculum argues that 'terminal "tests" should be rejected in favour of procedures that require students to engage in longer term, more complex and challenging projects, working in teams when it is appropriate to do so' (pp. 41–2).

Chapters on more knowledge-orientated subjects are attracted by more practical activity in pursuit of knowledge aims. I am thinking of their support for (a non-mechanical form of) enquiry learning in geography (p. 83), as well as in science. 'Other types of practical activity (than lab work) are readily identifiable (e.g. role play, drama, simulation, using the Internet and multimedia) but they have made little headway against a belief . . . that conducting "experiments" at the laboratory bench is really what matters in school science education' (p. 172).

The curriculum area where practical rationality is quite central is design and technology. Chapter 1 put forward the suggestion that D&T is one of the few subjects the details of whose curriculum closely fit the overall aims. This has been corroborated by Richard Kimbell's chapter. 'We are no longer the cuckoo, but rather the "model subject" for the new curriculum' (p. 56). It fits the aims partly because it is built around helping pupils to choose adequate means to ends, given the

> complex management demands on designers: managing (and optimising) time, cost, materials, production processes, technical performance and much more in ways that enable them to complete their task. At the end they typically have to bring together all the strands of thought and development into a single holistic solution.
>
> (p. 49)

But this is only part of the story. D&T is not confined to cultivating purely instrumental reasoning, i.e. about the most efficient means to an end *regardless of the value of that end*. It is not in the business of helping pupils to produce and realise exemplary designs for cigarette machines or instruments of torture. In the words of the National Curriculum documentation, it prepares pupils to 'learn to think and intervene creatively to improve the quality of life' (above, p. 47). As Kimbell points out, this leads the subject into the area of values (presumably aesthetic values as well as ethical) and involves pupils in the empathetic task of bearing in mind the differing values which various stakeholders in a project (e.g. the design of a school security system) may have (pp. 48–9).

Design and technology invites reflection not only on the efficiency of means but also on the value of ends (and of course other considerations than efficiency enter into the means which pupils learn to adopt – value-laden considerations like legality, considerateness to others, concern for safety). In this respect, the subject mirrors human life itself. True, not all human ends have to do with design and production: friendship doesn't, and neither does reading as distinct from writing poetry. But *every* department of human life depends on practical rationality in this value-laden sense applicable to ends as well as means. It is not surprising that Kimbell tells us that the real products of D&T are not furniture, hats or computer mouses, but 'empowered youngsters' (p. 51).

It should be obvious, I hope, that when I am referring to 'practical' aspects of the curriculum, I am not associating these particularly with vocational goals, but with something much wider. D&T is often seen as a 'vocational' rather than an 'academic' subject (see Chapter 4 above, p. 55), but to my mind this is mistaken as its significance goes beyond the world of work. This said, the wider sense of 'practical', with its focus on means-ends reasoning, is *also* applicable to all but the most routinised forms of employment. Equipping pupils for occupational choices is an important aspect of equipping them for a flourishing personal and civic life and as such is rightly present among the new aims of the curriculum. *All* curriculum activities have some role in this work-related aim. There is no longer – if indeed there ever was – a place in general education for dividing 'academic' subjects from 'vocational'.

There are several signs that the school curriculum is now moving closer to practical concerns in the wider sense. The three other subjects, apart from D&T, which most closely match the new overall aims, are ICT, PSHE and citizenship (see above p. 9). All these are practical subjects, but not all in the same way. ICT, like D&T (and also like aspects of music, science and art and design), is partially hands-on, in the sense that pupils operate on the material world in order to bring about certain results. PSHE and citizenship, the newcomers after 2000, are still practical areas insofar as they are concerned with reflection about means and ends, whether in one's personal life or in the life of states and other institutions. In this they differ from subjects like mathematics or science. Although as areas of human activity both mathematics and science are goal-directed and involve at many points flexible choices among means, they do not embrace the wider reflectiveness about human ends and means found in PSHE and citizenship – and also in history, literature and human geography. None of this is to deny that any of these subjects does and should include more direct immersion in practical projects.

Neither do I want to deny the important role of the curriculum in fostering knowledge and understanding of truths about the world in such areas as mathematics, science, history, geography and knowledge of oneself and other people. All I have said is that knowledge is not its first aim, not that it should not be an aim at all. As practical beings, livers of a life, we human beings need huge amounts of knowledge to sustain us in various ways. This is *not* to say that that we need huge amounts of knowledge as possessions in themselves, disconnected from our interests. Quite the contrary: the knowledge we need is a function of our concerns, goals, projects. Again, the D&T chapter illustrates this in microcosm. 'Since the demands in any task may vary considerably, designers need to develop robust, self-confident strategies for informing their designing by acquiring appropriate resources of knowledge and skill' (p. 49). The word 'appropriate' is where the stress falls.

So, the task for the main knowledge-centred curriculum subjects is to sift through their traditional content and reshape this in line with personal and social requirements. What this means differs according to curriculum area, not least according to whether human concerns constitute its own subject-matter. This book has shown how this reshaping should take place. The geography chapter alludes many times to the subject's relevance to economic, social and political concerns – encapsulated in the quoted remark that geography is 'a prerequisite for watching *Newsnight* intelligently' (p. 84). The history chapter has the same civic thrust in its call for the past to be more firmly linked to the present and for contemporary issues to be included in the syllabus: 'if we want politically literate citizens, they will need to integrate their political understandings of the past with present-day political issues and problems' (p. 98).

Some aspects of biology apart, mathematics and science do not examine human concerns as their subject matter, although their importance for human affairs in the world we live in is beyond dispute. Insofar as children need to understand something of these fields, there is no alternative to initiating them into the non-human subject matter of mathematical symbols and operations, as well as, as Edgar Jenkins says, 'the key features of how scientists understand the material world' (p. 175). This should be the core, as Jenkins says, rather than any more direct links with socio-political issues that have a scientific dimension. There is a good case for leaving the discussion of such issues primarily to the citizenship part of the curriculum.

More student choice

A further message from previous chapters is about introducing more student choice, especially from Key Stage 3 onwards. Kevin Williams' careful assessment of arguments in favour of modern foreign language learning leads him to conclude that pupils 'should not have to do a language as part of a compulsory curriculum for more than at most one year' (p. 124); and that 'it is misguided to insist that all young people spend more than one year at a subject in which some have no interest or for which they show no aptitude' (p. 125). For similar reasons of lack of interest and inclination, Peter Gill suggests that some students be allowed to opt out of mathematics at Key Stage 4. As he says, for mathematically weaker children 'the existence of the Foundation programme of study for Key Stage 4 as a re-run of Key Stage 3 is an admission that the curriculum has failed the pupils forced to follow it' (p. 114).

Other chapters recommend constrained options from Key Stage 3 rather than the opportunity to opt out altogether. In art and design 'there should be more opportunity to specialise within the discipline at Key Stage 3 and greater opportunities to make a well-informed choice about whether to continue with it as an examination subject at Key Stage 4. The choice and type of study available across all forms of art and design must be broadened without the present implied hierarchy that places "fine art" at the apogee. There should be opportunities to choose to study a range of media and technologies' (p. 41). Interestingly – given that the chapters were written independently, recommendations about music follow similar lines. 'Schools might coordinate access to a range of authentic and viable instrumental and vocal groupings led by general class teachers, instrumental teachers and community musicians. Students above primary level could then elect into at least one of these projects. Within the context of such specific activities they would be able to perform, compose and listen to and discuss music from many sources' (p. 135). The chapter on PE also favours more flexibility. 'It is possible to consider a physical education curriculum in which the choice of activities is entirely a matter for schools, teachers and pupils to negotiate. Is experience of any particular specific activity something that is essential to stipulate in a National Curriculum?' (p. 147).

The recommendations for more student choice from Key Stage 3 make sense in light of wider considerations about aims. I have already commented on the overall aim that 'the school curriculum should develop enjoyment of, and commitment to, learning' – an echo of Matthew Arnold's remark, quoted in Chapter 5, that subjects should be taught in a 'less mechanical and more interesting manner [to] call forth pleasurable activity' (p. 60). If we want to do more in England to reverse our abysmal record – twenty-fifth out of 29 developed states – of young people continuing in education and training at age 17, it makes overwhelmingly good sense to make education more enjoyable and interesting for them.

I do not have comprehensive – only partial – data for England about pupil percep-tions of their curricula, but full data do exist for Key Stage 3 pupils in Northern Ireland and may to some extent be valid this side of the Irish Sea. Pupils' largely positive opinion of the NIC (Northern Ireland Curriculum) in the first year of secondary school 'nosedived' in the second year: 'their enjoyment of the curriculum and their perception of its relevance, breadth and manageability all declined' (Harland, 2002, p. 277). In the second year the subjects least enjoyed were, in order of increasing enjoyability: French, RE, maths, and music. Those most enjoyed, in the same order, were technology, art, IT, PE (op. cit., p. 201).

Recently published data on the perceptions of second year secondary students suggest that something like this is true for England as far as enjoyability goes. The three subjects enjoyed least, still in the same order, were found to be mathematics, French and RE. The three enjoyed most were art and design, drama and PE/games (Stoll *et al.*, 2003). All this may support the idea of more student choice in MFLs and maths. As for RE, Michael Hand's chapter neatly undermines the currently most favoured justifica-tions of it as a compulsory subject, leaving only a currently *un*favoured justification in terms of equipping pupils 'to make informed, rational judgements' on the truth or falsity of religious propositions' (p. 161). Whether this, as he himself holds, 'constitutes an adequate justification for separate and compulsory RE, at something like the cur-rently recommended level of provision' is a further question. There may be a case here, too, for reducing the amount of compulsion that children face (White, 2003).

What place for subjects?

The recent history of design and technology prompts a more radical thought. Richard Kimbell describes it as 'deliberately and actively interdisciplinary. The "design" label leans towards the arts, and the "technology" towards the sciences. But neither will do as a natural home. It is a restive, itinerant, non-discipline' (p. 51). How interdisciplinary should the *whole* curriculum be?

We have seen how the National Curriculum has perpetuated the idea that the latter should be planned around school subjects. These have tended to remain discrete enti-ties, backed by discrete professional associations and often competing for curricular space. Links across the curriculum have been built into the system only once these main building blocks have been put in place. There is plenty of evidence from this book that this system, at least in the form we have it now, is multiply defective.

Most of the book's chapters have suggested reforms to the largely subject-based framework which reduce compulsoriness and/or make subjects more responsive to the new overall personal and civic aims. For the most part this has meant *preserving* the traditional subject framework.

Yet at several points in the book there have been indications of something beyond this. For one thing, the case of D&T shows that a subject in the National Curriculum can see itself as firmly *interdisciplinary* in its essence. PSHE and citizenship are other offi-cial 'subjects' which draw from different sources. ICT, as a curriculum area concerned with applying technology, is non-subject-like in a different way. Could other curricu-lum areas, at present discrete, move towards interdisciplinarity? D&T has arisen from previously segregated subjects like woodwork and cookery. John Steers' chapter shows how Ken Robinson's case for the inclusion of 'the arts' rather than specific arts disci-plines in the new National Curriculum in 1988 very nearly made the grade. 'A vigorous debate ensued that was eventually resolved in favour of separate disciplines by a narrow majority in the House of Lords on the eve of the enactment of the Education Reform Act' (p. 37). As should be clear from his chapter, John Steers is personally in favour of an extended vision of art and design rather than a more global 'arts' conception. David Lambert entertains the brave thought for a Chief Executive of the Geographical Association that geography educationists should stop merely defending their 'subject tribe' as an end in itself and that subject associations should begin to work more together, not least on local solutions.

> Geography may become, or remain, a strong and successful single subject in some schools, a contributor to science in another, a member of the arts and humanities faculty in another, a key organiser and contributor to citizenship in another.
>
> (p. 84)

The arrival of citizenship and PSHE suggests further breaches in old battlements. Ethical and civic concerns unite not only these two subjects, but also the remodelled geography and history favoured in this book. Could we begin to think more explicitly of an ethical/civic area of the curriculum? If so, a question mark would hang over RE. Should this belong to such an area? At present many of its proponents see it as a vehicle of moral education, but Michael Hand's chapter raises important doubts as to whether this should be so.

Chapter 2 suggested, following the IPPR paper *A National Curriculum for All*, that curriculum planning should begin with overall aims and then work *downwards* to sub-aims, thence to broad groupings of curriculum areas, and only then – if and where appropriate – to discrete school subjects. If future policy is to work from where we are now rather than from the more idealised stance of the IPPR paper, we may well find ourselves working *upwards* from discrete subjects towards similar broad areas.

Government's and schools' responsibilities

How, more globally, should curriculum policy proceed? I conclude with a thumbnail sketch.

First, it is rightly becoming accepted that central government control of the school curriculum must be loosened. Control should be of the broad framework, not of the details. The broad framework consists of the overall aims plus the specification of these aims in different areas – first in whole school processes (see Chapter 2, p. 27) and then in curriculum areas such as ethical/civic matters, health and fitness, practical competencies, the arts, literacy, mathematics, science. The extent to which the framework should include sub-aims within existing subjects rather than within broader groupings needs further investigation.

At all events, government's role is *not* to enter into the curriculum world as just another interest-group alongside industry, universities and so on, pressing, as it did in the early 1990s, for a certain kind of history syllabus, or, as it is still doing in the early 2000s, for easily quantifiable pupil attainments as a means of winning elections. Its proper role is to stand aloof from interest groups as the guardian of liberal democratic values. Its job is to *restrain* the interest-groups, to prevent their biases from warping the curriculum away from coherence and adherence to underlying values. This said, it would be good to see teachers having a greater role than now in central decisions on the curriculum – as compared, say, with government advisers, given teachers' knowledge of the pupils on whom a curriculum will be inflicted.

A first task for government is to initiate a global review of whole school processes and curriculum areas so as to improve their coherence under the aegis of the broad aims. The review should concentrate on fundamentals and not go into all the specific content and objectives found in the present documentation. The task is to get a far clearer picture than we have now of what government should properly demand of schools and where the boundaries of its jurisdiction should run.

If central authorities have a tight grip on the aims and broad framework they can leave more of the details to schools. We can extrapolate to the whole curriculum David Lambert's suggestion about local variations in ways of meeting geographical objectives. The less central prescription there is about requirements within school subjects, the more room there can be for imaginative and locally-responsive patternings at school level. Schools could indeed be *required* to work out their own whole school processes and ways of grouping curriculum areas and activities.

The last point brings us to ways of holding schools to account. At present this is done from the wrong end. It focuses on the most specific items in the curriculum and sees how well a school does, especially via SATs, in getting them into children's heads. Where it should start is with overall aims. These are, as has been said, the touchstone for whether curricular offerings are adequate. A combination of school self-review and external monitoring involving a national inspectorate among other agencies is required to see that schools are conforming – in their own ways – to the aims and broad framework of sub-objectives that government lays down (Richards, 2001).

References

Harland, J. (2002) *Is the Curriculum Working? The Key Stage 3 Phase of the Northern Ireland Curriculum Cohort Study*, Slough: NFER.

Johnson, S. (2001) *Teaching Thinking Skills*, Impact No. 8, Philosophy of Education Society of Great Britain.

Richards, C. (2001) *School Inspection in England: a Re-appraisal*, Impact No. 9, Philosophy of Education Society of Great Britain.

Stoll, L. *et al.* (2003) *Preparing for Change: Evaluation of the KS3 Pilot Programme*, London: DfES.

White, J. (2003) 'The last rites for Religious Education?', *Ethical Record*, Vol. 107, No. 10, London: South Place Ethical Society.

Index

Main references are in **bold** type

eBooks

eBooks – at www.eBookstore.tandf.co.uk

A library at your fingertips!

eBooks are electronic versions of printed books. You can store them on your PC/laptop or browse them online.

They have advantages for anyone needing rapid access to a wide variety of published, copyright information.

eBooks can help your research by enabling you to bookmark chapters, annotate text and use instant searches to find specific words or phrases. Several eBook files would fit on even a small laptop or PDA.

NEW: Save money by eSubscribing: cheap, online access to any eBook for as long as you need it.

Annual subscription packages

We now offer special low-cost bulk subscriptions to packages of eBooks in certain subject areas. These are available to libraries or to individuals.

For more information please contact webmaster.ebooks@tandf.co.uk

We're continually developing the eBook concept, so keep up to date by visiting the website.

www.eBookstore.tandf.co.uk